T0113919

DETERMINING THE FUTURE'S TRUTH THROUGH

Bible Prophecy

PETER GALARZA

WESTBOW
PRESS®
A DIVISION OF THOMAS NELSON
& ZONDERVAN

WestBow Press books may be ordered through booksellers or by contacting:

WestBow Press
A Division of Thomas Nelson & Zondervan
1663 Liberty Drive
Bloomington, IN 47403
www.westbowpress.com
844-714-3454

ISBN: 978-1-6642-4736-9 (sc)
ISBN: 978-1-6642-4738-3 (hc)
ISBN: 978-1-6642-4737-6 (e)

Library of Congress Control Number: 2021921019

Print information available on the last page.

WestBow Press rev. date: 10/21/2021

CONTENTS

INTRODUCTION

What is prophecy? Is it the foretelling of future events? Some people seem to think so, but in reality prophecy is the utterance of God's Word through the Bible, a messenger, or a medium; usually it is a man or woman. This person is called a prophet or prophetess, and the person's job is to deliver or interpret the divine will of God. Prophecy is not a prediction (guess); it is the truth, which is the infallible Word of God.

The Bible, whose author is God Himself, was written by prophets. The scripture was given to them through the Holy Spirit, who is God Himself, and their job was to speak it or put it in writing. We know this from 2 Timothy 3:16, where it reads, "All scripture is given by inspiration of God, and is profitable for doctrine, for reproof, for correction, for instruction in righteousness" (NKJV).

Some prophets were given futuristic events to write about, and others were given truths or righteous doctrine to write about. In this book, we're concerned with futuristic events only because with all that is unfolding in the Middle East and across the world, many are asking questions relating to the "end-time."

Operation Desert Storm back in the early nineties and "Shock and Awe" in 2003 give us a very scary scenario of war tactics never before used in war. These tactics came about because of the superior technological advances that Western nations have in today's modern military. Though our troops were outnumbered two to one, that didn't matter.

With the growing labor pains of society's struggles, one must wonder whether there will ever be peace. The truth of the matter is yes, there will be peace, but first some (or many) will have to go through a dark period or a purging process, which we will call the Tribulation or the time of Jacob's trouble (Jeremiah 30:7). This Tribulation period, which will impact the whole world and not just Israel, is a response to sin. The purging process, which will take almost seven years, will separate the righteous from the unrighteous; or should I say the sheep from the goats.

Let's keep an open mind and watch with the guidance of God's Word, or prophecy, as to what God's ultimate plan of salvation is for humankind. My intention and purpose for writing this book is to teach those who are looking for answers on humankind's future, destiny, and events dealing with the end-time.

The Persian Gulf wars of Operation Desert Storm and Shock and Awe, which we will call a continuance of the destroying wind, were the culprits for interest in humans' future destiny, at least in America. This interest has sparked worldwide curiosity in prophetic material, both biblical and nonbiblical. My intention is to guide those believers who are interested in the biblical aspects of the Bible, and to hopefully spark an interest in the Bible itself to those who are looking for answers in the secular sense, such as those looking at Nostradamus's predictions.

CHAPTER 1

A Destroying Wind

August 2, 1990—Iraq (Babylon) invades Kuwait.

Days later, the United States warns Saudi Arabia of a possible attack by Iraq.

US ally troops prepare for war under the code name Operation Desert Shield, under General Norman Schwarzkopf's command.

The allied forces were the United States, Britain, France, Italy, Saudi Arabia, Egypt, Syria, and Kuwait, among others.

The enemy was Iraq.

January 15,1991—The air campaign begins, with the United Nations (the world) versus Iraq.

February 23,1991—The predawn ground war begins.

February 28,1991—President W. H. Bush orders a cease-fire.

The allies' intention at the time was to free Kuwait from Iraq. Although many were in favor of the allies' continuance into Iraq to take down the regime of its dictator, Saddam Hussein, that did not happen. Twelve years later, the allies had to go back into Iraq, this time under the code name Operation Shock and Awe, to take down Saddam Hussein and also destroy weapons of mass destruction. The weapons were never found, but they did capture the dictator, who later was tried and hanged to death by his own countrymen.

These were the headlines that dominated the news during conflicts that many thought would lead to the greatest war of our time—"the war to end all wars," recognized as Armageddon. However, that wasn't the case. Operation Desert Storm was just a restart, or continuance, of what the prophet Jeremiah called the "destroying wind," terminology used in the first verse of his book in chapter 51. In this verse, God spoke through His prophet and said: "Behold, I will raise up against Babylon a destroying wind" (Jeremiah 51:1 NKJV). That destroying wind started with Operation Desert Storm, it was followed by Operation Shock and Awe, and it will end with Armageddon.

Babylon, which is present-day Iraq, was a great empire in its day until it was brought down by the Persians. The great king who represented this empire was Nebuchadnezzar, a name that Saddam Hussein resurrected and made popular among his countrymen and peers. He imagined himself to be this great king reincarnated.

What we witnessed in Iraq during the Persian Wars was not a complete destruction as emphasized in Jeremiah's prophecy, but it was the beginning of things to come. God, in His right time, will stir up the destroying wind again and put Israel's enemies to rest. As for Iraq, had the Lord desired it, the allies would have made a parking lot out of it. But it wasn't His wish, because Iraq has a big role in the last days, according to scripture.

True, Iraq did suffer a massive blow against its military, not to mention its pride as a military machine in the Middle East, but the blow was not enough to fulfill the future prophecy, which reads, "Babylon shall become a heap, a dwelling place for jackals, an astonishment and a hissing without an inhabitant" (Jeremiah 51:3 NKJV).

Because this prophecy has yet to come to pass, we might conclude that a disaster of great magnitude still awaits Iraq. We might even discern that Operation Desert Storm and Operation Shock and Awe were simply dress rehearsals of things to come in the not-too-distant future. Only time separates the true destruction of Iraq (Babylon), for once Iraq and its allies attack Israel, God's wrath will be kindled, and His vengeance will liberate His people.

With a study in Bible prophecy, we can almost visualize foreseeable events yet to unfold in the Gulf region. Unfortunately, Iraq and the rest of the Muslim world are not yet finished with Israel. The animosity and hatred, going back ages into biblical times, is too great to be ignored. Prophecy warns us that there is yet a great war that must be fought—one that will only be stopped by the appearance of the Messiah Himself.

The alignment of nations has already been molded. One can already see, from the Persian Wars, which nations will align with Israel and which will align with the Muslim world. There will be sheep nations and goat nations contending for high stakes in the next Gulf war.

Why do I say "the next Gulf war"? Because it is no mystery for the Bible student to know what catastrophes lie in the latter days, especially in the last seven years of this present-day structure—or should I say dispensation (chapter 5 will explain). It was Jesus Himself who spoke of nations rising up against nations, wars and rumors of war, and famines and pestilences before His second advent.

The Bible does prophesy about a great futuristic war in the Middle East, which will claim the lives of hundreds of thousands, if not millions. Those who thought the two Persian Wars in 1991 and 2003 were the wars that would end all wars were dead wrong. We must yet experience quite a bit before the wars of the end-time comes to pass. What we saw in Operation Desert Storm and Operation Shock and Awe was just the beginning of the real thing.

Let's not forget the US war in Afghanistan that started right after 9/11, when America was attacked by Al-Qaeda, led by Osama bin Laden, a world-renowned terrorist from Saudi Arabia. With the Twin Towers already laid waste, America, under President George W. Bush's administration, launched a campaign against this terrorist organization in Afghanistan. Later on, during the Obama administration, bin Laden was finally found and killed.

Upon seeing the unfolding events as prophesied in the Bible come to pass, one must wonder whether the Messiah is virtually at the door. The truth of the matter is yes! He is that close to making His second debut in biblical history. The birth pangs have already begun, and they'll continue to progress until they magnify to the point where the Messiah will have no choice but to make His spectacular reentry back to planet Earth.

For Christians, this will mark the most awaited time in Christendom. To the Jews, who still awaits the Messiah's first coming, this time will not only be joyful but also mournful, for they will realize whom they sent to be crucified almost two thousand years ago (Zechariah 12:10). Unfortunately, not recognizing Him at His first advent caused them much turmoil and distress throughout the centuries. But it was God Himself who hardened their hearts, just as He hardened the heart of Pharaoh during Israel's exodus from Egypt.

Let me tell you, friends, that God is, was, and will be in control right through eternity. That is the point I will be stressing throughout this book, for I know that our God is an awesome God who is omnipotent and omniscient. And let's not forget that our God is a jealous God. He will avenge and destroy any nation or kingdom that comes against His people of Israel. He is the alpha and omega, the beginning and the end. Praise His name forever!

In determining the future's truth, one can totally rely on and trust the Word of God as a guide to the prophetic message. Prophecy, by definition, is the inspired, divine utterance of God's Word via a prophet or God Himself in the person of Jesus Christ, His Son. I don't want to repeat myself, but it's important to know the difference between prophecy and a prediction, which is only a guess. Prophecy (the Word of God) is truth and is therefore trustworthy. What the Lord has planned, He has forecast through His prophets. For example, in Isaiah 7:14 (NKJV) we read, "Therefore the Lord Himself will give you a sign: Behold the virgin shall conceive and bear a Son and shall call His name Emanuel." (Emanuel means "God with us.") Here, we have a prophetic message that was written approximately seven hundred years before Jesus was born, and yet this scripture specifies an occurrence that comes to pass in the books of Mathew and Luke.

Knowing both your biblical and secular history will validate the authenticity of a prophetic message. For example, just as Jesus's birth was prophesied, so was His crucifixion, death, and resurrection. Each occurrence has been validated either by biblical or secular records. The secular records I'm referring to are the writings of Flavius Josephus, a Roman Jewish historian priest of the first century AD.

The return of Christ has been prophesied also, for as He left us, so will He return to rule the nations of the world from a reconstructed temple in Mt. Moriah, the same location as Herod's Temple of old in the city of Jerusalem; it is also the same location where Abraham almost sacrificed his son Isaac. Today, we find in this piece of real estate the Dome of the Rock, which was built around AD 700 and has caused much turmoil and animosity between the Arab Muslims and the Jews. Not just the temple grounds but all of Jerusalem has caused turmoil. In fact, all of Israel is a target and will continue being a target until the Palestinian issue is totally settled and Jerusalem is returned to the Arab Muslims. Unfortunately for the Muslims, this will never happen without a fight, for Israel is there to stay.

The rivalry that we see here is one that dates back to the time of the pregnancy of Rebecca, Isaac's wife, where it was evident that two struggling nations were in her womb. These were the twins Jacob and Esau. If you recall from your Genesis reading, the Lord told Rebecca that the older would serve the younger—that is, the nation of Esau would serve the nation of Jacob, who is Israel.

In Genesis 36:8, we are told that Esau is Edom, which along with Ammon and Moab constitutes present-day Jordan. It is where a large percentage of Palestinians resided and still reside. They lived there for many years prior to the peace talks, which gave the Palestinians the old city of Jericho in the west, and part of the Gaza, which is known as the Gaza Strip, in the east of Israel.

Back in 1948, the Palestinians were forced to leave their homeland (Palestine) when the United Nations divided it into two separate states, Israel and Transjordan. What ensued was an eruption of violence when the Islamic Arabs attacked Israel to reclaim their territory. They failed.

Prior to 1948, Palestine was controlled by Britain under a mandate awarded to them by the League of Nations in 1920. It was Britain's support of a separate state that drew a UN vote to make Israel a reality with its own sovereign government. It was America's vote that made the difference for the resolution to be enacted. Without it, Israel would be a nation without a homeland; such was the plight of the Palestinians prior to 1994. At present (2021), a two-state solution is still in the works to give the Palestinians their own sovereign nation.

Who are these Palestinians? We've already mentioned Edom as being Esau. And because Edom is part of Jordan, we must assume these people to be part of the makeup of the Palestinians who reside in the Gulf region. One might even contend with the fact that Palestine was inhabited by several, if not many more, nomadic Arab tribes after the destruction of Jerusalem by Rome in AD 70. If you want to get speculative about it, one might even contend that the Palestinians are directly related to the Philistines of the book of Judges in the Old Testament.

These Philistines were a very dominating and powerful force that never got along with the Israelites. They had a very powerful military force, which took credit for pushing the Canaanites off the land. Even though Israel's first king, Saul, tried his hardest, it wasn't until King David's time that the Philistines were handed enough blows to dissipate them.

We must also acknowledge the fact that these Philistines were very involved in idol worship, an act that had to trigger God's wrath. That was exactly what happened when God inflicted a blow by the hand of Samson, who took the jawbone of an ass, giving him supernatural strength to kill a thousand Philistines (Judges 15:15). This episode, along with Samson's destruction of Dagon's temple (Judges 16:30), inspired Israel to puncture the Philistines and inflict them with a wound that probably still hurts to this day.

These Philistines and Canaanites, among others, were the inhabitants of the land of Palestine prior to King David's reign, and probably they were the inhabitants after the Romans' destruction of Jerusalem in AD 70. It wasn't until after AD 700 that the Muslim Arabs became the true inhabitants of the land, and they remained so until 1948, when Israel became a nation again, thus fulfilling a Bible prophecy (Ezekiel 37).

Can we therefore dare to say that today's Palestinians are an intermingled group of Muslim Arabs, Philistines, and Canaanites? Maybe so, but without Jerusalem, they'll always feel unsuccessful about putting their sovereign land back together, and they will still feel as a scattered nation. True, Jericho and Gaza have been given to them with their own governance, but without a true solution to this problem, the next Gulf war is inevitable, for they blame Israel for their plight. Unfortunately, the rest of the Arab world supports them, thus hindering or slowing down a more peaceful solution.

It won't be until Messiah's coming that this issue will be resolved completely, for the Messiah will deal with Israel's enemies in a very harsh way. Scripture tells us that "Jerusalem will be a heavy stone burdening the world. And though all the nations of the Earth unite in an attempt to move her, they will all be crushed" (Zechariah 12:3 TLB). This is God's warning given to all nations through His prophet Zechariah, who conveys the message that God is in control and has the final say in His infinite wisdom over Jerusalem.

Historically speaking, Babylon overran Jerusalem, and so did the Romans in AD 70. Even the Turks had control over it, and much of the Middle East, for about four hundred years (1516–1917). World War I changed all that when the British took control over the Middle East and carved it up, thus allowing part of Palestine to be returned to the Jewish people in 1948.

Known as Judea (or Judah) during Rome's control, its new name became Israel again, the name given to Jacob after he wrestled with a man all night long who apparently was God Himself (Genesis 32:24–28). That was also the name of the land during the reigns of Saul, David, Solomon, and Rehoboam. Afterward, a civil war broke it into two separate kingdoms, one to the north (Israel) and one to the south (Judea). The one to the north, Israel, was invaded by the Assyrians under King Shalmaneser in 732 BC, which was finally taken three years later by Sargon II. The one to the south, Judea, was finally destroyed by the Romans in AD 70 when they totally destroyed Jerusalem and scattered all the Jews. Known as the Diaspora, the Jews were scattered all over the world until they came back together in 1948, thus fulfilling Ezekiel 37's "valley of the dry bones" prophecy.

Can we therefore dare say that a predawn of the "destroying wind" begins emerging into the real thing by 1991 (Desert Storm), when Iraq (Babylon) is approached and questioned by the allies: "Have you come to Kuwait to plunder them and take their booty?" "Beware Israel! You might be next," would have been the allies' thoughts. As it was, Saudi Arabia was their next intended target. Their next-door neighbor to the west, Israel, might have also been an intended target. I believe a similar scenario was seen in 1938 when Poland was invaded by Hitler. Unfortunately, Hitler didn't stop there but continued invading other European nations, which climaxed in a world war.

Let's thank God for His protection toward Israel during this time between 1990 and 2003, for a cataclysmic event could have easily sparked an uncontrollable war that would have taken us into an Armageddon scenario. But it didn't happen that way. As we proceed with this book, you will see God's plan of salvation, which will take us from these Persian wars to the Armageddon scenario in the book of Revelation. Certain things must take place first in history before this battle called Armageddon is initiated before the second coming of Christ.

For now, let's concentrate on God's salvation and the second coming of Christ. If you don't know Him, hopefully this writing will lead you to Him, and salvation will be established in your life. It was such a writing as this, in Bible prophecy, that led me to the Lord. Praise His holy name!

CHAPTER 2

Setting Boundaries and Blessings

As we already know from Genesis, twelve sons were born out of Jacob's seed, who later became the twelve tribes of Israel. These twelve tribes were scattered all over the world after the final destruction of Jerusalem in AD 70, and they remained so until 1948, as mentioned before, thus fulfilling Ezekiel's prophecy of the "Valley of Dry Bones." In this prophecy (Ezekiel 37), the bones that had been scattered came together with flesh for the prime purpose of putting the house of Israel back on the map and back in their place and destiny. Even as I write, this prophecy continues to be fulfilled, especially with migrations coming into Israel from the old Soviet Union, Eastern Europe, and Africa. Even those who made their homes in America are leaving for the Promised Land. "Son of man, these bones are the whole house of Israel … I will open your graves and cause you to come up from your graves, and bring you into the land of Israel" (Ezekiel 37:11–12 NKJV).

What God has spoken through the prophets, God has done and will continue to fulfill. Not only has He given this land back to the twelve tribes of Israel, but He has extended their borders, especially with the reunification of Jerusalem in 1967. Still later on, the borders will be extended even farther at the time of Messiah's arrival due to the acquisition of other grounds at the time, for it seems that the map carved up by the British doesn't quite agree with the map of Genesis, where God told Abraham, "To your descendants I have given this land, from the River of Egypt (Nile) to the Great River, the River Euphrates" (Genesis 15:18 NKJV).

Let's take a careful note here, for where some say this prophecy has yet to be fulfilled, 1 Kings 4:20–21 tells us otherwise. Unfortunately, because of Israel's disobedience to God, they lost it all. But because we know scripture's prophetic language that Babylon will be utterly destroyed, we can only speculate that Israel will again inherit this promised land sometime in the future—that is, the land that borders the River Euphrates to the River Nile in Egypt. That means Iraq, which is the Babylon of the Old Testament, will be dealt with in a most harsh way, along with the rest of the goat nations upon the Messiah's arrival.

The goat nations I'm referring to are Israel's enemies. Let me explain. Matthew 25:32–33 (NKJV) tells us of the Messiah, "All the nations will be gathered before Him, and He will separate them one from another, as a shepherd divides his sheep from the goats. And He will set the sheep on His right hand, but the goats on His left." Then He goes on to say to His sheep that they have inherited the kingdom prepared for them. To the goats he says, "Depart from Me, you cursed into the everlasting fire prepared for the devil and his angels" (Matthew 25:41 NKJV).

All I can say to that is, Ouch! The inference made here is about the goat nations literally going to hell due to God's wrath against them, whereas the sheep nations will inherit the rewards promised to them. With this in mind, one can almost foresee, and logically evaluate, that boundaries in the Middle East will be radically changed at the Messiah's arrival. This will give Israel, or the meek, the inheritance promised in Matthew 5:5 (NKJV): "Blessed are the meek, for they shall inherit the Earth." Let's all agree that the gospel of Matthew was written to a Jewish Christian audience. One thing is for certain: once the new boundaries are established, they will remain so through the end of the millennium, only because the Messiah will be in charge. For anyone disputing these boundaries, they will have to deal with the Messiah directly.

Now, what about the Arab Muslim people who have survived thus far during these times? Do they also inherit the promises made to Abraham because they are of his seed? The answer is simple. But first let's elaborate. In Genesis, starting in 35:11, we read, "God said to him [Jacob] I am God Almighty. Be fruitful and multiply: a nation and a company of nations shall come from your body. The land which I gave Abraham and Isaac I give to you; and to your descendants after you I give this land" (NKJV). God also told Jacob earlier that his descendants would be "as the dust of the Earth," implying a countless multitude of people. Again, we have proof that only through Israel would the covenant be fulfilled.

When reading the book of Genesis in the Old Testament, one can see that a covenant, or contract, was passed on to Isaac, son of Abraham (Genesis 26), then to Jacob (Genesis 28), son of Isaac. This covenant was not passed on to Ishmael, Abraham's first son, born of the bond woman (Sara's concubine) Hagar, or Esau, Isaac's firstborn son of the twins. True, Ishmael was blessed also, in that his seed multiplied exceedingly. He too had twelve sons who became twelve princes with twelve tribes. And true, Esau was blessed in that he became the nation of Edom (Genesis 32:3). But remember that Esau did sell his birthright to Jacob (Genesis 25:29–34), thus allowing the inheritance to go to Isaac's second born, who is Israel. This made Esau Jacob's servant, thus fulfilling Isaac's prophetic blessing to Jacob of being master over his brethren (Genesis 27:29). Later on, Esau married Ishmael's daughter (his cousin), thus carrying on the blessing bestowed upon Ishmael that he would become a nation (Genesis 21:13). These are apparently our Arab friends of today. They also regard themselves as partakers to the inheritance, for Abraham was their father too.

Today, Arab Muslims are scattered all over the Middle East. The Arabian peninsula is mostly of Arabic descent. Jordan, located east of Israel, with its Palestinian Arabic population numbering over half its people, is also Arabic. Other nations with Arabic influence include Syria, Lebanon, Iraq, and others; there are over twenty in all. Today, we see Israel with a population of over eight million, not counting the ones that are in foreign countries, such as the United States, which has a population of at least seven million more Jews. But, as compared to other populations in the world, Israel's numbers are comparatively much lower, which in my opinion doesn't account for the number implied to "as the Earth's dust." How is it, then, that the population number will match or exceed that of the "dust of the Earth"?

What we have here is an enormous multitude of people who will, or want to, share in the inheritance. But who? As I said before, the answer is simple. There is another multitude, other than Israel, that can account for such numbers. These are the believers, or those who come to know the true God of the Bible and His Messiah, Jesus. This multitude includes anyone willing to accept the message in John 3:16, "For God so loved the world, that He gave His Only begotten Son, that whoever believes in Him should not perish but have everlasting life" (NKJV). These include our Arab friends, Asian friends, African friends, European friends, and any others who want to make the Lord Jesus Christ their Savior, Lord, and friend. If they want to share in this inheritance and enter the kingdom prepared for all believers, they must be, as John 3:3 puts it, "born again." In other words, once they believe in this simple message, their spirit man, which is dormant, awakens or quickens, to be joined with the Spirit of the Living God. This has nothing to do with religion; it has everything to do with having a relationship with God and His Son, Jesus, who is the Messiah. If our Arab Muslim friends follow this simple doctrine, they too will be inheritors of God's blessings.

Now, what about blessings that have been bestowed in this Middle East region of the world thus far? As they stand today, many have enjoyed certain blessings, even from their beginnings, for they have their own sovereign nations, including the Palestinians, who are almost there. They have been multiplied exceedingly in population. They also have been supplied with much prosperity, in that they have abundant oil supplies, which alone puts them in a most respectable place with the rest of the world, especially the Western world. Their food supplies are adequate with their known staple foods and spices. It's not often that you hear about hunger in the Middle East, but just as any other country in the world, I'm sure there must be hunger with a small segment of the population.

Getting back to oil supplies, one nation that comes to mind is Iraq, for it has more than adequate oil supplies. Unfortunately, we already know from our current events what their profits have supplied them with, and it seems that some Third World nations believe that if they beef up their military programs, it will bring about respectability to them. It pains me to see the waste involved here. Why not take the profits to better the nation in other ways, helping others to prosper in economics, health, education, and more.

If we take a close look at the book of Genesis, we can find approximately where the Garden of Eden might have been located. It was located where the Euphrates and Tigris Rivers meet. This meeting place is in southern Iraq by the port city of Basra. If you recall from Operation Desert Storm, this port city took a tremendous pounding by allied bombers. Just south of Basra lies Kuwait, the country the allies rescued during the war. If we're not mistaken, we can say that Eden was located approximately in this region, but then again, there are two other rivers to be considered from Genesis: the Gihon and Pishon Rivers (Genesis 2:10-14), which I'm sure have shifted positions due to erosion and the meandering of the waters. To be honest, no one really knows the exact location of the garden because God doesn't want modern humans to have that information. That is why He drove Adam and Eve out from the garden and "placed Cherubim at the east of the garden, and a flaming sword which turned every way, to guard the way to the tree of life" (Genesis 3:24 NKJV). Not only that, but with geological movements of the terrain for thousands of years, who can actually locate the garden?

Can you see why this region is so abundantly supplied with oil? It was abundantly filled with vegetation and greenery during biblical times. Noah's flood was the culprit for burying this whole area under tons of sediment and debris. Just ask any geologist, who can tell you the result of such a geological event happening where organic debris is buried under intense pressure for a long period of time. The result will be either gas or oil. Iraq has been blessed with this treasure, but like the former Soviet Union, it chooses to build weaponry not just for defense but also for offence.

Will nations ever take heed to Jesus's words when He said, "For all who take the sword, will perish by the sword" (Matthew 26:52 NKJV)? Did Iraq learn from the two Persian Gulf wars? According to the Bible, prophecy's answer would be no, only because they'll be warring with Israel and the allied forces again at a later time in history.

What about Kuwait? Can you believe that at one time during the sixties, it had one of the highest gross national products (GNPs) in the world solely because of its petroleum-based economy? I'm sure they now know who their true friends and enemies are for the present, especially after Operation Desert Storm. That in itself is a blessing to them, and they prove it by providing the world with a much-needed oil supply. It shows their appreciation and thankfulness.

Just think: If Hitler had been stopped when entering Eastern Europe just as Saddam Hussein was stopped from further aggression in Kuwait, do you think World War II would have been as bloody and messy with killings and genocides? I don't think so. Unfortunately, it didn't happen that way.

I'm sure that by now, you're getting a glimpse of what's going on here concerning the boundaries of nations, as well as the blessings and cursings of nations in the prophetic picture. Sooner or later, these same nations will be involved in a war to end all wars. The pieces to the puzzle are fitting right into place, and the Word of God will determine this truth.

In concluding this chapter, to get an overview picture as to where the Middle East is heading, one must consider all biblical and secular historical data, current events and prophecy. This will again determine the future, especially the prophetic message that can be relied on. For now, let's view the map of the Middle East and consider its boundaries. Examine carefully the boundaries of nations north of, south of, and east of Israel. Some of these nations are oil-rich nations. Sometime in the future, their boundaries will change drastically, for God Himself will expand Israel's boundaries and shrink the boundaries of some of these oil-rich territories. Then the people of Israel will enjoy their inheritance from God.

The truth of the matter is that God is in control of all situations in the Middle East and in the world. Maybe it's time for the world to respect and accept what God has in store for them. Please don't hesitate to choose God's love in your lives. He is the King of kings, Lord of lords, and Prince of peace. Believe it, and be saved.

CHAPTER 3

Purging Israel

Jerusalem is probably the most popular and most explosive city on the planet. Biblically speaking, it is God's city, and it will be the Messiah's dwelling place at His return, for from this city He'll rule all nations on Earth. Jerusalem will be the headquarters, or the capital of the new world. And out of His mouth, He'll strike the nations with a sword, and then rule them with a rod of iron (Revelation 19:15).

Going back to the time of King David, Jerusalem was inhabited by the Jebusites. King David took it and made it Israel's capital. He reigned there thirty-three years after reigning in Hebron for seven years over Judah. It is this same Hebron, which is one of the oldest inhabited cities of the world, where Abraham's traditional burial site rests. In all, King David reigned for forty years over Israel and Judah. His successor, King Solomon (his son), also reigned in Jerusalem for forty years. It was he who gave the order to build the temple for the name of the Lord (1 Kings 5:5). Once built, only the Levites, or the priestly tribe of Levi, were allowed to enter it to make daily sacrifices and offerings to the Lord. Also included in it was the Ark of the Covenant, which was kept in the Holy of Holies (an innermost shrine of the temple, behind closed curtains).

Nebuchadnezzar, king of Babylon, is credited for destroying Solomon's temple when he carried Judah into captivity around 586 BC. It was the prophet Jeremiah who wrote, "Thus says the Lord: Behold I will give this city into the hand of the King of Babylon and he shall burn it with fire" (Jeremiah 34:2 NKJV). These words were spoken from the mouth of the prophet Jeremiah to King Zedikiah, Judah's last king. And so this prophecy was fulfilled.

Looking at historical biblical data, we find in Jeremiah 39:8 (NKJV) where Nebuchadnezzar besieged the city of Jerusalem with all his armies: "The Chaldeans burned the king's house and the houses of the people with fire and broke down the walls of Jerusalem." These walls were enlarged by King David (originally built by Canaanites) for the purpose of fortifying the city. Most biblical cities were fortified with walls. Take for instance the walls of the great city of Babylon. It is said that they were eighty feet wide—wide enough to ride chariots atop of them.

Again, through prophecy, God warned Israel and Judah of consequences for their unrighteousness. They didn't repent, and as a result they paid the price. They were taken away from their homeland in captivity, put into exile in a land full of idol gods, and stripped of their dignity. This was God's chastisement on them.

When reading the Bible, one can observe God's warning being repeated over and over. True, He is slow to anger, but there is a limit as to how much a father can take from defiant children. In Jeremiah 30:11 (NKJV), He warns, "But I will correct you in Justice and will not let you go altogether unpunished." This was God's message to Israel, who either received it or ignored it, for it came from a man's (prophet Jeremiah) mouth. Once Judah committed itself to be totally disobedient, God had no choice but to inflict it with pain, and as we know, that pain came in the form of Israel's and Judah's breakdowns.

In His merciful ways, God will always chastise. In Israel's and Judah's case, He didn't just correct or punish them—He took actual corporal punishment against them for their misconduct. Through an invader, He captivated them and afflicted them in order to discipline them. He then later brought them back to their homeland as promised, only to later repeat the process once again for their misconduct.

For those of you who have children, I'm sure you have chastised or punished them at times—that is, if you love them. Let's use an example. A small child goes shopping with his parents; let's call him Johnny. Johnny repeatedly has temper tantrums. This goes on time and time again because he wants a toy or candy. His parents repeatedly give him warnings, but he doesn't take heed. Finally, the father takes control of the situation and whacks him where it hurts, across his rear. This shocks Johnny to the point where he says, "I'd better give it up, or else I'll be getting more." Johnny's father did not chastise him because he wanted to stir up Johnny's anger. He did it as a purpose of discipline so Johnny would mature with the moral behavior that is expected of him. In other words, the father corrected him because he loved him.

God will also chastise His children so they will reach that maturity level expected by Him—a level that is considered righteousness before God. Once this level is achieved, rewards will be reaped. In Hebrews 12:6 (NKJV) we read, "For whom the Lord loves He chastens."

In John 3:16 (KJV), God shows that "everlasting life" is the ultimate reward, or gift, once chastened, for chastisement will purge out unrighteousness and fill in the void with righteousness. To believe means to do God's will. Therefore, to believe in a gospel message that can be summarized in a simple gospel verse, like John 3:16, is reward enough for now, because the promise has been made. And that promise is everlasting life through Jesus Christ, the Son of God, who resurrected from the dead after being set in a tomb for three days and three nights. Now, if Christ resurrected from the dead, how are we believers not to resurrect also if we believe in this gospel message.

Scripture reminds us that we've been appointed once to die, and then afterward is the judgment (Hebrews 9:27). That means human beings alive today will have a share in the judgment, for they will all stand accused before God. Satan will make sure of that. For those who have already passed away, they too will be resurrected to share in the judgment. The only exception might be those who will resurrect at Christ's coming (first resurrection), for they will already be cleansed or purged of all impurities (sin). These are the dead in Christ, who have already been washed in the blood of the Lamb and who stand with their advocate, Lord Jesus.

In chastising Israel, God gave them more than ample opportunities to repent so life, in an everlasting sense, could be made more abundantly. Sending them into captivity to Babylon, after destroying Jerusalem, was God's plan in the chastening process, because later on He gave them another chance by having Cyrus, king of Persia, issue an order to the Jews to start the rebuilding of the Temple in Israel and, later on, the walls of Jerusalem (Nehemiah 2). This led to the rebuilding of Jerusalem and the return of the captives to the Holy Land.

Chastisement again played a big role when Jerusalem was besieged and destroyed by Rome in AD 70, thus scattering the Israelites (or Jews) all over the world. This time, the purging process lasted almost 1,900 years, a time known as the Diaspora, because they were without a homeland, wandering again in the wilderness (world), as they did in the book of Exodus.

In the last days, Israel again will be plagued with more chastisement, for in purging unrighteousness and wickedness out of her, God will send His final plagues on not only on Israel but also the whole world. If you don't think He can plague the entire planet in one moment's time, just look what happened with the coronavirus (COVID-19) pandemic that started in December 2019, stretching into the early 2020s all over the world. He did not instigated it, but allowed it to happen. Believe me, that is nothing compared to what He can do in a moment's time. Just brace yourselves, because chastisement comes with a price.

Known as the "time of Jacob's trouble" (Jeremiah 30:6–7 NKJV), or the Tribulation, what will ensue will be the most devastating time in the history of the world. It will be a time of great anxiety and distress. "For then shall be great tribulation, such as was not seen since the beginning of the world to this time, no. nor ever shall be" (Matthew 24:21 KJV). Again, Gentile nations will overrun Israel and try to wipe it off the face of the map. The last three and a half years will be the most devastating. Thank God that the believers in Christ will not be around to witness it to the end; they will have been raptured, or caught up to heaven to be with the Lord; more on this later.

With an antichrist ruler coming into the scene and leading the charge against Israel, he will attack not only the Jew but also anyone associated with godliness and righteousness. Here, we are being tested by God to see just how we will endure. "Blessed are they who Endure," says the Word, for the purging process will be on a worldwide scale. Our main focal point, or place at the time to perceive what's going to happen, will be Jerusalem. That is why scripture describes Jerusalem as a "Heavy stone burdening the world" (Zechariah 12:3 TLB). Unfortunately, those loyal and faithful to God in Israel who will have to go through this time of trouble will also have to endure suffering until the Messiah's arrival. But this endurance will prove their worthiness for entering God's kingdom, and they will be rewarded with everlasting life with Christ Jesus. Praise His name!

In closing this chapter, let's remember that God will do as He says. He is in control (not humankind), for there are rewards for those who choose to follow Him. Tomorrow might be too late, for we never know what might transpire between now and then. "God is not slack concerning His promise as some men count slackness, but is longsuffering towards us, not willing that any should perish, but that all should come to repentance" (2 Peter 3:9 KJV). Enduring to the end is a race that must be finished. Reaching the finish line has to be everyone's goal. Let's run the race well.

CHAPTER 4

Messiah to the Rescue

The end? What exactly does it mean? Will I have to die? Why not just live it up now if we're all going to die?

Many Christians and non-Christians who are uninformed about Bible scripture tend to think that the end of the world will come with a big bang that will obliterate humankind off the face of the planet Earth. Little do they know that God has a plan, and that a new millennium is around the corner. When Jesus said in Matthew 24:12 (NKJV), "And the end will come," He was speaking of the end of this present world structure as we know it today, the end of this present dispensation.

Today, we live in a society that is corrupt, sinful, wicked, and full of hatred. Illnesses, diseases, and infestations prevail without cures. People throughout the world go hungry while governments spend millions buying weapons of mass destruction rather than feeding their poor and taking care of them. In other words, this world is in shambles.

What this world needs is a superhero, one who will take charge and do away with all its wickedness and unrighteousness. The book of Revelation shows us such a hero. In chapter 19 verse 11, we see Him coming on a white horse. "And He who sat on him (horse) was called Faithful and True and in His righteousness, He judges and makes war" (NKJV). This superhero is Jesus (Yeshua), for He comes for a second time in history as a conquering Messiah, unlike the first time two thousand years ago, when He came as a suffering Messiah who humbled Himself and was led as a lamb to the slaughter. It was through this suffering that He gave His life as a ransom (1 Timothy 2:6) and bought us, or should I say redeemed us, with His blood.

It is the belief in Christianity that He died, was buried in a tomb, and rose again from the grave after spending three days and three nights in it. This almost sounds incredible to believe, but not for the believer, because the believer has accepted it in faith, and that in itself accounts for righteousness.

Back in Jesus's day, in the days of early Christianity, it was the intention of the Jews to make a mockery of the resurrection, especially when Jesus's disciples ran and hid themselves because they were afraid of the same torture the Romans gave to Jesus. But after witnessing Jesus alive after the three days, which He prophesied, they came out of hiding and shared by witnessing what they experienced. This witnessing began fifty days after the resurrection and ten days after the ascension into heaven by the Lord Jesus, when the Holy Spirit descended upon the disciples during the feast of Pentecost. What the disciples witnessed two thousand years ago is still being witnessed to this day all over the world, for "Jesus Christ is the same yesterday, today and forever" (Hebrews 13:8 NKJV).

Jesus Himself prophesied His death and resurrection when He said, "Destroy this temple and in three days I will raise it up" (John 2:19 NKJV). Many thought He was speaking of Herod's temple, but He was speaking of the temple of His body. He also said, "For as Jonah was three days and three nights in the belly of the great fish, so will the son of man be three days and three nights in the heart of the earth" (Mathew 12:40 NKJV).

These two prophecies, spoken from Jesus's own mouth, were fulfilled to the fullest. He showed himself to His disciples after resurrecting from the grave, and even to five hundred more witnesses according to 1 Corinthians 15:6. It wasn't until His ascension to heaven that the apostles put together Jesus's words to realize just exactly what He was trying to teach them, because Jesus spoke in parables (allegories) that made it hard for them to understand their meaning.

As for His second coming, upon leaving Earth and giving His disciples instructions to preach the gospel to the world, He gave charge to two white robed men, who were probably angels, to prophesy and say, "Men of Galilee, why do you stand gazing up into heaven? This same Jesus who was taken from you into heaven will so come in like manner as you saw Him go into Heaven" (Acts 1:11 NKJV). This verse proves without a doubt that it will be Jesus who will return as Messiah. This is the promise that believers are waiting for. In contrast, the Jews are still waiting for His first arrival.

When you think about it, there isn't much of a difference between Christian and Jew, for they both believe in the same God. They both believe in the Messiah's arrival in the last days. And they both believe in the resurrection, or at least the Orthodox do on the Jewish side. In fact, it was Jews who first believed Jesus as the Son of God and became Christians. Jesus walked with twelve Jews, who became His disciples. They were people like Matthew, a tax collector; Simon Peter, a fisherman; Simon's brother Andrew; John and his brother James; plus seven more. Saul, who persecuted the early Christians, later became the Apostle Paul when he was converted. Many more became disciples of Jesus, who ministered to them for three and a half years. These people were brought up in the Jewish faith, laws, and customs and later accepted the teachings of Jesus. In the latter days, which are now, this same Jesus will become a household name in Jewish homes, and many will accept Him. Praise God for that.

It is the return of Jesus the Messiah who will save Israel from a terrible nightmare in history called the Great Tribulation. Hitler's Holocaust during World War II won't even compare to what they will go through. It will be so bad that they won't have any choice but to call for God's intervention, and God will give them that intervention in the person of Jesus the Messiah. Little does Israel know now that the Messiah they wait for is the same Messiah they rejected two thousand years ago, when they had Him crucified—oops! But, that's okay because that's the way God planned it.

When looking through the Old Testament, one can read many prophecies pointing to Jesus as Messiah. Let's take Psalm 22 for instance. Here, the psalmist, who is David, describes a suffering individual whose bones are out of joint and whose hands and feet are pierced. The individual claims that God has forsaken him. All this, plus more, happened during Jesus's crucifixion. He is the one whose bones were out of joint, whose hands and feet were pierced, and who shouted from the cross, "My God, My God why have You forsaken Me" (Matthew 27:46 NKJV). Even the casting lots for his clothing can be found in the Psalm. It's no wonder most scholars agree that this is a prophetic message written about Christ about one thousand years before it happened.

I'm amazed by some of these prophetic scriptures. Let's take Isaiah 53, where a suffering Messiah is described as being bruised (marred) beyond recognition, totally disfigured, whipped, and led as a lamb to the slaughter. Again, this describes what Jesus endured just hours before the crucifixion, which was prophesied and written approximately 750 years before the fact. Keep in mind that we have a suffering Messiah prophesied on the Old Testament side, and a conquering Messiah on the New Testament side. Both Messiahs are the same person.

It even gets more exciting as we proceed. The Bible is not a science fiction book predicting things of the future. It is a book of truth whose author is God Himself. Scripture tells us that God is the "same yesterday, today and forever" (Hebrew 13:8). He never changes. Whatever He prophesied thousands of years ago still applies today and will still apply tomorrow.

The return of Christ will be the most glorious sight to watch. His feet will touch the Mount of Olives just outside of Jerusalem, causing a split in the mountain that will make a great valley (Zechariah 14) during a time when Israel is fighting for its survival after being invaded by outsiders. It will be Messiah Himself who will put an end to the chaos. He will come with His army of angels and saints (book of Jude) to shorten the tribulation, for if He doesn't, no flesh would be saved. In Matthew 24:22 (NKJV) we read, "And unless those days were shortened, no flesh would be saved; but for the elect's sake, those days will be shortened."

It almost appears that a great war will be going on when the Messiah makes His second debut, for if no flesh would be saved or spared, the implication is that of a thermonuclear war. God help us if that is the case. It was Jesus Himself who said, "But woe to those who are pregnant and to those who are nursing babies in those days" (Matthew 24:19 NKJV). Why would He say that unless He was warning us, and those in Israel, of impending nuclear radiation? That is my thought. I hope I'm wrong, but again I stress that God is in control.

True, the reality of such a war taking place is no shock, for humankind has the destructive devices needed for such a war to take place. Just think, if given the opportunity, what a third world zealous terroristic nation would do given this destructive force. It was for this reason that the George W. Bush administration went after Saddam Hussein in Iraq during the Shock and Awe campaign in 2003.

The last thing the world needs is to be intimidated by some crazy lunatic with nuclear capabilities. I believe the United States did the right thing at the time. Unfortunately, this will not be the only encounter in this century because there are other fanatics who have the same desire in mind—that is, to rule the world. If Iraq had used a nuclear device at the time, there's no telling how much destruction the world would have experienced and suffered.

In the not-too-distant future, more nations will be equipped with such devices, which will cause much world friction and turmoil, thus leading to a catastrophic war that can be defined as the "war to end all wars." The war I'm referring to can be found in the Bible. It is the war that will terminare with the battle of Armageddon. At that time, the Messiah will make His historic reentry to Earth and deliver Israel and the rest of the world from the hands of a demonic world leader, the antichrist.

Upon the Messiah's arrival, He will not be as humble as He was at His first Advent. This time He comes as a conquering Messiah to deal with the forces of unrighteousness, who are Israel's enemies. His brightness alone will crush many who will try to hide from Him, especially the antichrist (beast) who will be ruling the world at this time. Their hiding will be unsuccessful because there's no hiding from God.

The significance of His coming will be to usher in the new millennium and restore the Earth. This new millennium will be a peaceful, one-thousand-year period that will become the seventh dispensation in God's plan of salvation at this time. One can therefore conclude that there will be no end to humankind or the planet, as some had perceived, but rather an end to an ungodly and unrighteous world system that has been around since the fall of Adam and Eve. Intervening in a world that is corrupt, sinful, and full of blasphemers will be the aim of the Messiah as He comes to rescue humankind.

Let's praise the living God of heaven, who will send back His Son for the second time in history. His name is Jesus. Believe in Him, and you shall live. Deny Him, and He will deny you. It's your choice. Praise God!

CHAPTER 5

The Seven Dispensations

By now, you are probably wondering what I mean by dispensation. It is a term used by many theologians depicting God's orderly plan of salvation. By definition, it is a specific plan or order of dispensing, or distributing, in portions. Also known as an economy, it is a divine plan for administering God's affairs; that is, God Himself has set aside certain arrangements or time frames to fulfill His plan. We might even call them eras that, when completed, will purge out all unrighteousness.

You see, God has a plan for humankind. To carry out this plan, He must purge out, or cleanse, all wickedness from the world. Because we're presently in the dispensation called grace (the sixth dispensation), we know that it won't be long before we enter the seventh dispensation. That means the Messiah is virtually at the door and waiting to make His entrance. But before making this entrance, God will plunge the world into its most intense, chaotic, tragic moment yet. The moment I'm speaking of is the Tribulation, which is reserved for the last seven years of this present dispensation. Here, the believers will be tested and then raptured, hopefully before the antichrist's takeover. As for God, We're speaking here of a time in which He will eliminate all evil, unrighteousness, and wickedness, including drunkenness, drugs, nonbelievers, corruption, apostasy, witchcraft, and more. All sin will be dealt with.

Thanks to Satan's deceptive tactics, many will fall during the

Tribulation years, but the elect of God won't because they will be well informed and ready for the trickeries of "That old serpent, called the devil and Satan" (Revelation 12:9 KJV). That is why scripture tells us to be ready at all times with wisdom, understanding, and knowledge. Also, we can put on the full armor of God and beware of anything thrown at us by the great deceiver, Satan (Ephesians 6).

If you recall in your Bible readings, back in Noah's days, Satan managed to deceive all but eight people who entered the Ark. These eight were Noah's family. The result of this deception was death to all but the eight. This was God's plan: to purge the wicked and unrighteous of the time. The remaining eight who survived repopulated Earth.

The seven dispensations we'll be discussing show a progression in God's plan that will lead to and explain why God must purge out the wicked and cleanse the elect. When we look at the book of Revelation, it speaks about the Seven Seals, the Seven Trumpets, and the Seven Bowls (judgments). Each category spells disaster upon humankind, but there is something unique about it, and that is the number seven. With this in mind, we can see that God works in sevens because it represents completeness. If you study your Bible, you can see that seven is used throughout to express God's eschatological framework.

The Tribulation is one of these sevens because it is a seven-year purging event that will climax with the return of the Messiah, Jesus. This return will fulfill God's revelation and open the start of the seventh dispensation, often referred to as the new millennium. Here we'll experience a time of total peace and rest on the planet Earth.

It's taken almost six dispensations to bring us this far in history. The remainder of the sixth will take us right through the Tribulation years. Then the new millennium will be ushered in, and a rest period will be bestowed upon all. This is why an emphasis is made to rest on the seventh (sabbath) day, for that is the way God planned it: work six days and rest on the seventh day. This is His guideline that should be practiced by all.

Presently, we are in the sixth dispensation of God's master plan. It is called the dispensation of grace, which is really a timeout period from law so that the Gentiles and Jews can come into God's kingdom simply by accepting Jesus Christ as Lord and Savior. This timeout period started at the cross when Jesus was crucified at Calvary, and it will continue until the end of the Tribulation, when He returns. The beauty about grace is the fact that not only are Gentiles being saved, but Jews all around the world are also saved. Praise God!

Today, Israel as a nation is not ready to accept Jesus as Messiah. But that doesn't mean they won't, because later on in the Tribulation period, many Jews will accept Him as Messiah, for God will raise an army of 144,000 evangelists, along with two other special witnesses, who will take Israel by storm and witness to the Jewish people the salvation message (we'll study this later).

Let's take a look at these seven dispensations because by now, you're probably wondering what they are. Keep in mind that we've already touched upon the dispensation of grace.

1. Innocence—This is the Adamic dispensation that lasted an unknown number of years. It is the time when God's creation looked perfect in the eyes of God. It was so perfect that He gave Adam dominion over the whole Earth, over every living creature, fish, and fowl. This even included giving names to every creature God created.

The term *innocence*, by definition, means "free from guilt, or harmless." We can therefore say that this dispensation was a time of freedom. Unfortunately, all this freedom came to an abrupt end when the woman Eve took the forbidden fruit from the Tree of Knowledge of Good and Evil and shared it with her husband, Adam, after being deceived by the serpent, who we all know as Satan, the devil.

This act of disobedience took dominion away from Adam and transferred it to Satan, who to this day still has dominion over it. True, Christ's crucifixion defeated Satan's claim, but Jesus the Messiah, after ascending to heaven, has not returned to Earth to take back the claim. He's saving it till the end of this present dispensation.

Please note that upon eating the fruit, Adam and Eve saw their nakedness, which forced God's hand to curse the snake and send it crawling upon its belly (Genesis 3:14). This is when God's purging process for humankind began: by inflicting Adam with punishment, and cursing the ground so that he would have to work all his days (Genesis 3:17). Likewise, God cursed the woman by multiplying her sorrow and her conception. "In pain you shall bring forth children; your desire shall be for your husband, and he shall rule over you" (Genesis 3:16 NKJV).

The inflictions brought about by these curses would have made humans think twice about disobeying God, but it didn't. In time, the rebellion against the Almighty became so intense that God began to rethink and question the creation of humans. This is only because He gave humans the power of choice. Too bad they made the wrong choice. Even today, they continue to make wrong choices. As for Adam and Eve, I perceive they made the right choice to later repent of their wrongdoings.

2. Conscience—This dispensation lasted over sixteen hundred years and was known as a time of unrest. It was unrest in that murder was introduced by Cain, Adam's son. Then the world was plunged into a violent mode. It was this very violence that led God to make a decision on humankind's destiny. His ultimate decision was to purge the world by flooding the Earth, thus destroying it, and starting all over again from scratch.

As we already know from our Bible history, God destroyed the Earth by flooding it and sparing only eight human beings. These eight were Noah and his wife, and his three sons with their three wives. If you recall, two of each unclean animal, and seven of each clean, along with seven of each bird of the air (male and female), were saved along with Noah and his family. This was so the Earth would be repopulated and restored. Unfortunately—and this is the opinion of many scholars—the dinosaurs became extinct at this time.

Again, the purging process became a most powerful tool on God's behalf. Some might ask, "Why did God even bother with creation if He is omniscient? After all, He should have known that His creation would go sour."

This is not so, my friends. God created us in His own image, thus giving us independent choice, or free will, to make up our own minds as to whom we would serve. We could serve Him, and that was His intention from the beginning. Or we could serve the adversary, who is Satan, the one who desired God's throne in heaven. Unfortunately, the world chose the adversary, bringing them closer toward ultimate destruction.

Even though God promised never to flood the Earth again, there will come a time in history when He will utterly destroy it with fire. "The heavens will pass away with a great noise, and the elements will melt with fervent heat; both the Earth and the works that are in it will be burned" (2 Peter 3:10 NKJV). The word *fervent* implies a very hot situation, so hot that any known element will actually melt. It almost makes one wonder why God let humankind invent nuclear toys.

3. Human Government—This dispensation introduces humans to organized government, for it was Nimrod (Genesis 10:8–12) who established the first known government and became the first known world leader. How long did this dispensation last? No one really knows, for the Bible is not specific with this time frame or arrangement. We do know that its climax was at the Tower of Babel (Genesis 11), for it was there where God confused humankind's language.

Confusing humankind's language was God's way of purging, for the one-language society was getting too smart for its own good. What God did here was confuse the language so as to create more languages, which forced people to scatter all over the known world with different ideas and different directions. What got the Almighty so upset was the fact that humans were erecting a tower to reach heaven for the purpose of getting closer to the stars and making a name for themselves. Now, ask yourselves why they wanted to get closer to the stars. Believe it or not, humankind figured that the stars would talk to them and guide them through all endeavors in life. In other words, they wanted the stars to become their gods. Little did they know that the reading of stars would infuriate the true God of heaven, who happens to be a jealous God.

This worship of stars introduced what we now call astrology. Sound familiar? Just pick up your newspaper, or even look on the Internet, to read your daily horoscope of the day. This is what millions do every day when reading the paper or browsing the Internet. They do it out of ignorance, not knowing that they're serving the same gods the Babylonians served in Babel. Reading your daily horoscope can be considered practicing this ancient religion. In Jeremiah 10:2 (TLB) we read, "Don't act like people who make horoscopes and try to read their fate and future in the stars! Don't be frightened by predictions such as theirs, for it is all a pack of lies."

I don't mean to get sidetracked in this dispensational review, but we must emphasize the fact that this religion, which is ancient and occultic, is part of the New Age syndrome that has enveloped the masses of the world and distracted the minds of those who are searching for the truth. Why don't we start our mornings by reading the word of God in the Bible instead of reading the horoscope of the day? When reading the Bible, my motto has always been "A chapter a day, keeps the devil away."

Let's get back to Nimrod. He is credited for building city after city, especially the great city of Nineveh. Remember the story of Jonah in the belly of the great fish? Well, it was Jonah whom God sent to evangelize the people of Nineveh, and they repented of their wrongdoings, thus keeping the Lord from destroying the city. These people knew about the God of Israel. They knew that if God said it, He would do it.

Nimrod represented a "one man, one world" ruler situation, and God saw danger in this type of government, especially because he promoted a one-world religion (astrology). In other words, Nimrod was a dictator. The danger imposed here was one that would lead the whole world away from the true God of heaven. The answer to this threat was to scatter the people all over the world by confusing their one language, thus preserving humankind's will of choice. Eventually, the scattering led to other types of rule, which were more of a family type than a clustered, tribelike rule. This purging process was God's answer which, as time went by, sorted the righteous from the unrighteous.

4. Family Rule—This dispensation dealt with the family type rule, which developed after the confusion of languages. It lasted from Abraham to the time of the exodus of Israel from Egypt.

As we already know, Abraham was the father of two great nations, Israel and the Arabic Muslim nation. We also know that Ishmael, who had twelve sons, led them to become twelve tribes, or in reality twelve nations. Likewise, Israel (or Jacob), whose father was Isaac, also had twelve sons, which eventually became the nation of Israel.

In ruling the family, the rule had to be passed down from one generation to the next. Abram, who was a rich man, passed his rule down to Isaac, who in turn passed it down to Jacob, who eventually passed it down to each of the twelve tribes so as to rule themselves independently as a family clan. Unfortunately, in this dispensation, one might say a family feud developed to create an animosity that has been carried on to this present dispensation (grace), and it will continue until the Messiah's return. The animosity referred to here is the rivalry between two brothers and two nations. The two brothers are Jacob and Esau, both sons of Isaac. The two nations are those who were born of the freewoman Sarah and those who were born of the bondwoman Hagar, Sarah's concubine (Genesis 16).

If you have read the book of Genesis, you can see where Hagar was thrown out by Sarah (Abraham's wife) but still blessed by God, for a great nation was promised to her (Genesis 16). The great nation promised to her was the nation of the Arab Muslim people. In contrast, Sarah conceived Isaac, and Isaac begat Jacob and Esau, who also were blessed with promises of becoming great nations.

Jacob became Israel and had twelve sons who became the nation of Israel. But what about Esau, who displeased his parents by marrying two Hittite women, and who also married his great uncle Ishmael's daughter? Here, he tied in with the bondwoman's seed and defected from the freewoman, which caused a greater animosity between the two brothers. We can therefore say that the animosity portrayed here is between the Jewish nation and its relatives, the Arabs (Muslim nations). In the book of Genesis, we see this breakup of family leading to individual or family rule caused by family feuding. Esau, after losing the blessing to Jacob, became his own ruler under his own domain. Likewise, Jacob did the same. On the other side of the family, Ishmael, born of the bondwoman, raised twelve sons who themselves also became nations with individual rulers of their own domain. It seems that each family became an individual nation with individual family rule instituted by the previous generation, which taught them well. That is how they learned to govern themselves, from Abraham to Isaac and Ishmael, to Esau and Jacob and Ishmael's twelve sons, to Jacobs's twelve sons and Esau's offspring. It was like climbing a stepladder with individual rungs of rulership. Each rung represented its own sovereignty, unlike Nimrod's rulership, which represented a one-ruler situation.

As for Israel, they became God's chosen ones, chosen to carry on the mission of preserving God's word—something Esau couldn't do because he was a freeman of the wilderness who loved to hunt. On the other hand, Jacob was a mild man, dwelling in tents, and tending sheep, which reminds me of David, a type of Jesus who also tended sheep. Even our Lord Jesus, our Shepherd, referred to His disciples and followers as sheep. It was Jacob's descendants (Moses, the prophets, the psalmists, etc.) who carried and preserved the Word of God.

5. Law—This is the dispensation where law is introduced. It was instituted for the purpose of giving humans guidelines by which to live. Why? Because of their transgressions (sins) against the Almighty. It started after the exodus of Israel from Egypt (note that Israel was in captivity for 430 years by Egypt) and lasted until the crucifixion of Christ Jesus.

It was the Ten Commandments, handed to Moses at Mt. Sinai, that initiated the law. This law came directly from God and was given to the Israelites by Moses. Ironically, Israel wasn't ready to follow any laws, because while Moses was up on the mountain conversing with the Lord, the Israelites were busy building a golden calf to serve as a worshipping idol. What ensued afterward was God's wrath upon the camp after sending His servant Moses back to it. After separating out those unrighteous ones responsible for leading the flock astray, as punishment, God killed 250 people responsible for the rebellion. As for the rest of the camp, God withheld their reward for the promised land for forty years, thus using a form of negative reinforcement as the purging tool.

Did they learn from their punishment? Maybe, but as the forty years progressed, there wasn't much excitement going on at the camp except for complaints that Moses had to endure and deal with. As a result, all but a few (except the offspring) died in the wilderness and never got a chance to cross the Jordan River to the promised land. Even Moses was not allowed to cross it, and he died in the plains of Moab. This dispensation continued with many laws being enacted, but it ended at the time of Jesus's crucifixion when the veil of the temple was torn in two, thus signifying an interruption of law in the dispensation and the initiation of the next dispensation, which was grace.

6. Grace—This new dispensation is our current one and will last through the Tribulation years, then the new millennium will come into view. Grace is where salvation is presented to humankind in gift form—in other words, free of charge. All humans have to do is accept the fact that Jesus died for them on the cross, was buried, and on the third day rose (resurrected) from the grave. Accepting this message and surrendering one's heart to Christ with the acknowledgment that Jesus is the Son of God will quicken one's spirit (born-again concept) and make one a member of God's kingdom.

The dispensation of grace, as I mentioned before is a timeout period that will terminate at the end of the Tribulation. It is during this Tribulation time that the Jews in Israel will reestablish the sacrificial rituals that were used during the law dispensation. To do this, the temple will have to be rebuilt, either before or during the Tribulation. Let's get one thing straight here: it's not grace that will terminate. It's the dispensation of grace.

As compared to the other dispensations, this one has an advantage in that both Jews and Gentiles can be saved and enter the kingdom of God together. True, this was not in agreement with the Jews during the establishment of the church in Jerusalem, and arguments erupted over this issue. But the apostle Paul set the record straight, for he taught the doctrine of "salvation through grace, not by works." It was he who brought the Gentiles into Christianity and reprimanded the newly converted Jew for not accepting the Gentiles into the newfound faith. He taught that grace is a gift from God for all, not just the Jew. He also taught that circumcision wasn't necessary, for it represented works. His doctrine of "salvation by grace and not by works" offended many of the Jews, thus causing many scandals that led to a division in the church even at its onset. Even the apostle Peter questioned Paul's message at first. Later on, Christianity would be divided even further by breaking up into denominations, and for good reasons. You see, just as God confused the language at Babel to discourage a one-ruler situation that would eliminate choice, He did it to the Church to prevent a one-doctrine situation, which was already marred with false teachings that would dominate as the only philosophy. That is why there are so many denominations today, and some are true to the Word of God, but others are not. Those that are not are those who have compromised with past pagan religions so as to bring about a flock into their church buildings. Unfortunately for these, God will make them suffer one way or another. When reading the letters to the churches in Revelation 2 and 3, one can see why certain churches failed: they did things their own way rather than God's way.

Today, many don't understand what salvation is, and they ask, "What are we being saved from? After all, life is pretty comfortable. Why bother with God and religion?" Let me tell you, friends, God has a plan for all of us. To be included in this plan, we must believe and have faith, because without it, we'll be counted in along with the wicked. You see, God created us to be His companions and friends. This was His intention right from the beginning when He created Adam and Eve. Had they remained perfect, this world would be perfect. But because of the fall, due to their disobedience to God, Satan, who is the devil, took over this world, and still controls it. That makes him the god of this world.

Now, ask what you'll be saved from, for in God's wrath, all nonbelievers will have to experience damnation and be sent to a place where they do not want to go: hell (lake of fire). I don't know about you, but I don't want to experience God's wrath. So let's get with it, take advantage of this dispensation called grace, and make a commitment to turn to the Lord.

These six dispensations that have been touched upon—and I mean just touched upon, for so much more can be said about them—have taken a great deal of work on God's part. Today, we are still in this dispensation called grace, and a great deal of work is still needed for the accomplishment of God's work of salvation.

Jesus said in Matthew 24:14 that this gospel message has to be taken all over the world, and then the end will come. To accomplish this feat, humans have invented tools of communication such as TV, radio, and the Internet. Other means have come in the form of books, tracts, churches, and even door-to-door witnessing. The truth of the matter is the message is getting across and being relayed all over the world with the exception of some nations known as 1040 nations, but in time these nations will tumble. That is why we know that the end is just around the corner, for the Lord Himself has prophesied this message: "Then the end will come." Let's keep it in prayer so that doors will open for the opportunity to propagate the gospel Message.

7. The New Millennium—When God created the universe and all things, including humans, He rested on the seventh day. This was an illustration to show humans that they too must rest on the seventh day, or the Sabbath. Once initiated, during Law, the Sabbath was set aside as a day of worship. God's number of completeness is seven, so we must discern the millennium (seventh dispensation) to also be a time of rest, peace, praise, and worship because God Himself in the person of Jesus (Messiah) will be here on Earth with us. By this time, all wickedness and unrighteousness will have been purged out. This is God's ultimate plan of salvation for the believer, for it is a gift of God to the saints (us) and those who have endured the Tribulation. Enduring the Tribulation means survival. It also means becoming born again during this time, for this is the ultimate means for survival and entering the kingdom of God.

If you remember back in chapter 2, I mentioned this born-again concept. Let me elaborate on it now. To be born again, one's spirit must be quickened, or made alive again. We're all born with dormant spirits because of the inheritance of sin going all the way back to Adam and

Eve. The concept includes believing in the one who sacrificed Himself for us for the purpose of removing our sin. In other words, He died for your sins by His crucifixion on a cross. But guess what? After three days in a tomb, He resurrected, thus defeating death. Believe it and accept the fact that He's God's Son, and you'll have a new life and a relationship with the Lord. The Holy Spirit will reside in you, and you'll have a direct line, or connection, to God Himself through His Son, Jesus Christ. That means that you and I and every believer can communicate one-on-one with God through the Holy Spirit. With that in mind, our faith in God will increase. Jesus is the one who said, "Most assuredly, I say to you, unless one is born-again, he cannot see the kingdom of God" (John 3:3 NKJV). The kingdom of God, or the Earth, is the inheritance that Jesus will claim upon His arrival, as well as the inheritance that He will share with His family of believers.

Once this inheritance is claimed by Jesus the Messiah (Christ), the world as we know it will be totally changed, and the new millennium will begin. This, my friends, is the seventh dispensation, for which all believers are waiting. It will be a time of total peace and rest, as well as a blessed time for those mentioned by Jesus in the Sermon on the Mount in Matthew 5: "Blessed are the poor in spirit, blessed are the meek."

This is a time, as prophesied by the prophet Isaiah, when "the wolf shall dwell with the lamb, the leopard shall lie down with the young goat, the calf and the young lion and the fatling together; and a little child shall lead them. The cow and the bear shall graze; their young ones shall lie down together; and the lion shall eat straw like the ox. The nursing child shall play by the cobra's hole, and the weaned child shall put his hand in the viper's den"(Isaiah 11:6–8 NKJV).

Just imagine having lions graze in your backyards like the deer, or watching your small child play with a grizzly bear. What would you do today? Shoot them to protect your young ones? You probably would, but God has assured us by the prophecies that harm will not come during this time because a transformation will take place, even among the wild beasts. They will all be tamed as household pets, and humans again will have dominion over them just as Adam had in the Garden of Eden.

We can also be assured that the weapons of destruction will be done away with during this time. Again the prophet Isaiah prophesies, "They shall beat their swords into plowshares and their spears into pruning hooks, nation shall not lift up sword against nation, neither shall they learn war anymore" (Isaiah 2:4 NKJV). In other words, there will be no more need for weapons because humans will repent of war. The Lord will make sure of that.

When looking at Joel 3:10, we see just the inverse, or opposite, of Isaiah 2:4. In Joel 3:10, we read of strategies of war and weaponry as men "beat their plowshares into swords, and pruning hooks into spears." This is the scenario of previous dispensations, whereas in the new millennium, there is no need for weaponry.

When mass-producing weapons, one must consider the expense involved in its production. True, some countries like the United States have to produce these weapons solely for the purpose of defense and preserving peace through what we term as a balance of power. They can also argue that it brings about jobs for thousands of workers. But in reality, it can also bring death to countless thousands, if not millions, if war was to break out. Take the United States and Russia for instance. They both have a nuclear arsenal that can destroy the planet over and over again, leaving no human alive—and this is precisely where the world is heading. That's why we need a Savior who will stop this incoming destruction.

In the new millennium, alignments of nations will be nonexistent, weapons will become nonexistent, and war will be nonexistent. This will cause a shift in world economics. The funds used to beat plowshares into weapons will now have to be used for the advancement of human needs, especially the rebuilding of homes, buildings, offices, and food markets, because all these things will be destroyed due to war all over the world. The Messiah, who is Lord Jesus, will be in the midst of it all. And all said amen to that.

I can't imagine where nations such as Iraq and Iran would be today if they had taken their defense (or offense) money and pumped it into their economies to feed and clothe their people and to build housing for them instead of concentrating on nukes. The same thought goes to the former Soviet Union, China, and the Far Eastern countries. Look at North Korea. Where has their economic concentration gone?

Iraq had a GNP of fifty billion dollars per year prior to the Desert

Storm campaign, during which Saddam Hussein used a large bulk of it to build his military just as the USSR did. Now ask yourselves, What profit did it serve him? None? You're right, because the United States and its allies demolished over 50 percent of his arsenal in forty-two days. This included 80 percent of his five thousand tanks. A tank is not a cheap piece of machinery. The cost of one can feed and clothe several families for a lifetime.

Jesus said, "For what will profit a man if he gains the whole world and loses his own soul, or what will a man give in exchange for his soul?" (Mark 8:36–37 NKJV). I often wondered during Operations Desert Storm and Shock and Awe why Mr. Hussein was so willing to kill off his country's population just to gain the exalted respect he desired. His ultimate aim was to become the greatest leader the Arab World has ever known. I don't believe God let him get that far, because he never achieved that goal.

What we saw during the Desert Storm and Shock and Awe campaigns, we'll see again sooner than later. Time is running out, and the Messiah is waiting for His grand reappearance so He can introduce the seventh dispensation, which is peace. The sixth dispensation will be leaving us soon, but not until we experience the Tribulation, or at least part of it for the believers (we'll discuss this later). This will be a time when God will pour out his wrath upon unsaved humankind. Once complete, the Messiah will usher in the millennium. Let's be ready for it. Praise God!

CHAPTER 6

The War of Ezekiel 38–39, Part One

By looking at specific prophecies in the Bible, one can see events that have already occurred, events that are presently happening, and events that will yet occur at a future time. In this chapter, we'll be concerned with a major event that has yet to occur. This major event is a war that will be fought in Israel and will involve practically the whole world. I'm referring to a war described by the prophet Ezekiel written approximately six hundred years before Christ in the book of Ezekiel, in chapters 38 and 39. It is often referred to as the War of Ezekiel 38–39.

When we look back to the Persian Gulf crises (1991 and 2003), in which the United States and its allies had to intervene in Kuwait and later in Iraq, we saw that a major strategy on Saddam Hussein's part was to mobilize Arab Muslim nations against Israel. He wanted this to guarantee himself a victory and become a hero among the Arab people. Fortunately, the Arab people did not go along with it, or else World War III would have become a reality.

Still, had Israel broken its restraints during Operation Desert Storm and attacked Iraq, Saddam's tactics might have worked. But thanks to US insistence, Israel restrained itself and left the allies to fight the war. It was the Scud missile attacks on Israel that enraged the United States and its allies to the point where continuous bombardment of Iraq and Iraqi positions in Kuwait were necessary to repel Iraq's aggression and bring the war to an end. It took six weeks of this pounding before the allies were able to advance with ground troops, but to their surprise, the Iraqis were not willing to fight any further, for they were tired and hungry, exhausted from sleepless nights caused from the bombardments, and humiliated from all the lice crawling on them. In other words, surrender was a relief.

As in Germany during World War II, the allies were surprised at the unnecessary destruction of war that was inflicted upon Kuwait by the Iraqis. Hundreds of oil wells were set on fire. Hundreds if not thousands of Kuwaitis were beaten, tortured, and dragged into captivity. Many women were raped. It was even rumored that Iraqi soldiers entered hospitals to kill infants, an ancient practice to keep the next generation from seeking revenge.

The scenario depicted in Kuwait seemed like one that will prophetically occur in Israel during the end-time when the Tribulation is in full force. It is Jesus who reminds us today (Matthew 24:19–21) about the times and what tactics (nuclear war?) the enemy will use when war breaks out in Israel and the Middle East, for it seems that Iraq has already demonstrated that truth in the present day by going after the infants. When looking at Zechariah 14:2 (NKJV), we see signs of what happened in Kuwait City. "The city shall be taken, the houses rifled, and the women ravished." True, the city spoken of here is Jerusalem in the future, but note the similar pattern of events: "Half the city shall go into captivity, but the remnant of the people shall not be cut off from the city."

Can it be foreseeable that the Lord is preparing us to witness these events now so as not to be shocked later when they occur in Jerusalem? One must wonder. One might even contend that Zechariah's prophecy occurred in AD 70 when Rome invaded and destroyed Jerusalem. But if you recall, that was a complete destruction, for it sent the Jews into captivity for 1,900 years, Therefore, this prophecy (Zechariah 14:2) cannot be referring to the Jerusalem of AD 70, for the remnant of the people were cut off, whereas in Kuwait City the remnants of the people were not cut off; only forty thousand were taken into captivity and led to Iraq. Had Saddam desired it, his army would have destroyed Kuwait

City right down to its last inhabitant, for they came to kill, steal, and destroy as a roaring lion ready to devour its prey. But thanks to the rapid deployment of America and its allied troops, the advance was halted.

In Ezekiel chapters 38 and 39, we read of a futuristic time when Israel will be attacked by outsiders who will trample Jerusalem. This happens during a time when Israel is dwelling safely with unwalled villages—in other words, at a time when Israel thinks they are at peace. Let's keep in mind that in biblical times, cities were surrounded by walls as protection against outside intruders. With today's modern technological weaponry, it would be senseless to put up walls as a defensive measure. But literal walls is not what the prophet meant, for in his own terminology, he was describing a situation by which Israel would feel completely safe from harm and therefore lower its protective shields, or defenses. I can see that happening because of peace talks. Sooner or later, something has to give in so peace in Israel can be achieved. But the peace achieved will be a false peace, for once this situation exists where countries like Israel and others will lower their defenses due to talks of peace and peace treaties, then all hell will break loose. You can count on it.

First Thessalonians 5:3 warns us of this very situation: "For when they say 'peace and safety'! then sudden destruction comes upon them as labor pains upon a pregnant woman" (NKJV). Sudden destruction implies just that, and the implication here is that of a surprise attack that will leave Israel totally defenseless or unable to immediately fight back. Such was the plight of the United States when attacked by the Japanese at Pearl Harbor in 1941.

The prophecies revealed in Ezekiel 38–39 are mind-boggling, for they name the nations that will be involved in this great war. They name the bad guys, and they name the good guys who will help Israel out. They even let you know in advance who will win and lose. Of course God is the primary winner, but He will still set the motion for the involvement of many nations. The motion I'm talking about has already begun with the Persian wars I described in previous chapters. This is what excites me, for I can utter these same prophecies to anyone and know for a fact that I'm 100 percent right, because the true Word of God says so.

Watching these prophecies come to pass will be the true test of the prophet Ezekiel. Not that we're doubting him, for he has proven himself already, especially with his prophecy in chapter 37 about the "Valley of Dry Bones," which represents Israel's rebirth. Only the Almighty could have revealed this to him. Therefore because it came to pass as uttered, Ezekiel must be a true prophet.

In Ezekiel 38:2–3 (NKJV), we read, "Son of man, set your face against Gog, of the land of magog, the prince of Rosh, Meshech and Tubal and prophesy against him, and say 'thus says the Lord God: Behold, I am against you, o Gog, the prince of Rosh, Meshech and Tubal.'"

Gog, from what most scholars believe, is a futuristic evil leader whose main ambition is to destroy Israel. His home is in the land of Magog located to the extreme far north of Israel. According to the prophecy, and according to scholars, it has been concluded that Rosh and Tubal are both linked to the former USSR, which lies to the extreme north of Israel. Ezekiel 39:2 (NKJV) verifies Gog's northern location when God speaks to Gog through His prophet Ezekiel and says, "And I will turn you around and lead you on, bringing you up from the far north, and bring you against the mountains of Israel." Most Bible scholars believe this far north refers to the uttermost distant north, which points to Russia itself. Some even think this northerner is Turkey, but it doesn't quite qualify to be at the uttermost north.

It is also believed that Russia derived its name from Rosh, and Tobolsk, a region in Russia, is from Tubal. These tribes, along with Meshech and other nomadic tribes, are apparently the Scythians of Scythia, which is the name given to this northern territory in Ezekiel's time. These Scythians, who resided in what is called Siberia (Russia), scattered and settled in northern Turkey, Iran, and southern Russia and are apparently the northerners spoken of by the prophet. They are also briefly mentioned on the New Testament side in the book of Colossians (3:11).

To further analyze this location, set your eyes on a world map and pinpoint Israel. Now look to the uttermost north of that location and see what lies there, for it is Russia, or the former Soviet Union. For those who say that Ezekiel wrote his prophecies from Babylon (Iraq), Russia is still to the extreme north of that location.

Up to this point, we have stressed Russia as the culprit, but what about the rest of the breakaway republics of the former Soviet Union? Aren't they still armed with weapons of mass destruction? One must take into view the fact that they are still located north of Israel and are heavily populated with Muslims. With this in mind, who is to say that Russia is Magog? But do these breakaway republics fit the location of the extreme north?

It's no secret that Jews and Muslims repel each other like the same poles of a magnet. Aligning the breakaway republics to make war with Israel would therefore be of no surprise. Israel's real threat has always been the former Soviets with its heavy Muslim influence. In contrast, Middle East Muslim countries, even though a threat, have proven not to be as real a threat only because Israel outweighs them in military superiority, at least for the present. And let's not forget Israel's big brother who is always ready and able to help them out: the United States.

In previous wars, Israel has shown its military superiority. I'm referring to the 1967 and 1973 campaigns, as well as other skirmishes in Lebanon and with the Palestinians. If it had not been for the allied forces restraining them during Operation Desert Storm, I'm sure Israel would have taken the challenge to take on Iraq, because they admitted after the war that they had a plan to enter Iraq with troops, tanks, and planes had the need occurred. Also, let's not forget that Israel is supposedly equipped with nukes, which I'm sure they would use if their backs were against the wall.

Other nations to the north of Israel that might become a threat would be Syria and Turkey. When looking at Syria, one must realize this nation has been Israel's adversary since biblical times. It was as recent as 1967 that these two nations fought, with Israel getting the upper hand. It was in this war that Israel took the Golan Heights area, an area that has caused much friction between the two ever since.

Turkey, which sits to the north of Israel, is a member of NATO at time of this writing. Just how long this membership will last, God only knows, because this country, or at least part of it, will be aligned with Magog according to Ezekiel's prophecy. How do we know this? Let's read: "Gomer and all its troops, the house of Togarmah from the far north and all its troops—many people are with you" (Ezekiel 38:6 NKJV).

From what most scholars can gather, Togarmah is northern Turkey, or even Armenia (southern Russia), because they border each other. Believe it or not, Gomer might be Germany (the Eastern European Germanic tribe). It almost sounds preposterous that Germany, which is now unified with East Germany, will conspire along with other nations to plan an evil plot against Israel. But that is what the Bible is showing us. Just remember where Germany stands today, for at the time of this writing, they are still a member of NATO and the European Union (EU). A few years back, one might have thought this Gomer to be East Germany, but with unification, this state is now nonexistent. What is it, then, about Germany's alliance with Magog? What will they gain from it?

If you recall, back during the Desert Storm campaign, Germany did not want to contribute any troops but was very boisterous in defending Turkey when Russian troops massed at her border. This ordeal drew much attention from other NATO members who were busy with the Desert Storm campaign. Luckily, the Russians restrained themselves, for if they had not, Armageddon might have become a greater reality at the time.

Now, ask yourselves, "Was God's hand in this?" Sure it was, for the Russians had their greatest opportunity then to take advantage of the situation in the Middle East and use it for a distraction to do their own damage in Turkey and beyond. Thank God it failed. I believe that God made sure that the Russians were busy also with their own internal troubles at the time. If you recall, Russia and the former Soviets were tied up with revolution at home. Six months later, a coup attempt, which failed, brought Boris Yeltsin into the picture, only to force Gorbachev to resign months later. Presently (2021), Vladimir Putin is president of Russia.

Why the discussion of Germany and Russia? Because they play a big role in Ezekiel's war. Germany will align itself with Russia. Others will follow, such as Turkey and nations of the former Soviet Union. If you look at history, it's no mystery that alignment of nations goes back thousands of years, even as far back as the book of Genesis. They form and break up. Let's take the Warsaw Pact as an example, for they broke up thanks to the failure of communism. If the Warsaw Pact dissolved itself, what is to stop NATO from doing the same? After all, isn't there a "New World Order" in the works. Can it then seem awkward that Germany and Turkey will break away from NATO? Not so, for the Bible has already prophesied that Germany (Gomer) and Turkey (Togarmah), along with other nations of Muslim descent, will align themselves with Magog for the purpose of invading Israel. Who are these other nations? Ezekiel 38:5 (NKJV) calls them by their names: "Persia, Ethiopia, and Libya are with them with shield and helmet."

Libya (northern Africa) is by no means a friendly nation, so that is no surprise. Persia is Iran and Iraq combined—again, no friend of Israel. Ethiopia (northern Africa), with its Marxist government (at time of writing), constant revolutionary turmoil, and Muslim influence, will come out of the woodwork and aid in the invasion. Keep in mind that borders in Ezekiel's time were different than today's borders. In all probability, they were much larger, thus allowing room in the prophecy for other northern African nations to be called Ethiopia or Libya. After all, most of northern Africa is of Muslim descent.

So far we've named Persia (Iran and Iraq), Libya and Ethiopia (African nations), Gomer (Germanic tribes), Togarmah (northern Turkey with southern Russia), and Magog (Russia?) as the ones coming against Israel. Now, listen to what God has in store for them and their leader, Gog. According to Ezekiel 38:4–7 (TLB), God says to Magog, through His prophet, "I will put hooks into your jaws and pull you to your doom. I will mobilize your troops and armored cavalry, and make you a mighty host, all fully armed. Peras [Persia], Cush [Ethiopia], and Put [Libya] shall join you too with all their weaponry, so shall Gomer [Germanic] and all his hordes [former Warsaw Pact nations?], and the armies of Togarmah [Turkey] from the distant north, as well as many others. Be prepared! Stay mobilized. You are leader, Gog!"

Putting hooks into Gog's mouth and dragging him into Israel shows us that Gog has no freewill intention of invading Israel. But God has other plans, for He will force an issue that will make Gog want to invade Israel whether he wants to or not. You see, God wants Gog in His arena. There, He will judge and destroy him and his armies.

Now, if Magog is Russia, one has to consider the fact that they have been suppliers of arms to most of Israel's and America's enemies for years. They have also murdered millions throughout their communist history. They have persecuted countless Jews in the former Soviet Union. And they have supported all Muslim and Arab causes against Israel. What I'm trying to say here is that God has a score to settle with the hard-liners of the former communist system, even if communism doesn't exist anymore. The damage has been done, and someone has to pay for it. It's judgment time for the bad guys. To attack Israel is to attack God Himself. That is why God calls upon Israel's enemies to come into His courtyard so as to deal with them there in His own terms. Once there, the Almighty will be glorified, for He will do the impossible and show the world that He is God.

Most scholars have joined the bandwagon in concluding that Russia is this Magog spoken of in the Old Testament book of Ezekiel. With all that the Russians (communist hardliners) have contributed in terrorizing this planet in the twentieth century, many would have to agree with these scholars. Even I am more than partially convinced that Russia (old Soviet Union) is Magog.

Communism, which has taken somewhat of a downfall, is or was considered a religion by those who practiced it only because it was implied that the state was worshipped in place of the true God of the Bible. Because the practice represented an abomination to God, its downfall to the believer was more than satisfying. It was justified because since 1917, the Russians had been practitioners of this religion. Spreading it faithfully all over the planet was their goal thanks to the writings of their mentors, Karl Marx and Friedrich Engels. With this anti-God philosophy in mind, and the fact that the former Russian empire (Soviet Union) and modern-day Russia is heavily populated with Muslims, one must adhere to the theory that present-day Russia will someday subdue or overwhelm the Jewish state of Israel after taking sides with Islamic nations that promote vengeance and the annihilation of Israel.

Consider the fact that there is too much against Russia with its communist background, which I'm sure is still alive and well, to simply let her go unpunished. As I mentioned before, for years they have supplied arms to most of the Islamic nations who stand against Israel and America. They supplied arms to Iraq during the Persian wars. It was their Soviet-made tanks that the allies destroyed during both campaigns. It was their Soviet-made war machines that the Israelis destroyed in the 1967 campaign against Jordan and Syria. It was Soviet-made equipment and supplies that were destroyed by Israel in the Yom Kippur War of 1973 when Egypt, under the leadership of Anwar Sadat, attacked and almost pushed the Israelis out to sea. Finally, it was massive Soviet arms that were discovered and confiscated from a cave in Lebanon after Israel invaded it in the early 1980s—enough arms to supply an army of over a hundred thousand.

These are but a few of Russia's divisive tactics against God's children. There are other countless atrocities that have occurred behind the Iron curtain that will never be revealed to humankind. Only God knows the minds of men that can do such harm, but in His purging process, all things will be revealed and dealt with. Look at Hitler's Germany. Was it not revealed how they exterminated six million people, mostly Jews, during World War II? It is rumored that Stalin was as brutal in Russia as Hitler was in Germany. Hitler thought by killing himself, he could escape what was coming to him. I don't think so. He might have escaped the Nuremberg trials after World War II, but he won't escape the trial set for all humankind when the second resurrection takes place at the very end (Revelation 20:5–15) of the millennium.

It almost seems like in the past sixty years, God has spared the Russians from destroying themselves and others. For instance, during the Cuban missile crisis of 1962, God spared them by having their navy turn back to avoid a confrontation with the US navy, thus averting a war with America. In 1973, again they were spared in that their minds were changed from entering the Yom Kippur War in Israel when the tide changed in Israel's favor. This change in mind was due to President Nixon's DEFCON order to arm the nuclear warheads when he learned of the Soviets' mobilization. Had there been a confrontation, only God knows whether Armageddon would have taken place that year. It's my opinion that God was waiting for the perfect opportunity to give Magog and his hordes a farewell party, and that's why He spared them the humiliation of defeat then.

In Ezekiel 38–39, the Russians will not back down. This time God will allow them to take the stand. It might be an alliance commitment that might make them attack, or it might just be greed for the spoils of war. No matter the reason, God will put hooks in their jaws and pull them down into Israel's territory to destroy them. In making a quick move, Gog and his hordes will surround Israel from all sides. From the north will come Magog and Togarmah (Russia and Turkey); from the south will come Libya and Ethiopia; from the east will come Persia (Iran and Iraq); and from the west will come Gomer and his troops (Germany and Eastern Bloc nations). Can you imagine what will go through Israel's mind? Will little David slay Goliath again, or will they need a superhero to intervene for them?

This is what God says through His prophet: "You will ascend, coming like a cloud, you and all your troops and many people with you" (Ezekiel 38:9 NKJV). The way Ezekiel describes the invasion, it almost appears that poor little Israel won't have time to react. The wars of 1967 and 1973 will seem like child's play compared to this one, for an enormous army will descend and surround them. But remember that God is still in control. He has his own plan at work.

Now, one has to ask oneself, What does Israel have to offer that a nation, or nations, should devise an evil plan against it? Could it be oil? Could it still be the Palestinian issue of acquiring more land? Could it be Jerusalem itself? Could it be their food supply because God blessed Israel with a land flowing with milk and honey? Or can it just be jealousy on the part of the Arab and Muslim people? If you said yes to all of the above, you're probably right. All we know from scripture is what God has to say to Gog from Magog: "On that day it shall come to pass that thoughts will arise in your mind, and you will make an evil plan" (Ezekiel 38:10 NKJV). I wonder who put these thoughts in Gog's head.

We've already focused on the Palestinian issue. And we already know the importance of Jerusalem. But what about oil, mineral resources, and other potential spoils of war? Israel isn't known for its enormous quantities of oil, but it does have oil. Several pipelines from the Port of Eilat on the southern tip (Gulf of Aqaba) extend as far as Haifa, supplying millions of tons of oil for domestic use, and also to Ashqelon for exporting.

The Dead Sea, the sight of the five biblical destroyed cities including Sodom and Gomorrah, is another gold mine loaded with all kinds of minerals that are, or will be, of great value in the aerospace industry (of which the Russians are a premier member) due mainly to its low density (two-thirds of aluminum). The highest quality magnesium in the world can also be found in the Dead Sea. Magnesium alloys are also used in aircraft, missiles, spacecraft, machinery, automobiles, and household appliances. This is just an example of what Israel has to offer an invader such as Magog. Other minerals include potash, bromine, and copper ore.

Food is another commodity an invader might have use for, especially for an invader that for years has been unable to supply its people with adequate supplies. Because of Israel's irrigation systems due to scarcity of water, they have been able to adequately supply themselves with food such as citrus fruits, peanuts, and sugar beets. Another food is fish. Fishing is also big, with the Mediterranean and Red Sea coasts supplying a limited quantity, but with trawlers traveling to the Ethiopian coast to rich fishing waters in the Atlantic, it makes up for the losses.

Another interest that an invader might have is the fact that militarily speaking, Israel is strategically located on the map, with three continents (Asia, Africa, Europe) on its sides. There are two major waterways: the Mediterranean Sea, and the Red Sea leading to the Indian ocean. With the immense size of the Russian navy, controlling these waterways would be a great military advantage. True, the Suez Canal is on the Egyptian side, but once in Israel, who is to say that a large invading force would leave Egypt untouched? After all, Egypt did side with the allied forces during the Desert Storm campaign. Not only that, but Egypt signed a peace treaty with Israel during the Carter administration in 1979. Two years later, Egypt's president, Anwar Sadat, was assassinated by his own people. Unfortunately, this incident goes to prove that any attempt toward a peaceful solution in the Middle East will always end up in shambles because of the animosity factor between Muslim and Jew. Therefore, once the Russians get to the Middle East, they intend to stay there. Or so they think.

Now, whether Egypt will take sides during Ezekiel's war or remains neutral is yet to be observed, for Ezekiel does not mention Egypt at all in these two chapters. But with the Desert Storm (1991) and Shock and Awe (2003) scenarios, one can almost visualize who will side with whom during this war. And that's keeping in mind the fact that some of the Muslim nations that sided with the Allies will defect and join the goat nations. I'm mainly referring to nations like Syria and Turkey, who were active in aiding the allies during Desert Storm but not during Shock and Awe. Let's also keep in mind that for years, Syria has been more than anxious to regain the Golan Heights area, which has been under Israeli dominance since 1967.

As we already know, Egypt did not defect during the Desert Storm campaign. As a reward, America forgave their debt, which amounted to billions of dollars. In contrast, America's promise on loan guarantees to Israel was greatly delayed due to political maneuvering. With this in mind, one must wonder just how far Western nations will go to preserve peace—or should we say, preserve their dollar interests. True, paying a dollar value for peace might be less expensive on the economic side, but God has a different plan. He will allow war only to show the world that He is in control of its destiny.

The war he allows has nations like Magog (probably Russia), Gomer (Germany), Togarmah (Turkey), Ethiopia (northern Africa), Persia (Iran and Iraq), and Libya as the enemy who will pounce on Israel. Now, let's look at those whom the Lord will send to rescue Israel and at the same time magnify His power and presence to show the world that there is a God in heaven. Let's not forget His name, for it is "Wonderful, Counselor, Mighty God, Everlasting Father, Prince of Peace" (Isaiah 9:6).

CHAPTER 7

The War of Ezekiel 38–39, Part Two

Watch what doom the Lord has in store for Magog and his hordes, for He plans to send a rescue mission to Israel. Those who will come are Sheba and Dedan, as mentioned in Ezekiel 38:13. Let's read: "Sheba, Dedan, the merchants of Tarshish, and all their young lions will say to you, 'Have you come to take plunder?'" (NKJV). First of all, let's identify Sheba and Dedan. Then we'll tackle Tarshish and his cubs. Who is Sheba and Dedan? In Ezekiel 27:15, we read about Dedan being a trader with Tyre, a merchant city of Phoenicia, which was located in present-day Lebanon. Dedan would bring ivory tusks and ebony as payment for their trade, and Sheba, mentioned in verse 22, would bring the choicest spices as payment for their trade.

We know from scripture that Sheba and Dedan are directly descended from Cush, Noah's grandson, who is also mentioned in Ezekiel 38 as Ethiopia along with Put, his brother, who is Libya. If you want to get technical about it, we can throw in Canaan, another brother who was cursed and was overrun by the Philistines and then by Israel. This might give us a general idea as to the location of Sheba and Dedan, for we know that Libya and Ethiopia are located in the northern part of Africa; and Canaan, in what is now Israel. We can therefore discern that Sheba and Dedan are located nearby—as nearby as the Arabian Peninsula—for this is what many scholars believe.

If you look at a map of the Middle East, you'll see that the Arabian Peninsula is made up of nations like: Kuwait, Saudi Arabia (which takes up most of the peninsula), Qatar, United Arab Emirates, Oman, and Yemen. The two eye-catchers here are Kuwait and Saudi Arabia. Why is this? If you recall, it was these two nations that America and its allies stuck their necks out for during Desert Storm. It rescued Kuwait from the Iraqis and prevented Saudi Arabia from becoming the next invasion victim. I'm sure these two countries were filled with gratitude and appreciation for what the allies did for them. Let's keep this in mind.

It is believed these Arabian and Middle-Eastern people are the same who brought ivory tusks, ebony, and spices into Tyre (Lebanon) for trade. It makes sense because access was easy for these Arab tribes to go to and from Africa, which is located right next door to the peninsula, to pick up their merchandise and transport it to their northern neighbors. As for the ebony, a trip across the Arabian Sea to India or southern Asia again made access easy.

Regarding the choicest spices, today spices are still being exported from Arabian nations, thus proving the authenticity of the Bible. It just happens that frankincense was its main trading commodity, for it was in great demand for medicine, incense, and ritual purposes. If you recall from the New Testament gospel readings, it was frankincense that was given to the baby Jesus as one of the gifts from the Magi of the east.

With this information in mind, one can conclude that Saudi Arabia and Kuwait are part of (if not actually) the Sheba and Dedan mentioned in Ezekiel's prophecy. Together, with the merchants of Tarshish and its young lions (cubs), they will align themselves to fight off an aggressor who has come to invade Israel—the same scenario as when Iraq invaded Kuwait and threatened to do the same to Saudi Arabia, but with a greater army this time. In all probability, Sheba and Dedan will play a big role in the rescue effort that will be led—and I'm only speculating here—by America again.

When the time comes, Kuwait and Saudi Arabia (Sheba and Dedan) will remember that Saddam Hussein of Iraq almost annexed them, but thanks to the United States and its allies, who interceded in their behalf, they were not, even though Saddam claimed annexation. I believe it was through the help of the Almighty that the allies were able to repel Iraq from Kuwait with ease. God wanted a dress rehearsal or a tune-up here before the real thing. Let's remember the "destroying wind" has not finished its job yet. There is a second part to his story; not the Shock and Awe of 2003 but the Ezekiel 38–39 War campaign.

Now, who is Tarshish, its merchants, and the young lions? First let's identify Tarshish. Also known as Tartessus, Tarshish was a commerce culture center with merchant ships, and it traded with many coastland nations along the Atlantic European and Africa coasts. Most scholars believe this commerce center was located in southern Spain by the Strait of Gibraltar as part of the Phoenician economic empire.

Tartessus had its own king, and secular history records that Arganthonios, a famous Tarshish king, died during the Battle of Alatia around AD 540. Tarshish is also mentioned in the Bible books of Psalms, Isaiah, Jonah, Jeremiah, and of course Ezekiel. This shows just how important this shipping network was, because it lasted approximately from King David's time (1000 BC) through Ezekiel's time (622–570 BC) according to the Bible's timetable, as well as into the sixth century AD according to secular history.

Its main commodities were metals, especially tin, copper, and iron. The ships of Tarshish would travel up and down the Atlantic coast looking for these metals and other commodities. Some scholars believe that some of these Phoenician Tarshish ships might have made it across the Atlantic and into North America, for there is speculation that artifacts have been found on the North American continent. Now, whether Tarshish artifacts have been found on North American soil, I can't say, but we know for a fact that they made it into Great Britain because artifacts from Tarshish have shown up in England. It was during this time period in Britain that small migrations came because of Britain's knowledge of iron and other metals. This time period is known as the Iron Age, which followed the Bronze Age (during which weapons and implements were made of bronze, which is an alloy of tin and copper). "The Phoenicians are believed to have played an important role in the spreading of the early bronze culture by their trade in tin, which their ships brought to the eastern Mediterranean from Great Britain and Spain as early as 1100 BC.

These merchants from Great Britain and Spain traded their commodities with merchants of Tarshish, or merchants from the Middle East, who acted as middlemen and transported all these goods all over the European coastlands, therefore providing a so-called Mercantile system of that day. In order for this Mercantile system to work, merchants would be needed—that is, one who would buy and sell his commodities for a profit. In Ezekiel 38:13, we read of the merchants of Tarshish" who will challenge Magog. These merchants are the merchants who did business with Tarshish. These are merchants such as Great Britain, Spain, and probably France and Italy. These were very dependent on Tarshish's merchant marine to transport their commodities. These same merchants, who did battle in Iraq during the two Persian wars, will again do battle during the Ezekiel 38–39 War. And because we know that Tarshish doesn't exist anymore, we know that it won't participate in the war, but we know from scripture that its merchants will.

By studying secular history, we already know that Great Britain was one of Tarshish's primary merchants because of its metals. Also, if you look at a map of Europe, you'll notice that the coast nations are Spain, the United Kingdom, the Netherlands, Belgium, and Portugal. These apparently were the nations or merchants that did business with Tarshish. Sound familiar? Here we are naming some of the member nations of NATO. If you're familiar with this organization of allied nations, you're probably asking why the United States and Canada have not been mentioned. Let's read part of Ezekiel 38:13 (NKJV) again: "Sheba and Dedan, the merchants of Tarshish and all their young lions will say to you ..." These nations are challenging Magog and his hordes after they attack Israel. They are the Arabian Peninsula nations—Sheba and Dedan (Kuwait and Saudi Arabia), the merchants of Tarshish (European Western nations), and their young lions (cubs), whom I will identify shortly.

To identify these young lions, let's go back to our elementary school history when we were studying the New World and exploration—that is, when European coastland nations such as, England, Spain, Holland, France, and Portugal were sending out explorers to seek out new frontiers and an easier water routes to the Far East. Europe was becoming a big commerce trading entity, so it was necessary to look for ways to expand their mercantile system. Reaching the Far East and finding the quickest way was their ultimate goal. But in their travels by sea, they stumbled into places like North, Central, and South America; the Caribbeans; South Africa; New Zealand; and many more places. These landmarks all became colonies of the European nations that were at one time Tarshish's merchants.

For those interested in heraldry, the symbol of the lion was emphasized on many European emblems, thus depicting themselves as lions, and their colonies as young lions. The British royalty emphasized these lions even on the coronation chair. In fact, some speculate that Queen Elizabeth herself is a descendant of King David, who represented the tribe of Judah (Lion), and that's why the lions are there. With this fact in mind, can we be so bold as to speculate that the young lions of Ezekiel 38:13 are descendants of ancient Israel? That is a point worth considering, especially when meditating on Jesus's words: "I was not sent except to the lost sheep of the house of Israel" (Matthew 15:24 NKJV). These colonies that became great nations, such as the United States, Canada, Australia, New Zealand, and others, are apparently the young lions of Ezekiel's prophecy. Now, ask yourself if America is mentioned in the Bible. In my opinion, it is. This makes America and Canada, along with other lion nations, participants in the War of Ezekiel 38–39.

If you recall from the Persian Gulf War (Desert Storm), the United States led the charge with the United Kingdom and other European nations following. If America remains as the number one superpower during Ezekiel's war—and I doubt it—it will again lead the charge to free Israel from its aggressors just as it did with Kuwait during Desert Storm. If for some reason America is not the superpower of the times, then another lion nation will take that lead. In all probability, it will be a European nation whose oil supply has been threatened, for again, oil might just play a big role in this war. This might just be arranged by God Himself, who is still in control of all things. Praise Him forever and ever!

Now, what about the Atlantic coast nations of Africa? Aren't these also former merchants of Tarshish? To answer this question, one must look at today's map of Africa, which is not the same map of 2,700 years ago during Ezekiel's time. Africa has been carved up many times, with new nations emerging and old ones folding. European nations, unlike African nations, have remained basically the same—that is, nations that traded with Tarshish. The only exception of African nations remaining the same are Egypt, Libya, and Ethiopia; even though their boundaries might have changed, their tribes have remained the same.

Africa's Atlantic coast nations have traded names and governments for hundreds of years. These nations are unstable and constantly fight the forces of Marxism and communism. They also have the forces of Mother Nature to contend with in the forms of drought, plagues, and famine. With this in mind, we can eliminate them from the Ezekiel scenario of war in the Middle East.

We already know that Ethiopia and Libya will fight alongside Magog against Israel. Egypt is a question mark, but like Saudi Arabia and Kuwait (Sheba and Dedan), if it decides to side with the Allied forces, rewards shall be reaped. But woe to those nations who go against Israel during this dark and gloomy time, for the Lord says, "It shall be in that day that I will seek to destroy all the nations that come against Jerusalem" (Zechariah 12:9 NKJV). God's warning in this passage is very explicit. Those nations going up against God's will, by siding with Magog and his hordes, will have to deal with God's wrath—and believe me, God will not be very nice about it.

It will be a combined effort from both Arab Muslim nations and the Western allies that will ask Gog, "Have you come to take plunder?" Wasn't this the same question posed in Iraq when it invaded Kuwait in 1990? As one may recall, Western nations didn't hesitate to take it to the United Nations and come up with resolution after resolution condemning Iraq's aggression. Finally, force was used to repel the aggressor out of Kuwait.

When Magog and his hordes, along with Muslim nations, attack Israel, I believe similar resolutions will be drawn against them, but with less response because many enemy nations will be member nations and therefore have veto power. Finally, without the aid of the United Nations, the forces described in Ezekiel 38 will take action against Magog. This combined effort will put the new world order, an organized police action, into war action against Magog and its hordes, therefore testing its authenticity. But stand by, because if this war is Armageddon, then Messiah is on His way. Either way, it will be God Himself leading the charge to save Jerusalem and His people just as He did in the Desert Storm and Shock and Awe campaigns. And let's not forget the 1967 Six-Day War and the 1973 Yom Kippur War, where the United States was instructed to help the Israelis. This has been the theme throughout the Old Testament, where God has rescued Israel time and time again. But after its rescue, Israel, in its complacency, has always fallen or taken a backward turn in disobedience; it is almost like a dog returning to its vomit, or like riding on a merry-go-round..

In an interview with David Frost, a TV show host back in the 1990s, General Schwartzkopf, commander of the Desert Storm forces, was asked if he thought God had a hand in the campaign, His reply was yes. He said, and I'm only paraphrasing, "After seeing all the planes arrived back safely without hardly any casualties, and seeing the minimal war dead, yes! The hand of God had to be in it." As the interview progressed, the audience got to know the godly side of the general.

As far as God having His hand on the Desert Storm campaign, I must agree with the general because never had I seen the spirit of the Lord move the country as it did with this forty-two-day war. People were turning to God everywhere. People were asking questions concerning the end of the world. *Armageddon* became a household word, and curiosity for Bible prophecy became a reality and a pastime—at least it did with me.

Scholars of prophecy such as Hal Lindsey were being questioned by leading national news magazines. Churches were packed with people, as they were also during 9/11, praying for God to intervene for family, relatives, and friends who were in the midst of the storm. The national spirit of patriotism was awakened, and everywhere the words "Support the Troops" were seen. The American flag with yellow ribbons became the nation's number one symbol. Even Nostradamus, a so-called prophet of the sixteenth century, became a household phenomenon.

The nation was scared about not knowing what Saddam had up his sleeve. Had a nuclear device appeared at the scene and been used against the allies, there's no telling what might have occurred. Saddam did say he wanted to force the "Battle of Armageddon." He called it the mother of all battles. Unfortunately, to his disgrace it turned out to be the mother of all retreats, with Iraqi soldiers surrendering by the thousands. This was so in the Shock and Awe campaign in 2003, where the Iraqis were forced to retreat, and it became more of a guerilla type of warfare. Unfortunately for Saddam, he was captured, sentenced by his own people, and executed.

During the Desert Storm campaign, I couldn't help but admire President H. W. Bush because he called the American people to pray for peace. He even spent the first day of the war with evangelist Billy Graham at the White House. After ordering the ground offensive, he was seen going to church with his vice president and several cabinet members. Not only did he encourage people to turn to God, but he himself served as an example. It was this show of courage and humility that moved the hand of God, for many followed the president's advice and example.

Not since World War II had this nation turned to God in the way it did during the Persian wars of 1991 and 2003. Just think how much more of a concern people will have when nations rise against nations in the Ezekiel 38–39 campaign, for in this campaign, the hand of God will move again, and a spiritual revival will follow. God will get the world's attention here and show His magnificence and glory. What will ensue here will be even greater than the parting of the Red Sea, for the world as a whole will witness it. Unfortunately, it takes a situation of great magnitude to move the hearts of humans. That was the plight of the Israelis in biblical times with its ups and downs with God, but God always showed them that He was in control. He also showed His love, faithfulness, and goodness toward them. But like little Johnny, as I mentioned in a previous chapter, little David too has to be reprimanded and punished at times. It all falls under God's purging process.

In that day of the war, humans will know what fear is and to whom it is due. Scripture tells us not to fear those who can kill the body, but to fear Him who can kill both body and soul in hell (Matthew 10:28). In Ezekiel 38:18–19 (NKJV), God shows His wrath against Magog and his hordes, but will they fear? Let's see: "And it will come to pass at the same time, when Gog comes against the land of Israel, says the Lord God, 'That my fury will show in my face. For in my jealousy and in the fire of my wrath I have spoken: Surely in that day there shall be a great earthquake in the land of Israel.'"

Imagine the fear factor involved here that will grip people's hearts on that day, for the prophecy continues to describe their shaking from fear at the mere presence of the Lord. They will hide in caves, shelters, and mountains. Even bunkers, such as were seen in Desert Storm and World War II, will not protect them, for God's illumination will penetrate through steel walls.

The prophecy on the judgment of Magog continues as follows: "So the fish in the sea, the birds of the heavens, the beasts of the field, all creeping things that creep on the earth, and all men who are on the face of the Earth shall shake at my presence, The mountains shall be thrown down, the steep places shall fall, and every wall shall fall to the ground" (Ezekiel 38:20 NKJV). It gives me the shivers just thinking about it. It almost sounds like the persistent bombing that took place in Iraq, for in that war, the grounds shook day and night, and had it not been for the humane side of it, even the walls of every dwelling would have touched the ground. Such was the plight of London, then later German cities, and finally Hiroshima and Nagasaki during World War II. But this is God Himself who will do all this damage. The former wars will seem like child's play compared to God's intervention in this war, for in His wrath, the whole eastern hemisphere will shake simultaneously because of His presence. Wow!, If you don't believe this by now, it's time you did because believing is your only chance for salvation.

Finally, God says, "I will call for a sword against Gog throughout all my mountains, every man's sword will be against his brother. And I will bring him to judgment with pestilence and bloodshed; I will rain down on him, on his troops, and on many peoples who are with him, flooding rain, great hailstones, fire and brimstone" (Ezekiel 38:21–22 NKJV). This is where the good guys come in—the allies and Israel itself. This is the sword that He calls against Gog and his hordes.

What God has in mind here appears to be nuclear warfare. That's my opinion. I don't believe He gave us these weapons of mass destruction in vain. He first issued them to His righteous nation, America, for He knew whom He could trust. Putting these weapons in the hands of the enemy would have meant disaster during World War II, but that was not the case. When you look at today's enemies with these weapons of mass destruction, It almost makes you wonder why God allows it, but again, let's remember who is in control. God is in control. There is a reason why the enemies of society have acquired these weapons. If God allows them to use these weapons, it's because of judgment on His part. How many times in the Old Testament did God send judgment to Israel every time they disrespected Him, especially when they served and worshipped idols? What God did was inflict pain so as to chastise His children. Today, Israel is a very prosperous nation in the upswing of things.

There is another reason why God would allow the weapons of destruction to reach the hands of the enemy. That is so it can backfire on them. An example of this can be found in the book of Samuel, chapter 5. Here, the Philistines took the Ark of the Covenant away from Israel after Israel lost a battle. This tool, which represented God's presence and contained the Ten Commandments, brought about victory after victory for Israel during battles. But when carried away by the Philistines, it brought them nothing but catastrophes, for it was used for unrighteous purposes. The end result was the ridding of the ark. They couldn't do it quickly enough. They had to give it back with a gift, for by doing so, it brought peace to the Philistine cities.

I'm not saying the Ark of the Covenant was a tool of destruction, but if used incorrectly and by the wrong hands, it could have been as deadly as a weapon. That's what the Philistines ran into. It almost reminds me of the movie *Raiders of the Lost Ark*. When the Ark was found, it got into the wrong hands: German Nazis and an evil French anthropologist. When the Nazis, who were eager to use its powers against the Allies, opened the Ark, a destroying angel appeared at the scene and consumed even the flesh of the evil-minded. True, this was only a fictional flick, but the reality of such an occurrence cannot be undermined. The producers and writers of this movie were almost on the right track. In the Bible, only the priestly tribe of Levi were allowed to touch the Ark; anyone else touching it would automatically be killed by God. I've always wondered how the Philistines got away carrying it. (The answer: very, very carefully.)

The falling of fire and brimstone, great hailstones, and rain has many scholars believing the possibility of a nuclear war. Whether the weapons of destruction will backfire and haunt Magog, or whether the allies and Israel, will nuke Magog, is a controlled situation that will be directed by God Himself.

When reading these passages, one must keep in mind that the prophecy was written five hundred years before Christ, at the time of Israel's captivity by Babylon. One must also understand the terminology used by Ezekiel, for the word *nuclear* wasn't even in their vocabulary. Therefore when breaking down Ezekiel's terminology, we already know what fire is and what destruction it can cause. But when adding brimstone to it, by definition we have a burning stone, or sulfur, which burns with a suffocating odor belonging to the oxygen family and is very reactive when mixed with potassium nitrate and charcoal. What we have here is black powder (gun powder) unheard of in Ezekiel's time, for it wasn't invented until the ninth century AD in China.

Some scholars believe that a thermonuclear war will erupt and that hailstones mixed with fire and brimstone describes such warfare. In Revelation 16:21, it speaks of hailstones the size of talents, weighing anywhere from fifty to one hundred pounds, falling from the sky on humankind. Can you imagine these rocks falling on you? It's no wonder they'll hide in caves. A thermonuclear blast will generate such intense heat that it will cause everything within its range to dissolve. It is said that the Hiroshima bomb's blast alone generated a temperature of ten million degrees Fahrenheit, or the equivalence of the sun's surface temperature. Can you imagine what damage a hydrogen bomb, which is hotter, can do?

In Zechariah 14:12 (NKJV) we read, "And this will be the plague with which the Lord will strike all the people who fought against Jerusalem: Their flesh shall dissolve while they stand on their feet, their eyes shall dissolve in their sockets, and their tongues shall dissolve in their mouths."

Can anyone imagine the scenery of this mass destruction? With this frightening passage in mind, just think of the intensity of heat and the quickness of this destruction, where a human will be standing and won't even have time to react or take shelter, and without blinking an eye, the person will be dissolved, melted, or pulverized. (Later on, we'll look at more evidence of a possible nuclear holocaust. But keep in mind this verse is a warning to those who come against Jerusalem or Israel.) If this holocaust is to take place, then we'll know why God gave humans such weapons of mass destruction. Because God is in control, He will induce the proper time of this massive destruction to do away with Israel's enemies once in for all. I'm thankful that America has remained a faithful and strong ally of Israel, for I hate to see America destroyed. But then again, God will also deal with the unrighteous ones in America unless they repent of all their sinful agendas. Such was the plight in Nineveh in the book of Jonah. Here, they repented, including their leadership, and thus God recanted his intentions of destroying the city.

Back in 1973, when Sadat of Egypt decided to attack Israel and draw the Arab world to war, the United States came to Israel's aid in the form of a massive airlift of military hardware. Thanks to that airlift, the Israelis were able to repel the Arab forces out of Israel. Again during the Desert Storm campaign, the United States protected Israel and kept it from entering the war. If this friendship continues because America has vowed to protect Israel, then God will save America from mass destruction during this time of doom and gloom. That is my opinion because those coming against Israel will be destroyed.

There is strong evidence that the United States will be saved during this time only because it is believed that America is one of the young lions in the prophecy. In contrast, Magog and its hordes will be destroyed. They will suffer a loss of 85 percent of their armed forces in the mountains of Israel. Some Bibles have translated it this way, whereas others translate it as a five-sixths destruction factor. Yet others might imply a one-sixth survival rate from the mass destruction. Any way you look at it, the death rate will be a staggering figure. Let's just take Tyndale's Living Bible's translation for instance: "I stand against you Gog, leader of Meshech and Tubal. I will turn you and drive you toward the mountains of Israel, bring you from the distant north. And I will destroy eighty five percent of your army in the mountain. I will knock your weapons from your hands and leave you helpless. You and all your vast armies will die upon the mountains. I will give you to the vultures and the wild animals to devour you. You will never reach the cities" (Ezekiel 39:1–5 TLB).

The reality of such a destruction taking place, where whole armies are being destroyed, is mind-boggling but can be taken seriously, especially with what we witnessed in Iraq during two Persian war campaigns where the reality of the "Battle of Armageddon" came into view. Thank God that it didn't yet occur, but it will happen sooner than we think.

Finally, in Ezekiel 39, Magog and his hordes are buried in Israel—a burial that will take seven months to complete. After the seven months, special search parties will mark the remaining skeletal remains for burial so other specialists can do the actual burials. Apparently, my thought is that a nuke or some form of biological war has taken place, leaving room for special precautions, for there will still be radioactive and biological contaminated debris left over after seven months of cleanup. Therefore anyone handling a radioactive or biological contaminated body part must wear special gear.

Another cleanup crew the Lord will prepare includes the birds and the beasts of the fields. In Ezekiel 39:17 (NKJV) He says, "And as for you, son of man, thus says the Lord God, 'speak to every sort of bird, and to every beast of the field' assemble yourselves and come; gather together from all sides to my sacrificial meal ... That you may eat flesh and drink blood." Verse 18 states, "You shall eat the flesh of the mighty, Drink blood of the princes of the earth."

It seems to me that because these animals will gorge themselves with flesh, blood, and fat, they too will become contaminated and probably die. Or maybe God will supernaturally cleanse them and spare them. After all, they might be needed for another mission later on. I'm referring to the battle of Armageddon in the book of Revelation—that is, if Ezekiel 38–39 is not this battle. In Revelation 19:21 (NKJV), at the coming of the Messiah (Jesus) we read, "And the rest were killed with the sword which proceeded from the mouth of Him who sat on the horse. And all the birds were filled with their flesh," and so the cleanup is accomplished.

In concluding this chapter, one must ask, Why does it get this far? After all, what is this new world order all about? Isn't it to prevent such catastrophes? The animosity built up against Israel will not cease until the coming of the Messiah. No world order will ever control this situation. It can try, but it will fail. The Bible tells us so.

It almost seems that the United States is the only world order at the present time (2020–21). Later on, we'll see another order rising with evil intentions to take over the world (in a later chapter). With the present order and its police actions, many catastrophes have been or tried to be averted. One can only recall that back in 1973–74, the Arab world revolted against America and Western nations with an oil embargo that was instituted to punish these nations, especially America. The idea was to deprive America of almost 50 percent of its imported oil. This led to enormous lines of cars waiting at the gas pumps. It also served as an excuse for oil companies to raise prices and keep them raised after the embargo was over. This led to double-digit inflation, which caused an economic recession.

This all came about due to America's aid to Israel. Little did the Arab nations know that the United States was trying to maintain a balance of power on the conventional side to avert the Battle of Armageddon. Aiding Israel didn't mean that the United States had an alliance with it, for Israel has never had an alliance with anyone, including America. True, America has contributed billions of dollars in aid throughout the years, and this is due to a good relationship and a strong Judeo-Christian influence in America. At the moment, Israel is a non-NATO ally that strategically faces three continents. That's an advantage to America if war broke out again. It's no wonder why Magog wants control of this region.

For years, the United States has been sandwiched between the Arab Muslims and the Jews. Though it tends to lean toward the Jewish state, it will not enter into a military alliance with it because it doesn't want to offend its Arab friends. Both Arab and Jew will get unedged if America was to officially side with one or the other. To solve this, America has supplied military arms to both sides, thus maintaining the peace at home with Israel's friends and keeping the oil flowing for its military, heating, and gas needs.

America is Israel's big brother no matter how you look at it, and it has always been there whenever Israel has called for help. During the Desert Storm campaign, America had Saudi Arabia side with it only because it was Saddam's next target, and also to help free Kuwait. But, at the same time, it had its eye on Israel, protecting and policing it from the enemy and restraining it from entering the war.

As in the Desert Storm campaign, both Western and Mid-Eastern nations will play a big role in rescuing Israel from its most grievous hour. That means putting, as President H. W. Bush called it, the new world order into perspective via an accredited United Nations, as in 1991. President Bush used this terminology when speaking about solidarity of nations against aggression and the seeking of peaceful solutions toward peace. The test of this new world order came during the 1991 campaign, when more than forty nations of the world participated in it. It was not that all these nations entered the physical fight, but they were still instrumental one way or another. Praise God for their cooperation.

This new world order came about right after World War I, when the League of Nations started it in 1920 in Geneva, Switzerland. It was President Woodrow Wilson who called for it at the time, because he had a vision for world peace and a way to prevent aggression. Ironically, America did not want to become a member then. Nineteen years later, Hitler invaded Poland to officially start World War II. Guess what? The League of Nations failed its mission to avert the catastrophe that followed for the next seven years, where seventy-five million lives were lost, including the holocaust, which took more than six million lives.

Some scholars believe this new world order (NWO) will become the ultimate formation of nations that will rule the world under a villainous ruler known as the antichrist. Only time will tell whether the NWO is the empire that most fear as the end-time empire of the Bible. Some look at Europe as this end-time menace, especially because they unified to become the European Union (EU). But let's be realistic: Why would prosperous economic powers want to attack Israel so the antichrist can take a seat in God's temple? (We'll discuss this later).

The Bible is the true Word of God, The prophecies in this book are not fairy tales. The war that awaits Israel in Ezekiel 38–39 will happen sooner or later. Take note that some of the prophecies I've used in this chapter may apply to the Battle of Armageddon. There are many similarities that can apply to both wars, as we'll see in the next chapter. Again, please don't hesitate to acknowledge its truth, for its reality will hopefully make a true believer out of you. Make Jesus your Lord and Savior today. He said, "I am the way, the truth, and the life. No one comes to the Father except through me" (John 14:6 NKJV).

CHAPTER 8

Perplexities of Nations and Two End-Time Wars

Historically and prophetically speaking, the Bible has been authenticated through archeology and scientific research. Many stories that were once thought of as myth have now been proven otherwise. For example, scientists have come to the conclusion that both man and woman have come from one common parent, thus focusing on the biblical truth of Adam and Eve (Genesis).

The War of Ezekiel 38–39 and the Battle of Armageddon (found in Revelation) are two biblical truths that have yet to occur and be authenticated. But with Middle East tensions and problems progressing the way they have been, who can deny these truths from occurring? Authenticating them would therefore be no problem, for it is the Word of God, and therefore it will come to pass. Now, a question comes to mind as to whether these two prophetic events can be segregated or be considered the same event.

Many Bible students have struggled with this very question for years. Some argue that Ezekiel 38–39 and Armageddon are the same occurrence, whereas others say they are not. Soon it will all fall in place, for scripture has it known that knowledge shall increase as we approach the end of the dispensation (Daniel 12:4). With this increased knowledge, thanks to the computer (Internet) and easy access to reading material, God's people will bear down and sort out the passages needed for certain subjects such as prophecy, which will lead to a more definite conclusion as to where this world is heading. This same knowledge also applies to the technology presently flooding the world in all phases.

If you study your Bibles carefully and compare scripture with other scriptures, you'll see that both Ezekiel 38–39 and Armageddon take place in Israel, occur in the end-time, have God's intervention, have enormous armies, and have an enormous casualty count. Just the mere mention of Armageddon scares many because they see it as the end of the world. In their lack of knowledge, they can't see that after the Messiah's return, they still have at least one thousand more years on this planet—that is, if they are in Christ, or born-again believers. Even if they have fallen asleep (died), they still have the promise of the first resurrection when Jesus returns to rapture the Church. The second resurrection comes later at the end of the millennium.

Revelation 16:16 mentions a place called Armageddon in Hebrew. Its location is in Megiddo, a valley located just north of the city of Haifa in Israel, which has been the setting of many battles in the Old Testament. Here, the forces of unrighteousness (Satan) will clash with the forces of righteousness (God). It will be the very last battle humans will ever fight, for after this battle, they will not know war anymore. Once this war or battle, takes place, many will be asking questions such as, Why did it happen? How did we ever let it get this far? What events led to it? Was it just God's doing? As we progress with this chapter and book, we'll try to answer these questions and more.

Unlike Ezekiel 38–39, the prophecy concerning Armageddon shows where the kings of the East will be involved in this conflict. In speaking about the River Euphrates, Revelation 16:12 (NKJV) mentions where "its waters was dried up, so that the way of the kings from the East might be prepared." For those of you who do not know where the River Euphrates is located, it is located in the heart of Iraq. It extends from the Persian Gulf through Iraq, through Syria, and into Turkey. Back in 1991 during Desert Storm, this river became very popular overnight to the Western world.

When visualizing the kings coming from the east of the Euphrates, one must look at a map to see what nation or nations are located in that region. By observation, one can see part of Iraq and the whole nation of Iran. But are these nations really a threat to Israel at the present? They may be troublemakers maybe, but they are too small in population to bring about an Armageddon scenario totaling two hundred million warriors (Revelation 9:16). That leaves us with the rest of the Eastern kings to contend with. And what other kings are east of the Euphrates if not the Asian kings?

Let's take a look at that map again. With nations like China, India, Pakistan, Afghanistan, and the rest of Indo-China, an army of two hundred million isn't hard to imagine. In fact, China alone could easily raise such an army, for its population exceeds the 1.5 billion mark, which accounts to about 18 percent of the world's population. India isn't too far behind with 1.4 billion according to the 2020 census. I believe that China has boasted in the past about having no trouble raising an army of two hundred million. I'm not saying that this army of two hundred million will be Chinese, or even of Asian descent, but it makes sense to speculate where such numbers can come from, for it would be an easy task for an alliance of Far East nations to come up with such numbers.

Regardless of which nations are involved in the battle of Armageddon, one-third of humankind will be killed (Revelation 9:18) by three plagues, fire, smoke, and brimstone, as stated in most translations of the Bible. On a planet with almost eight billion people in it, one-third translates to over 2.6 billion people. And that's just from this war, excluding the countless billions that will be killed because of judgments that will be levied on by the Lord Himself to the unsaved.

When comparing the Battle of Armageddon with Ezekiel 38–39, one can see that Armageddon will be fought in the plains of Megiddo, whereas 85 percent of Magog's army will be destroyed in the mountains of Israel (Ezekiel 39:2). Also, when looking at Ezekiel's war, one can see a confederacy of northern nations coming against Israel. Along with these nations, we see southern ones (Libya and Ethiopia). The only nations coming from the east in this scenario are Iran and Iraq (Persia), which can't possibly raise an army of two hundred million. Even if they incorporated every single man, woman, and child, they still can't raise such an army at this time. Therefore we have to look to the Far East to come up with such numbers.

The truth of the matter is we don't have all the facts as to whether these two occurrences (Ezekiel's war and Armageddon) take place at the same time. We do know they take place just prior to Messiah's return to Earth, therefore putting both wars within or before the Tribulation's time frame. We do know that the Battle of Armageddon will definitely be fought in the latter part of the Tribulation. But to definitely conclude that they're both the same occurrences requires much study on the part of the Bible student.

The two-hundred-million-man army of Revelation 9:16 is an army whose numbers are literal. This is what I believe, especially when looking to the Far East and witnessing an uncontrollable population explosion that has become so eminent, along with diminishing food supplies, that one must conclude these nations, in their quest to find answers, will get very restless, thus making war their prerogative and only alternative.

History shows that when governments get into trouble with their population, an easy way out is to start a war. This enables the population to become more nationalistic and regroup as a whole rather than go into civil unrest and oust the government. A classic example of this is Hitler's Nazi government just prior to World War II. Hitler was very successful in rousing Germany's nationalism when their economy faltered. He simply blamed the Jews by accusing them of taking away people's jobs, thus blaming them for the economic woes. Sound familiar? Look at immigration in America.

Unfortunately, by making the Jews their scapegoat, persecution ultimately abounded, thus creating a holocaust of great magnitude. Meanwhile, Hitler made war with all of Europe and America. The Soviet Union, in contrast, averted a civil war simply by giving in to its republic's demands of independence, thus breaking up the union in 1991. By doing this, the government was preserved, though not communist anymore, and a new confederacy of nations emerged with Russia as its head. The result of the breakup completed communism's downfall and destroyed its goal for world domination. But has war really been averted?

Let's ask ourselves a question. If Ezekiel 38–39 is a separate war from Armageddon, why wasn't there a lesson learned from Ezekiel's war? After all, another war of this magnitude would surely devastate the planet and kill off its population. With this in mind, let's assume for a moment that Ezekiel's war is this war described in the book of Revelation. Then let's look at why a nation would bring itself into this conflict.

As I've been stressing, God is in control. You see, just as He will put hooks in Magog's jaws to draw him into Israel's arena, so will He stir things up in the political scene to bring about a situation that will bring the world closer to an Armageddon scenario. It is He who has planned this from the beginning of time. It all started in the Garden of Eden in peace. Then the adversary came into the picture to steal away this peace. After many centuries of war, turmoil, and sin, God sent His only begotten Son to clean up the sin part of it. Jesus did this by defeating Satan at the cross, but the world remained in Satan's hand only because God wanted to give humankind a period to repent. Once this period, or dispensation of grace, is over, then the Lord will claim peace again. Satan will have to relinquish the kingdom and pay the price for his crimes.

Now, let's use Russia as an example. Assuming that Russia is Magog, what situations will God be throwing at them? First of all, let's look at Russia's present status in this world. We already know about the Soviet Union's breakup in 1991, and we know that it's been suffering an almost economic collapse for years since the breakup; though better now, it is still struggling. Its currency, the ruble, has dropped 50 percent in value this decade (2010–21). Thirteen percent of its population live in poverty, which is blamed on Western sanctions. The average monthly wage is $670 based on 2020 stats. They're very dependent on their oil and gas, which makes up 59 percent of their exports. With all this, they are still regarded as a superpower only because of their military might and nuclear arsenal.

Let's not forget that during the Khrushchev years in Russia (1960s), he swore in the United Nations that the Russians would bury the Americans someday. It was shortly afterward that the Soviet Union started their enormous arms buildup that has carried to this very day. It seemed for years that with the more money they borrowed from the West, the greater their arms buildup became. Did it ever occur to anyone why they wanted this buildup? Was it to conquer the world, or were they simply afraid of a Western takeover? The funny part of it is that they have nothing the West would want. Maybe their oil supply? Maybe their metal ores? Nowadays, some Western nations, like the United Kingdom and the United States, are becoming self-sufficient when it comes to oil and gas.

Unfortunately, without Western trade and aid, Russia will continue to struggle. Having sanctions against them doesn't help either. So where do they go from here? Will the formula shift to war with the former Soviets? Apparently, taking a lesson from history to preserve their sovereignty might be their only solution. Again, even though they might not want war, God will punish them anyway by drawing them to war, whether it be Ezekiel's war or the Battle of Armageddon. These same problems, or perplexities, could easily apply to any nation east of the Euphrates River, thus paving the way to Armageddon.

Let me ask a question here. What advantage would drive any nation into a conflict that for decades has existed between Arab Muslims and Jews? We know that the righteous sheep nations are there because the Lord has called them, but, what about the unrighteous goat nations that God has drawn into the conflict? Could it be possible that they are there to reap rewards or spoils of war? It would seem so. After all, some of these Middle Eastern nations want Jerusalem so bad, because of their religiosity, that they would even sell their birthright just as Esau did with Jacob, thus even driving the nations of the world into their conflict—and that's just what will happen. Even the antichrist will want Jerusalem for the purpose of sitting in the seat reserved for the Messiah.

The real issue here, as far as the Russians, Chinese, or others are concerned, is to become independently self-sufficient, and therefore they jump at the opportunity to get a piece of the rock, which in this case might be oil or a strategic place on the map. It might serve as a trading chip and lead to economic stability in the long run for them. Also, by gaining an upper hand with oil, they can perk up their economies, thus raising their GNP and standard of living, which they covet from oil-rich and Western nations. They might even, in their pride, look for world recognition and respectability now that they have conquered it all. My answer to all this is, "Stop!" and "No!". Stop looking for something that was never meant to be. And no, it will never happen because only God will determine the winners and losers of it all. I can surely tell you right now that only God will be that winner. It's His prophecy, not humans'. Humans cannot change God's truth.

Because history seems to repeat itself, Ezekiel's war and Armageddon are inevitable. The scriptures (God's Word) have announced, or let's say prophesied, these events. The students of the Word already know who will be involved in these wars and through analyzing current events and changes taking place on the planet, they discern approximately when these wars will take place. Jesus and the apostles gave us hints in the gospels and the epistles about these times. So how can we deny these catastrophes from happening on our planet?

The Word of God prepares us for such prophetic events. Knowing what's going to happen in the future without the help of a crystal ball can be very advantageous, because it can save our lives, if not our souls, from damnation. I can personally recall, from the Desert Storm and Shock and Awe campaigns, how many people were scared and frightened at the idea that the world might come to an end because of a possible nuclear war. When asked about this possibility, I assured many that these campaigns were not leading to the Battle of Armageddon even though Mr. Saddam pressed the issue at the time. By knowing my Bible, I was confident that these campaigns were going to be short-lived, because many events were still absent from the real thing. What's more, the alignment of nations was not right on the enemy's side. My biggest surprise of all was the casualty count on the allied side. It was very minimal, which led me to believe that God's hand was there to protect the allied troops. America as a whole turned to God for the safe and quick return of our troops.

Does God answer prayers? You bet He does. Not only did God answer America's prayer for victory and a safe return of troops, but He also answered Israel in that it was spared casualties, except for a few heart attacks here and there because of missile attacks. It almost seemed as if God had placed a defensive line of angels to block and thwart any missiles aimed at population centers.

As amazing as it may seem, Iraq, with its massive weapons supplied by the USSR, could not gain any ground or cause any serious damage to Israel during the Desert Storm campaign. In fact, Israel has never suffered a defeat by Soviet weapons of war, because Israel has always had the more sophisticated weapons thanks to its big brother America, who's always there to defend her or lend a helping hand. I'm not saying that the former Soviet Union's weapons wouldn't bring harm to Israel, but maybe its users needed either better training or a better technology to deal with what Israel or America could throw at them. And let me add that maybe if they had a God like Israel's or America's, who protects and saves its people, rather than themselves, that too would have been helpful to them.

In the past, the Israelis have beaten the user of arms to the punch and destroyed their weapons, or converted them for their own personal use. The user of the next war needs to import the merchant of arms (former Soviet Union and China) along with its weapons. This is precisely the scenario that we will see in the Ezekiel 38–39 and Armageddon campaigns, for in Ezekiel's war we'll see Magog (Russia) and its hordes in the midst of it. And as for Armageddon, we'll see Far Eastern nations such as China, North Korea, and Indochina nations that we saw during the Vietnam War. Included in these Indochina nations are Thailand, Cambodia, Laos, Vietnam, and others. With the exception of Thailand, these nations are communists nations.

A communist is an atheist, or someone who doesn't believe in the existence of God or gods. In communism, we know that atheism is their official doctrine or religion. With that in mind, the communist worships only himself or the state. The God of the Bible—that is, the God of Abraham, Isaac, and Jacob—is a jealous God, so what do you think He will do with the communists and the communist nations? He's already broken up the Soviet Union to deal with Magog later on. So what do you think He will do to China and the other communist nations of the Far East? Will He also put hooks in their jaws and draw them into his arena? I think so. God will deal with them in a very harsh way. The Bible says by the brightness of His coming, He'll do away with the lawless one, and by the sword in His mouth, he'll strike the nations to do away with them and all unrighteousness.

We know from scripture that Magog and its horde of nations, including Arab Muslim nations, are the goat nations because of their anticipation to enter and destroy Israel. These are the nations, according to Ezekiel's prophecy, whose armies will be mostly destroyed (85 percent).

On the Armageddon side, kings east of the Euphrates, including China, North Korea, Indochina nations, and maybe Japan, are, in my opinion, the goat nations coming from the Far East. These nations, with the exception of Japan, have a hatred for the West and especially America. It wasn't long ago (1960s70s) that America was involved in a war in Vietnam that affected other Indochina nations. And let's not forget the Korean conflict in the early 1950s, which left a split Korea, North and South. In both conflicts, China was there to help out their communist friends. Again, China is no friend to America. I guess the Chinese forgot that America helped them during World War II by defeating Japan, who was occupying them at the time. Today, China and North Korea are allies, which means that if there's a conflict with North Korea, the Chinese will come to their aid. Also, these nations, especially China, are guilty of supplying arms to the goat nations of the Middle East—arms that will harm Israel when the next war breaks out.

Japan, who is economically stable and wealthy thanks to America, who reinstated its economic world after World War II, has been (and still is) overly dependent on Middle Eastern oil supplies. Therefore they must remain friends with these nations, even if it means befriending America, who presently is an ally and protector of theirs. Let's note here it is no secret that for years, America has tried to push Japan into beefing up its military. This is so America can cut its defense budget and also cut down its defenses in the Pacific region, thus letting Japan patrol its own waters and police itself. The dangers involved in letting it build up its military, after limiting it to a militia-type military after World War II, is one of reminiscence. It was a little over eighty years ago, during 1937–45, that Japan tried forcefully to control all of Asia, including China. Its biggest mistake at the time was to attack a giant like America, for America struck back with such a blow that it will be remembered in world history. In humiliation, Japan had to surrender to America.

Unfortunately, this same blow will be witnessed in Armageddon—not necessarily in Japan, but in all nations that come against Israel and the Lord of lords, who is the Messiah, Jesus. The blow we're speaking of here is one that will involve, in my opinion, nuclear arms, for stars will fall from heaven in the form of bombs, which will darken one-third of the Earth (Revelation 8:12) and later kill one-third of whatever is left of humankind (Revelation 9:18). It is one-third only because other judgments of God will kill multitudes, which might even sum up to be another third or more of humankind. In all, this might translate to about two-thirds of humankind, or .666 if you put it into decimal notation. Just read the book of Revelation; that's where it is all laid out in God's Word. The death count will be so enormous and so unbelievable that people will have no choice but to repent. But will they? I believe many will, but still there are those who will not because they love their sin, their lives, their partying, and their drugs too much to give it up. Unfortunately, their addictions will take them right into the flames of hell itself.

I'm sure the dead involved will be people from all over the world, just as in the Persian Gulf campaigns of 1991 and 2003 where many peoples from many nations were involved in those campaigns—and many died, mostly on the enemy's side. In Armageddon, it almost seems like the entire world will be involved, and again, many will die of the plagues which God will inflict on them. The antichrist's empire, along with the Far East, will lead the charge to fight against God, to no avail. That in itself will be a losing situation for the world if that's the case, especially if the antichrist is leading it, which I believe he will. (We'll discuss the antichrist later.)

As for the Iraqis, they took the largest death toll from both Persian wars. But as some of them believe, they automatically go to paradise if killed in action. I'm sorry to say it is God who will determine where the dead will go. (It's certainly not paradise with seventy virgins, as some of them believe.) Let's thank the Lord for His protection toward Israel. Also let's also thank Him for Israel's preparedness, because it's no mystery by now that Israel has enough nuclear firepower to obliterate all the goat nations, plus more. I believe they will use it if their backs are up against a wall. But just like the United States, they must refrain from becoming the bully. Remember that Israel vowed never to be driven from their homeland again. If such an attempt is made to drive them out, then their only defense might be to use their nuclear arsenal. I remember when little David had to use his atomic stone to bring down Goliath. He had five atomic stones but used only one to bring down Goliath, and then he chopped off Goliath's head with Goliath's own weapon to give

Israel, under King Saul, a victory for Israel. I use this analogy to show what Israel might be capable of doing under pressure and under God's supervision.

Saddam Hussein was lucky in that had he used a biological or nuclear weapon on Israel during the Persian wars, I don't believe Iraq would exist today. Jeremiah's prophecy of Babylon becoming a desolate place would have instantaneously come to pass. What Iraq did use was Soviet-made Scud missiles to terrorize the Israeli population and harass them. The United States responded by bringing in their own Patriot missiles to shoot down the Scud missiles. Fortunately, as I mentioned before, a lack of training and technology (or the appearance of angels) kept Israel safe with minimal casualties. It was fortunate that these Scud missiles were not carrying biological or nuclear weapons. As was understood after the first Persian war, Iraq had a nuclear program and an arsenal of biological hardware. This is what led to the second Persian war in 2003 under the codename Shock and Awe. It was President George W. Bush, the son of President H. W. Bush, who opened the door for another campaign against Iraq, though it was a failure.

America and its allies practically embarrassed the Soviets by outdoing and outperforming the Iraqis' Soviet-made war machines during both Persian Gulf war campaigns. Thanks to US satellites, our eyes in the sky, Soviet-made war machines such as their T-62 tanks were sitting ducks for the allies who were able to destroy them with pinpoint accuracy thanks to better equipment with modern tech. I'm sure many lessons were learned on both sides during the two Gulf wars. I don't believe any one nation will ever try what Iraq tried by invading a country like Kuwait without backup, at least not while a big brother is watching. Iraq's mistake to ignore the UN's demand to get out while it still had time cost them dearly, and it set the new world order into action. That meant Iraq versus the World, which became a losing reality for them. I personally wouldn't want those odds. The lesson learned here will set the stage for Ezekiel's War and the Battle of Armageddon, and the tacticians of the next war will have to go in with a team of nations rather than alone. Still, once there, the world will demand or try to negotiate a withdrawal. If there is no withdrawal, then the world will be plunged into war to extract the invader just as they did to Iraq when Kuwait was invaded. It almost seems a shame that the League of Nations couldn't do the same—that is, go into Poland in 1939 when Hitler invaded it and take him out of the equation. Millions of lives would have been saved. As it is, World War II had a casualty count of about seventy to eighty million people.

We know from the Ezekiel 38–39 scenario that 85 percent of the enemy will be killed in the mountains of Israel, but a casualty count on the allied side is not mentioned. Again, I believe it will be minimal for the sheep nations as compared with the two Persian war campaigns of 1991 and 2003, where the enemy took a beating. That's because the Lord Himself was in total control of the situation. In contrast, just prior to or during the Battle of Armageddon, one-third of humankind will die as a result of three plagues mentioned in Revelation 9:18. These plagues are fire, smoke, and brimstone, which I believe to be atomic warfare. These plagues will kill both the bad guys and the good guys. Hopefully, the Church will be protected if it's still here during these plagues, although I don't believe it will be, because the Rapture (discussed in a later chapter) will take care of that situation with the Church. Later on during this battle, the Church will return with the Messiah, Jesus.

Even though Israel will fight back with everything it has prior to Armageddon, some scholars believe that many Israelis, if not all, will flee to the mountains, especially to a place called Petra, which was probably built around 5 BC in Jordan. In Matthew 24:16 (NKJV), Jesus tells the Jews, who are looking into the future during a time of storm that will befall them, "Then let those who are in Judea flee to the mountains." Fleeing to the mountains will ensure their safety in the physical sense.

Why Petra, and why Jordan? Maybe because of the difficulty factor by which an army would have following them there, for the mountains themselves would serve as a shield of protection. Not only this, but once the Israelis are out of Israel, why would the enemy want to follow them? Wasn't this their intention from the beginning—to kick Israel out of the Holy Land and retake it? But don't be fooled for a second, for God has a plan. He didn't set aside Israel without a reason.

Now, why would Jordan let Israel reside within her borders in Petra? Or will it? To answer this question, first of all, let's identify Jordan. In the Old Testament, Jordan is Edom, Moab, and Ammon. If you recall from an earlier chapter, I mentioned that Esau (Jacob's brother) is Edom, who didn't get along too well with his brother Israel. Today, many Palestinians still reside in Jordan. They migrated there in 1948 when Israel became a nation again, and they are now naturalized, but they are still looking for their own sovereignty. Yes, they inherited part of the West Bank, Gaza Strip, and Jericho in Israel, but they still consider themselves a people without a homeland. With this in mind, and the fact that Jordan will always side with its own Arab Muslim influence, we have to conclude that during the Tribulation, they will still have a problem with Israel. After all, it was the West Bank, Golan Heights, the Gaza Strip and the Sinai Peninsula that the Israelis took from Jordan during the 1967 war, but part of it was returned through negotiations.

Even though there was no military conflict in Jordan during Operation Desert Storm, they still sided with Iraq. They even threatened to shoot down Israeli planes if Israel entered the war. It just happened that Israel would have had to enter their airspace to attack Iraq (which never happened). When recalling the cheers coming from resident Palestinians in Jordan during Scud missile attacks on Israel: they were heard loud and clear around the globe.

Another interesting fact to remember is that in 1967, Jordan had one of the most powerful military forces in the Middle East, but that did not intimidate the Israelis, who destroyed Jordan's, Egypt's, and Syria's military machine with a destructive force—again, only because their Soviet-made war machines failed them. One might say that these weapons were inferior to American-made weapons used by the Israelis. This in itself embarrassed not only these Arab Muslim countries but also the Soviets.

No one knows at the moment where Israel and Jordan will stand with each other during the time of Jacob's trouble in the Tribulation. Regardless of their differences, Israel will be set in a safe place in what most scholars believe to be Petra, which is located in Jordan. Hopefully the Israelis won't have to take it by force, though no one knows but God alone. Only time will tell, and God is in control.

In concluding this chapter, one must realize where this world is heading, because it is not heading in the right direction. Perplexities will overwhelm nations to the point where war will be inevitable. Eventually, the Ezekiel 38–39 and Armageddon scenarios will become a reality. Then people will realize the Bible was correct in reflecting a prophetic message that was aimed at one's salvation. Unfortunately, these prophecies cannot be undone, for it is the Word of God and therefore truth; that means it will come to pass. Sooner or later, humans have to unlearn war, but before they do, God will show them the unprofitable side of it. God Himself will have to send His only begotten Son, Jesus, for a second time in human history to put an end to bloodshed and save humankind from this curse.

Many have struggled to bring about peace only to have it blow up in their faces—and sometimes they have lose their lives. A good example that comes to mind is the Vietnam War, where American servicemen lost their lives in an attempt to bring about a democratic system (to no avail) to a society that was plagued with a pending communist doctrine. Unfortunately, America gave up that pursuit because of tension at home and let Vietnam fall into the hands of the communists.

General Schwarzkopf had the right idea, during Operation Desert Storm, by hitting the enemy continuously and not letting up until they surrendered. Had the same approach been used in Vietnam, victory would have been achieved. As is, my local congressman told me that a Vietnamese colonel stated if America had continued its bombing for two more weeks, the North Vietnamese would have surrendered because they couldn't take the pounding anymore.

Another sad situation that erupted in the late seventies and the eighties was civil strife in Central America, for this region was plunged into civil war by Marxist groups whose agenda was to communize the region. El Salvador, for instance, fought a civil war that cost the lives of sixty thousand people. This guerrilla-type warfare drove many to seek refuge in nearby Mexico and America. Now that communism has diminished, Central America, along with the rest of the former communist nations, can utter a sigh of relief because now they have been given the freedom to choose. Hopefully, their choice has been one of Godly wisdom, for under communism, they were conned into believing a lie that promised a better lifestyle and standard of living with equal shares in riches.

Freedom of religion, which was nonexistent under communism,

also has come alive, and many who were deprived of this freedom are now experiencing and enjoying it to the utmost. Praise God for that. As is, the church was the only means for outside news for many in Central America and Eastern Europe. It has also been their only hope and comfort in times of despair and weariness. But even though humans have the freedom of choice to control his destiny, they will still choose war and unrest rather than God's peace. You see, humans have been cursed ever since God cursed them in the Garden of Eden. Therefore, choosing war over peace satiates their sinful nature.

That is why all of humankind, with the exception of those taken by God, will be gathered in a place called Armageddon in the Hebrew tongue. There, he will meet his ultimate destiny; and that destiny is the sword with which God Himself will send with His Son, Jesus Christ, to devour those who are in rebellion against Him. This war alone will claim one-third of humankind. And when incorporated with the Ezekiel 38–39 scenario, which will show a destruction factor of five-sixths, or about 85 percent of the enemy's military force, the loss of life will be horrifying. But this will be God's ultimate display of power in Israel, for He'll even shake the very foundations of the Earth.

Just how close are we to the end of this dispensation and the second coming of Christ? In Matthew 24:14 (NKJV), Jesus said, "And this gospel of this kingdom will be preached all over the world as a witness to all the nations, and then the end will come." At this present time in the twenty-first century, the gospel is being preached all over the world via satellite, television, the Internet, books, and radio. Any nation in the world has access to it, but not all nations want it, so they block it from the airways, bookstores, and the Internet. Sooner or later, the gospel message will reach these 1040 nations, as they're called, and deliverance will free them from their worldly ways and doctrines (or -isms). Once this happens, look for the end of the world as we know it, for all things will be changed and made new again when the Messiah makes His glorious reentry to Earth. His feet will be set on the Mount of Olives facing Jerusalem from the east. Then shortly after, the new millennium will be ushered in (Revelation 20:4; Zechariah 14:4).

Friends, are you ready for the Messiah's arrival? Do you know who He is and why He's coming back? His name is Jesus, the Son of God who visited us a little over two thousand years ago, but He was rejected by the religious leaders in Israel—something He already knew would happen because it was all in the plan that God had prepared. You see, Jesus came as a humble servant, was slain (crucified) as the ritual lamb was slain during Passover, was buried, and was resurrected from the dead three days later as He Himself prophesied. By doing this, He defeated death and also washed away humankind's sin so that humans wouldn't have to go to hell as long as they believed in Him. In other words, "God so loved the world that He gave His only begotten son, that whoever believes in Him should not perish but have everlasting life" (John 3:16 NKJV). That is a very simple message that needs to be repeated over and over again, and believed. Friends, let's get wise and take advantage of this very time period, also called grace. Call on Him today, for "whoever calls upon the name of the Lord shall be saved" (Romans 10:13 NKJV).

As we close this chapter, let's meditate on God's Word. Let's also concentrate on His prophecies. Knowing about the future, especially about two end-time wars, can be very scary, but at the same time it can be fulfilling because it will save you and your family. You don't have to be a scholar to teach about the prophecies. I'm not. All you have to be is obedient to the Word, and the Lord will take you places where you never thought you would go. The Lord said, "Go therefore and make disciples of all the nations, baptizing them in the name of the Father, and of the Son, and of the Holy Spirit. Teaching them to observe all things that I have commanded you; and lo I am with you always even to the end of the age" (Matthew 28:19–20 NKJV). The end of the age is not the end of the world but is the end of this present dispensation. Then, the Messiah (Jesus) will usher in the new millennium. Two world wars and much perplexity among the nations still await before this new millennium comes into fruition, but then again, that's how the Lord planned it, and that's how it's going to be. Praise His holy name!

Are you ready to know and accept this magnificent God of the Bible? Try Him. You might like Him. He is awesome in power, and today you can tap into that power simply by believing in Him. Don't let a moment pass by before becoming a member of the family of God.

CHAPTER 9

Approaching Judgments and the Four Horsemen

Contemplating whether this planet will survive through the twenty-first century is humankind's biggest worry today. With tensions in the Middle East and Afghanistan, famines in various parts of the world, civil strife all over the globe, and a world full of evil and violence due to drug usage, how can humans envision themselves in a peaceful futuristic situation? Something has to give.

The answer to this can be answered only by the Almighty Himself, for He is the only one who can foresee our destiny. He's the only one who has planned our destiny; and He's the only one who will bring humankind down to their knees if He wills it. You see, it seems like the human rebellion has gotten out of control; and to deal with it, God will bring this world to a terrible time in history, called the Tribulation. The question is when.

Jesus said, "But of that day and hour no one knows, no, not even the angels of heaven, but my Father only" (Matthew 24:36 NKJV). Did Jesus know the answer to this end-time schedule? I believe He did, for He said that He and the Father are one (John 10:30), thus making Himself equal to the Father. But why reveal it? For if one knew when the thief was going to strike, one would be ready to intercept him. Therefore through faith, we are supposed to be ready at all times because we don't know the time of our departure.

The consensus nowadays points to a "sooner or later" time in history for the Messiah's return. Again, it's hard to pinpoint with accuracy unless we have a guide or manual to steer us in the right direction. Our only guide is the Bible itself. Can we then actually discern this time table by focusing on the scriptures? I believe we can, and I'll try to show it in this chapter.

By prophesying and focusing about events that will take place prior to the Tribulation (the last seven years in this dispensation), one can generalize, or discern, as to the approximate time of the Tribulation and, once there, the approximate time of the Messiah's return to the earth. Let me clarify something here. The Tribulation has two parts to it. In part one, we have a Tribulation of seven years. In the middle of the seven years of Tribulation, or at the three-and-a-half-year mark, we have part two, which is known as the Great Tribulation. This is the part where all hell breaks loose, for the antichrist will be revealed and will literally take the Messiah's seat in the Temple. This is the hour referred to as the "time of Jacob's trouble." It's also the time when God, in His jealousy, attacks the antichrist (beast) and his kingdom and inflicts the unsaved with His judgments.

The events prior to the Tribulation are signs of His approach. To see this, one must read and study the Bible carefully along with history, for history will tell us whether or not these events have come to pass. For instance, let's think of what we are going through today with: political turmoil all over, environmental disasters, unpredictable weather patterns, earthquakes, sickness and pestilence, wars, and rumors of war. All these and more were prophesied to come prior to and during the Tribulation. Jesus Himself prophesied, "For nation will rise against nation, and kingdom against kingdom, and there will be famines, pestilence and earthquakes in various places. All these are the beginning of sorrows" (Matthew 24:7–8 NKJV).

In Mark 13:19 (NKJV) we read, "In those days there will be tribulation, such as has not been from the beginning of creation, which God created until this time, nor ever shall be." In Luke 21:25–26 (NKJV), we read a similar passage, but it is more intense: "And there will be signs in the sun, in the moon, and in the stars; and on the Earth distress of nations, with perplexity, the sea and the waves roaring. Men's hearts failing them from fear and expectation of these things which are coming on the Earth, for the powers of heaven will be shaken."

Oh, how true these verses are, for there are plenty of perplexities in the world today. The unpredictable weather has the sea roaring its waves (hurricanes, cyclones, tsunamis), and with scientific advances, we can finally witness the excitement and disasters that might come from outer space explorations upon this planet. This is due to increased knowledge in the sciences of the world and of Bible prophecy. Daniel 12 implies this very thing about increased knowledge in the latter days. Without this knowledge, especially biblical knowledge, it is impossible to discern the end-time timetable.

These three chapters in the New Testament—Matthew 24, Mark 13, and Luke 21—are known as the Olivet Discourse, also known as the Little Apocalypse. All three show Jesus's warnings to His disciples concerning what's coming in their future, and Israel's future, then and now in the latter days. These were Jesus's responses when asked by His disciples concerning the destruction of Jerusalem, the signs of His second coming, and the end of the age. His disciples knew that Jesus spoke the truth, especially Peter, James, and John, who saw Jesus transfigured before them (Matthew 17). These three disciples knew that Jesus was more than human. He was divine, a deity from the heavens, but Jesus told them to keep it to themselves. As for the rest of His disciples, He went on to tell them about futuristic things that weren't so pleasant to hear. The only pleasant thing Jesus had to say to them concerned His return to Earth.

Jesus went on to tell them that Jerusalem would be trodden down (Luke 21:24) by Gentiles (Romans) and that not one stone would be left upon another when speaking about the Temple. That prophecy by Jesus came to pass when the Romans entered Jerusalem in AD 70 to destroy it along with the Temple, which they took apart stone by stone thinking they would find gold between the stones. They also burned it down and killed Jews by the thousands, even up to a million as speculated by some, thanks to the writings of Josephus, a Jewish historian.

In the latter days, we might see this same scenario repeated, for again,

Jerusalem will be a target for the enemy. As for the rebuilt Temple, it will probably be destroyed in battle and then rebuilt again or refurbished for the Messiah. This second scenario of violence in Jerusalem gives us a twofold prophecy as many believe, the first being when Rome destroyed it in AD 70. The second time of its demise in the latter days, at a time when Israel will be fleeing to the mountains as instructed by Jesus in the gospels.

As I mentioned in an earlier chapter, the Tribulation is a time of purging not only for Israel but also for the whole world, Christians included (unless raptured). Here, God will test His elect during this chaotic time, either by purging them so as to bring them out of sin and preserve their family membership, or by testing their loyalty as He did with Abraham in the book of Genesis. The Jew will unfortunately get the worst of it, especially when Jerusalem finds itself overwhelmed with the forces of the antichrist. I doubt that at this time the city will be destroyed, but an earthquake will destroy a tenth of it (Revelation 11). The antichrist will enter the city and occupy the Temple. Unfortunately, many believers (Jews) will be persecuted and killed at this time, but still many will survive, probably through some supernatural protection, or simply by following Jesus's instructions to flee to the mountains. But most of all, they must believe and trust in the Word and the one who can save them. It all comes under the heading of faith.

It wasn't until 1967, when the Israelis reentered East Jerusalem (for it was on the Jordanian side), that the Jews got a glimpse of the western wall. This wall, also known as the Wailing Wall, was left standing after Titus, the Roman general, burned down the Temple in AD 70. For the Israeli entering East Jerusalem in 1967, this had to be one of the most joyous days in modern Israeli history, because they found a link that had separated them from God for many centuries. For those who witnessed this historical moment on television or on a documentary film, how could they not feel what the Israeli soldier felt in that very moment when entering the city's east side? It is this very same east side that the Lord Jesus will enter in, through the eastern gate, as He enters the rebuilt Temple.

As for this rebuilt future Temple in Israel, this feat will be accomplished, but with a struggle, for the Muslims have their Dome of the Rock mosque on the same grounds as was the ancient temple of the Jews. Prophetically speaking, the temple will stand again, and animal sacrifices will probably be reinstituted, for there is mention in the book of Daniel of the sacrifices and offerings coming to an end when the antichrist comes into the picture at the three-and-a-half-year mark of the Tribulation (Daniel 9:27). We can therefore assume that animal sacrifices will return as in the time before Jesus's death and resurrection.

As we can see, by following historical events, prophecy was fulfilled in that for almost 1,900 years, Gentiles (non-Jews) controlled Jerusalem. After the downfall of the Roman empire, Jerusalem fell into Muslim hands in AD 637. In 1099, the Christian Crusades retook it only to lose it again to the Muslims eighty-eight years later. It remained in Muslim hands until World War I, when the British took it over along with the rest of Palestine as a British mandate commissioned by the League of Nations. When the mandate was over, Jews and Arabs fought for control. The Jews lost Jerusalem but kept Palestine, which became the new country of Israel in 1948, thus fulfilling Ezekiel's prophecy of the "Valley of Dry Bones" in chapter 37.

Ever since Israel became its own sovereignty, thousands of immigrants from all over the world, especially Russia, began arriving into Israel, thus bringing an end to their Diaspora or scattering throughout the nations. Little did they know they were fulfilling Bible prophecy. After going through many events since becoming a nation again—events such as the 1967 Six-Day War, the 1973 Yom Kippur War, skirmishes with the Palestinians, Operation Desert Storm, and Operation Shock and Awe (in which they were restrained by the United States)—they still have to go through Ezekiel 38–39, one of the major prophecies that I believe will be next in line. Then there is the big one, the Battle of Armageddon, which will issue the Messiah's return for a second time to restore all things.

As mentioned earlier, God's number is seven. It is the number of perfection or completeness. In the book of Revelation, there are twenty-one judgments, subdivided into three categories of sevens. There are seven seals, seven trumpets of judgments, and seven bowls (or vials) of judgments. As each category progresses, the judgments get more intense and harder to deal with. Just remember these are God's judgments against the world, or against all of humankind. As He got tired of what He created during Noah's day and destroyed it in the flood, so will He destroy, by His judgments, a very large portion of humankind who will not repent of their sins. The grand finale is a great war that will destroy all flesh on Earth unless a miracle occurs. That war is the Battle of Armageddon. To the faithful, a miracle will occur—that is, the return of Jesus the Messiah. The Bible says that every eye shall see Him descending from the clouds of heaven (Revelation 1:7).

In the first four seals of the book of Revelation, we see what is commonly known as the Four Horsemen of the Apocalypse. The word *apocalypse* is just another term for revelation. The revelation that we're witnessing here is that of Jesus, commonly confused as the revelation of John because John wrote the book. It happens that the apostle John was a prisoner on the Isle of Patmos, located in the Aegean Sea between Greece and Turkey. There, in his old age, he was visited by an angel and taken in the spirit to heaven, where he was instructed to write everything that he witnessed and heard from the Lord Jesus. Without hesitation, the Apostle John obeyed, and he wrote the Revelation of Jesus Christ. Afterward he was returned to his imprisoned abode, where he finished his writing.

The book was written to the seven churches of the time, which were located in Asia Minor, or what is present-day Turkey. These churches, found in Revelation 2–3, were rebuked, admonished, or complimented by the Lord Jesus. He strongly warned five of them of their unrighteousness and lack of love for Him. The other two he considered as righteous unto Himself.

First Seal: In the first seal, we see a "White Horse and he who sat on it had a bow, and a crown was given to him, and he went out conquering and to conquer" (Revelation 6:2 NKJV). Immediately one must ask, Who is this rider who sits on a white horse? And why was he given a bow but no arrows? To understand this, one must see through the symbolic language that the Apostle John uses. First of all, the white horse represents royalty, so its rider must be a great leader, especially if he was given a crown.

Historically speaking, great leaders would ride on white horses, or maybe that is just an artist's depiction. Napoleon Bonaparte was an excellent example of this and was depicted as riding a white horse; so were George Washington and others. What these leaders from long ago did was lead and ride with their armies to the battlefield, but they wouldn't battle themselves unless in trouble. They would sit at a distance and direct the tactics of the battle from there. They wouldn't need the full battle gear, so they would only carry small arms, like a pistol (bow without arrows) or sword, which they probably would never have to use if the battle was going their way.

Some theologians believe this rider on the white horse to be the antichrist, a future powerful world leader (tyrant) who will terrorize the world and conquer as much as he can. This has been the plan for many tyrants since the beginning of the world starting with Nimrod. This particular rider wears a crown, therefore representing kingship. Also, he has to be a well-known world leader, or as some believe, this rider might be the reincarnation of Alexander the Great. I'm not advocating a belief in reincarnation; I am simply stating how some look at this picture.

There are those who think this rider to be Jesus, or the Messiah, for again He rides a white horse, wears a crown and represents royalty. True, the Lord will come on a white horse and wear a crown representing royalty, but this particular person is not Jesus. And true, Jesus comes as a conquering Messiah, and He comes with an army of saints and angels. He also has a sword protruding out of His mouth (again symbolic), but His appearance comes later, toward the end of the Tribulation during a time of war (Battle of Armageddon). If you are a student of the Word, then you must see that many things need to happen yet before His triumphant reentry. The white horse is introduced in Revelation 6. Jesus doesn't appear on the scene (Earth) until chapter 19 of this book—that is, if we're assuming a chronological order of events beginning with the first seal. As we proceed, we'll try to show events that must happen before Messiah's reappearance on Earth.

Throughout history, there have been many antichrist leaders. But if this leader is the prophesied antichrist of the end-time as many believe, then this person riding on the white horse of the first seal is a tremendously strong leader who will show up just prior to the Tribulation. He will show such strength that many will believe he is the

Messiah, the anointed one Himself. In reality, this leader is an imposter and a counterfeit of the real Messiah. His primary mission is to steal, kill, destroy, and deceive the people of the world to exalt himself above the Almighty. He comes to steal the hearts of humans, including God's people. He comes to kill those who are still true to God. He comes to destroy anything that has to do with God, and he comes to deceive the nations and lead them to war. Do we now get an idea of who this person is? He is, as I mentioned before, a counterfeit to Jesus the Messiah. He will answer only to Satan, his master. He is the beast of Revelation 13. He might even be Satan himself. Unfortunately, to accomplish his agenda, blood will have to be spilled, and many will have to die.

Second Seal: This seal represents the prophecy of the Red Horse, and as we know, the color red depicts blood. "And another horse, fiery red, went out. And it was granted to the one who sat on it to take peace from the Earth, and that people should kill one another, and there was given to him a great sword" (Revelation 6:4 NKJV). This is the warhorse who travels all over the Earth to bring war and bloodshed to its inhabitants. With this horse and its rider, there can't be any peace.

Throughout the 1980s, there were forty wars, and at times some were fought simultaneously. Prior to that, including World War I, America alone was involved in World War II, the Korean conflict, and Vietnam. There was the Cold War with the Soviets and conflict in Panama and Grenada, and let's not forget the war on drugs. That in itself can count as World War III. Then came the conflicts in Iraq with Operations Desert Storm and Shock and Awe, and also Afghanistan. We can go on and on with military conflicts on this planet. What we see here is an unending struggle of nations fighting against other nations. There is also civil strife in the form of ethnicity, labor issues, and anarchy. Normal people simply want peace in this world. Unfortunately, there are no answers or remedies to stopping this plague.

Because the Red Horse plays a big role in the money profits of war, many countries compete in a bidding war for defense contracts. It is countries like America, China, Russia, and European nations that produce weapons of mass destruction to distribute directly or indirectly to Middle Eastern, African, and South and Central American nations.

It's also fascinating to see these same countries, who distribute arms, at each other's throats to see who would get what contracts for rebuilding after the fact. Ask yourself if there are those who enjoy the company of the Red Horse. Scripture teaches that the love of money is the root of all evil. Oh, how true that statement is.

The Red Horse is definitely here to stay with us today until the Messiah returns. The wars we see today will become more numerous and more intense by the end of this present dispensation. It's just what Jesus said about "wars and rumors of war": they will intensify as we get closer to the Tribulation. The final outcome will be a meeting of all nations at a battlefield in Megiddo in the land of Israel. This meeting place will serve one purpose only, and that is to fight the last fight and get rid of this Red Horse forever, which has been granted authority from above to terrorize and harass people into warring with themselves.

Ask yourself, How long can humanity endure this punishment without destroying itself? It was said of World War I that it was the "war to end all wars" because of the destruction and deaths that came about from it. Guess what? Not so, because twenty years later, another white horse leader (Hitler) was starting, with the help of the Red Horse, another war that would plunge the world again into a world war. That war alone caused the deaths of over seventy-five million people. Our ultimate prophetic war (Armageddon) will cause not millions but billions of deaths.

A lesson is learned from reading the book of Job, for here he had to endure that which God allowed Satan to throw at him. Satan thought that Job could be brought into submission to curse God. He didn't, so as a reward, God blessed Job immensely. But as God allowed Satan to bring Job into a state of almost submission, He will also allow the Red Horse to bring the world into the same situation, where of course Satan will want the nations of the world to curse God. Unfortunately, many people who love their sin will want to keep it and will do just that. They will curse the Almighty. But God will have the last say and the last laugh. For those who endure till the end, God will reward them, just as He did with Job. Scripture says, "He who endures to the end, shall be saved" (Mark 13:13 NKJV). With God's approaching judgments, how can people still express such arrogance and ignorance in the Word?

Third Seal: This prophecy deals with economic woes due to scarcity of food caused by famine. "And I looked, and behold, a Black Horse, and he who sat on it had a pair of scales in his hands" (Revelation 6:5 NKJV). The scales are the balances for weighing the scarcity of food with the cost factor. That is, how much are you willing to pay for a loaf of bread? A day's wages? Let's read: "A quart of wheat for a denarius; and three quarts of barley for a denarius" (Revelation 6:6 NKJV). Two thousand years ago, a denarius was approximately a day's wages. Today, it probably represents a very large percentage of a day's wage for the average worker.

In economics, when the demand of a commodity goes up, so does the price. It's like back in the early seventies when, during an oil embargo, the price of gas skyrocketed. The demand was there, so people were willing (with disgust) to pay the price at the gas pumps. Due to inflation, every consumer can foresee prices climbing year after year, especially with food. When wages go up, consumer costs also go up due to higher production costs. Unfortunately, the cycle is never ending, for businesses have to cover their costs plus make a profit. That's what businesses do; that is their nature. I can always remember my boss saying that he was in business to make money.

I can also remember, as a boy back in the sixties, going grocery shopping with my guardian aunt and helping her fill up a grocery shopping cart at the cost of about twenty-five dollars. With today's inflated prices, one cannot do that. In fact, one is lucky if that same amount of money can fill a shopping bag. Filling up that same cart of groceries over fifty years ago, at today's prices, would easily cost between two and three hundred dollars depending on what you're buying. That translates to 800–900 percent inflation in that time period. Just think what this same cart of groceries will cost twenty years from now if inflation continues to rise—and it will. Can the average consumer keep up with these rising prices? Look what happened in Eastern Europe and the former Soviet Union back in the early nineties: people had to stand on lines to buy food, which was in short supply due to famine, mismanagement in distribution, or simply a lack of modern technology in farming. Sad to say the Russians at the time proclaimed themselves as a famished state, thus seeking help from the European community and America. Upon realizing that their only hope for survival laid in Western hands, they disintegrated their communist ways. Even their leader at the time, Mikhail Gorbachev, realized this before his counterparts did, and he prepared himself as a friendly comrade so as to blend in with the West. Had this famished state continued, God only knows whether the Red Horse would have unleashed a war so Russia could take the spoils of food from other nations. As it was, the Black Horse had its say, but with the West's help, they survived.

Now, because a lack of rain is usually to blame for famine, weather becomes the enemy. But why blame the weather? Why not blame man for turning away from God? Isn't it easier to pray for rain just as Elijah did in 1 Kings? Unfortunately, during famine the demand for food goes up, and so does the price, but the demand for prayer doesn't. I feel very fortunate to live in a country that recognizes a creator who blesses His children. As long as we continue to recognize, bless, and worship our God, He will continue with His blessings. That includes sending rain for crops to grow. In contrast, as I mentioned before, many nations do not want to recognize the God of the Bible. Instead, they want to worship themselves, or their governments, and that's why God sends the Black Horse in their direction as a purging tool against them.

The world has finally come to the conclusion that famines will ultimately kill millions. Such was the plight of certain African and Asian nations in the eighties and early nineties. To cope with it back then, several programs of relief or rescue were initiated, such as UNICEF, CARE, benefit concerts, and others. The Church, which is always actively at work and has relief programs of its own, took care of what they could for the hungry and needy at the time. Unfortunately, you hardly ever hear on the news about churches jumping in to help. A scripture that comes to mind from the book of Matthew is Jesus speaking: "Inasmuch as you did it to one of the least of these my brethren, you did it to me" (25:40 NKJV).

Here, Jesus teaches humankind to reach out and lend a helping hand to those in need, especially those who need to eat due to famine. An economic disability or a disaster of great magnitude such as a hurricane, typhoon, tsunami, or earthquake can be very devastating. Therefore, helping those in need would be the same as helping the Lord, for by doing so, you've invested treasure in heaven. The Lord pleads to the world to help one another for the sake of salvation. Unfortunately, many do not care because they are into themselves. These are the ones who will be condemned on Judgment Day.

Like the Red Horse, the Black Horse is here to stay until the coming of the Messiah. Jesus prophesied of the beginning of woes, or birth pangs, prior to the Tribulation. The Black Horse, who I believe has been here for centuries, is one of these woes who will be working overtime before and during the Tribulation. To see this Black Horse at work today, all you have to do is check the newspaper, TV news, or the Internet to see him galloping all over the globe, for even though this rider seems spiritual and can't be seen, his works are very evident. As it is, many will face death due to famine and other judgments during this time. For those who are in Christ Jesus (believers), I'm sure He will deliver them from these judgments.

The third seal also mentions "oil and wine," for a command seems to have been issued for keeping the oil and wine safe from harm. Ask yourself, What does oil and wine have to do with this prophecy? Why does the angel say "do not harm the oil and wine" (Revelation 6:5 NKJV)?

To answer this question, one must see what symbolism these two commodities stand for. As you know by now, the book of Revelation is loaded with symbolism, for the apostle John was very careful not to offend the Roman Empire. That's why the Lord kept stressing, "For those who have an ear, let them hear what the Spirit says to the churches."

First of all, oil in biblical times was used for anointing. This anointing, or smearing on of oil, was reserved for God's elect, like King David when Samuel the prophet anointed him at a very young age to become Israel's second king. The anointed represented something, or someone, which is holy, or sanctified in nature. Because the Word of God is holy, it is therefore anointed (with oil). "In the beginning was the word, and the word was with God, and the word was God" (John 1:1 NKJV). Without the Word, there is no sanctification and therefore no anointing. To harm the Word is to harm the oil, which would be unwise, for God will either bring the plague unto the abuser or erase his name from the Book of Life (Revelation 22:18–19). I believe the command not to harm the oil (and wine) is issued to Satan himself. As the story goes, he was commanded not to kill Job in the Old Testament book of Job, but only to bring distress and turmoil to his life. He has also been commanded not to harm the oil and wine.

Ask yourself, What about the wine, which is also not to be harmed? When looking at the Last Supper, after taking the cup and giving thanks, Jesus said, "Drink from it, all of you, for this is my blood of the new covenant, which is shed for many for the remission of sins" (Matthew 26:27 NKJV). This was the Passover, so one must assume the cup was full of wine, for wine and unleavened bread was part of the traditional meal during Passover. Wine was also used in other festive occasions like wedding feasts. Also, for those of you who think Jesus didn't drink wine, in Matthew 11:9, He was accused of being a winebibber, or a drunk.

The wine represents the shed blood of Christ. Without its cleansing power, one cannot enter the kingdom of God, for the blood washes away sins. To enter the kingdom of God, one must be cleansed from sin. The only way this can be accomplished is to accept Jesus as your personal Lord and Savior, for it was at Calvary where He shed His blood and gave His life as a ransom. Accepting this message with the fact that He also resurrected from the grave will wash your sins away and make a new creature out of you (2 Corinthians 5:17).

The gospel message might be tampered with, and so it will in the latter days by false preachers with false gospels, "but the word of the Lord endures forever" (1 Peter 1:25 NKJV). That is God's assurance by His inspired Word, and to assure it further, He has given the command not to harm the oil (true Word) and the wine (washing process by Christ's blood), for many false prophets will come on the scene deceiving many and leading them to darkness. That is why we must all educate ourselves with the Word of God by reading the Bible on a daily basis.

To further illustrate this salvation process by oil and wine, let's take one of Jesus's parables found in the book of Luke (chapter 10) and analyze it. The parable here is that of the Good Samaritan. Here, Jesus speaks of a man who had been beaten, mugged, wounded, and left to die. A priest passing by totally ignores him. Likewise, a Levite does the same, but a Samaritan, hated by Jews, walks by and has compassion on the battered man. "He went to him and bandaged his wounds pouring

'Oil and Wine'; and set him on his own animal, brought him to an inn and took care of him" (Luke 10:25–37 NKJV).

Even though this parable deals with a good Samaritan situation, we're mostly concerned with the oil and wine that was used in the healing process. What the good Samaritan did was pour oil and wine on the battered man to heal his wounds and "save" him. This is what God does in our lives. He pours out the oil (gospel message), and then He saves us by Jesus's shed blood (wine). A lesson has to be learned from this parable; and that is all believers (good Samaritans) must spread the good news, or gospel message (oil), so that seed may be planted. If planted on good ground, it will bear fruit (new believers). Once saved, they will be washed in the blood (wine) of the Lamb to complete the salvation process.

Symbolically speaking, the oil and the wine are two important tools used in the salvation process, not to mention also for medicinal purposes. Since the Last Supper, its use will continue the salvation process right through the Tribulation era. How do we know this? From Revelation 7:13–14 (NKJV), where a conversation takes place between a heavenly elder and the Apostle John: "Who are these arrayed in white robes and where did they come from?" asked the elder. The apostle John's response is, "Sir, you know." The elder continues: "These are the ones who come out of the Great Tribulation, and washed their robes and made them white in the blood of the lamb."

With this passage in mind, one can see that people will still be saved during this dark hour. True, many will be persecuted and killed, for in Satan's desperate attempt to disrupt God's plan of salvation, he will devise many tactics to deceive even the elect if it were possible. Therefore, our aim as believers is to "resist the devil, and he will flee from you" (James 4:7 KJV), for he "walks about like a roaring lion seeking whom he may devour" (1 Peter 5:8 NKJV). Also, we are to pour out the oil and wine, as the good Samaritan did, to heal those in sin and bring them out of bondage so Jesus can be Lord of their lives. By doing this, the old person will be put out, and the new one will be brought in (2 Corinthians 5:17). Next time you have communion in church, remember why the Lord doesn't want the oil and wine harmed. It's also a testimony of remembrance for what He did for us.

For those of you who think the oil mentioned in the passage is Middle East oil, just remember what happened in Kuwait during Operation Desert Storm, when the Iraqis were being evicted. They didn't hesitate to set seven hundred oil wells and fields on fire to destroy the oil. Was the oil harmed? Yes, for millions upon millions of gallons were burned and, as a result, deposited tons of soot into the atmosphere. This went on for about ten months (February—November 1991). Thanks to American and allied efforts, these oil wells were extinguished long before anticipated.

Now, let's ask ourselves, If this occurred today again (burning of oil wells), would such a harm bring about the Black Horse in full force? You bet it would! After all, this type of terrorism might just be the weapon of the future. Terrorists don't care whether they destroy their own people or their own land; after all, they think they have seventy virgins waiting for them if they die in battle. If a terrorist attack on the oil fields occurred tomorrow, one of a greater scale than that of Kuwait in 1991, wouldn't this tip the scales of productivity? Keep in mind that farm machines run on petroleum products, namely oil and gas. Take away this energy source, or limit it so that prices are driven up to an unbearable level, and you'll see the balances tipping and witness nineteenth-century farming all over again, which won't produce enough food for the enormous population of this world. Also, let's not forget the enormous amount of fuel needed for the transportation of goods. Any way you look at it, the Black Horse has the upper hand, and famine will become inevitable.

Fourth Seal: This seal shows us the Pale Horse and its rider. It is the fourth horse of the Apocalypse, and it represents death: "And the name of him who sat on it was Death, and Hades followed him, and power was given to them over a fourth of the Earth, to kill with the sword, with hunger, with death and by the beasts of the Earth" (Revelation 6:8 NKJV).

The rider of this horse has the makings of the Red Horse and the Black Horse, for again we see the sword, which represents death by a weapon (war). We also see hunger, which signifies death by famine.

And we see death by the beasts of the Earth, which can be interpreted in several ways.

The sword, which represents war in the second seal (Red Horse), is not just war (nation against nation) in the fourth seal. In my opinion, it is also death by violent means, such as crimes and drug-related murders, which are very prevalent today in America and abroad. Take the drug war for instance, termed as sorceries in the Bible. It is probably the #1 cause of crime related deaths in America today. It seems as if every time we pick up a newspaper, watch the local news on TV, or browse the Internet, we are confronted with violent crime news, many of which are related to drugs. America and nations abroad have tried to stop the trafficking of drugs but have failed. Many governments, such as those in South America, cannot prevail over the well-armed forces of drug lords. In fact, many in the governments are corrupted and paid handsomely by these drug lords. It's a cycle of sin that cannot end until the Messiah Himself puts an end to it.

What is the answer? How can America and nations abroad deal with this drug situation? They can't. As long as there is a demand for drugs, the profiteers will find a way to keep it moving. We're talking about a multi-billion-dollar business here. Again, scripture teaches us that "the love of money is the root of all evil" (1 Timothy 6:10 KJV), and how true that is, for there are those who will gamble with their own lives for profit's sake. The employment of this disease stretches from the drug lords to the middleman and to the vendors, which include even children selling to other children.

It pains me to see this drug situation continue all over the world. It even hurts to see sin abound all around us. But the Lord has already warned us about this situation in 2 Timothy 3:1–4 (NKJV), for here we read, "But know this, that in the last days perilous times will come: For men will be lovers of themselves, lovers of money, boasters, proud, blasphemers, disobedient to parents, unthankful, unholy, unloving, unforgiving, slanderers, without self control, brutal, despisers of good, traitors, headstrong, haughty, lovers of pleasure rather than lovers of God." Should I continue with this list? It's amazing to see the reality of this scripture message, for even household family members fall into this category of corruptness, selfishness, and ungodliness. I see it even in my own family members. They do it out of ignorance because they have kicked God out of their lives, or they never knew Him.

The problem is society has accepted it as today's norm. Even governments throughout the world have legalized some of these drugs, such as, marijuana, labeling it as medicinal or recreational. What's next is the legalization of harder drugs like cocaine, heroin, and meth. Back in 1920, prohibition became law, but it lasted only until 1933 because of the intensity of crime that came from it. Today, we see the same situation happening. It's like history repeating itself. Unfortunately, the Pale Horse will prey upon these ungodly situations to bring about violence and death.

Schools in America are a perfect example of this ungodliness only because prayer has been totally abolished, and God has been kicked out of the schools. This has brought a downfall upon our schools and children, for some of today's kids get hooked on drugs, alcohol, smoking (vaping), and sex at a very young age. The end result is death. Drugs kill, alcohol kills (drunk drivers), and even sex kills if unsafe (STDs, AIDS). "For the wages of sin is death" (Romans 6:23 KJV).

Jesus Himself spoke of these days, implying that as we get closer to the end of this dispensation, each generation will become more unrighteous than the previous generation. Why is this? Can it be because of all the technological toys that have been invented throughout the years? How many can say that they start their day in prayer, devotions, or reading their Bibles? Not too many. I would dare to say of this generation it is minimal, and I'm talking here about Christians and Jews alike. They should know better. It's no wonder why "God will send them strong delusion that they should believe the lie, that they all may be condemned who did not believe the truth but had pleasure in unrighteousness" (2 Thessalonians 2:11-12 NKJV). Jesus wondered whether any faithful ones would even exist on Earth at His second coming. This goes to show just how ungodly the world will become. But let me tell you, friends, there is time yet, because you have until that very last hour to make peace with the Lord. Don't say in your heart that it can wait till tomorrow, for tomorrow might never get here. You never know when your time's up. It can happen at any age and at any time. Let's face it: now is the time for salvation.

For those of you who are still miraculously alive at His coming at the end of the Tribulation but are still unsaved, He will destroy you with the sword protruding from His mouth, or by the illumination of His brightness. For those of you who died unsaved, He will resurrect you to be judged at the end of the millennium and then send you to the lake of fire. Are you scared yet? I hope so, because that's how I became saved: by reading a book on Bible prophecy. It scared me to the point where I gave my heart to the Lord that very hour in 1984. It was *Countdown to Armageddon*, written by a very popular evangelist, teacher, and author, Hal Lindsey.

Let us get back to our discussion of the Pale Horse. We see hunger, which reflects famine. We also see death, which probably comes in the form of pestilence. These two, among others, are top priorities in world problems today. Let's take hunger for instance. Hunger is still very prevalent today. Perhaps the party has no money to buy food, or maybe stores ran out due to a pandemic. Or maybe the land is famished and can't grow food due to a drought. Or prices are so high that people can't buy food (Black Horse). Whatever the reason, the final result is starvation and death.

Pestilence is another of the Pale Horse's characteristics. Its plagues can kill millions in no time. By definition, we're speaking of a fatal epidemic disease, or we can just call it a pandemic. An example of such a fatal disease was the coronavirus known as COVID-19, which hit the entire planet in 2020 and killed hundreds of thousands. Also, let's not forget AIDS, which has also killed hundreds of thousands since its discovery in 1983. Today the death count of this disease has been cut in half due to the medications that have worked on some but not all people. It was projected at one time that AIDS could surpass the death count of the Black Death, also known as the bubonic plague, of the fourteenth century. This worldwide plague cost the lives of twenty-five million people in Europe alone, or over 30 percent of its population. In 1918, during World War I, the Spanish flu, which lasted two years, took the lives of about one hundred million people worldwide. Other diseases throughout the world can be identified as cholera and hepatitis, which are very prevalent during times of war where dead bodies remain unburied for a long period of time, and because of sanitary conditions.

What about heart disease, the number one killer in the world, followed by cancer? I believe that these two diseases are brought about due to people's carelessness in polluting the environment, cigarette smoking, and not watching their nutritional eating habits. Will humans find a cure for these diseases and plagues before the Messiah's return? I pray they do, but I doubt it, for I believe this plague of diseases is also part of this prophecy of the Pale Horse. Again, this Pale Horse is here to stay until the Messiah's return to Earth.

The last part of this prophecy involves the animals, or death by the beasts of the Earth. Exactly how this is to occur, no one really knows for sure. I've watched many sci-fi flicks concerning this phenomenon. Maybe Hollywood has the answer, but I doubt it. I do like when they find solutions and the good guys win. The only good guy in this prophecy is Jesus Himself. He's got the answer, but the purging process has to run its course. Have you noticed how today's rise of killer viruses have become immune to the antibiotics that doctors prescribe? Who is to say that these viruses are not the "beasts" spoken of here in the book of Revelation? Aren't viruses single-cell biological organisms by definition? Scary, isn't it? I believe they call the deadly ones the "invisible enemy."

What comes to view here also is the process of survival of the fittest, for it will take its toll among animals too. Humans will even fear for their lives when famine hits and there's nothing to eat. A carnivorous animal will be a dangerous animal because what's going to stop it from attacking humans for food? Remember Alfred Hitchcock's movie *The Birds*, or movies with swarms of killer bees or killer ants? Can this scenario actually happen in real life? What about the locusts eating everything in sight? What about humans? Will people become cannibals just as the residents of Jerusalem did when under siege by the enemy, where babies and children became meals? There are many questions but no answers until the Messiah's return.

Because the fourth seal's judgment includes death for one-fourth of the Earth, we can conclude that one-fourth of the world's population will die in these judgments. Along with the one-third of the Armageddon scenario and other scenarios like Ezekiel 38–39, earthquakes, famines, pestilences, and other wars, we can estimate that billions of people will die. With a world population approaching eight billion (2020 census), we might be looking at five to six billion dying from God's judgments. In Zechariah 13:8 (NKJV) we read, "And it shall come to pass in all the land, says the Lord, that two-thirds in it shall be cut off and die." I don't think this verse is speaking primarily of national Israel alone. My perception leads me to believe it's the whole world because of the judgments inflicted on all humankind. It is sad to say that two-thirds of this planet will have to die unless it repents its sins and gets right with God. Prophecy tells us that it will not repent because it loves itself and its sin more than it loves God. That in itself is a real shame. The number two-thirds is a significant number, for it is 666/1000 in fractional notation and .666 in decimal notation. It is also the number of a man (the antichrist?) as stated in Revelation 13:18, and it is the number of humankind.

As stated in scripture, one-third of the angels in heaven fell with Satan. Michael the Archangel and His forces kicked Satan and his army out of heaven and threw them to Earth. We also know that one-third of humankind will be saved; refined "as silver is refined, and test[ed] them as gold is tested" (Zechariah 13:9 NKJV). Can we then be bold enough to speculate that the one-third who is saved will take the place of the one-third who have fallen from heaven? This is only speculation on my part, but it is worth considering to rouse the thoughts of those who take numbers seriously.

Unfortunately, believers, along with nonbelievers, will have to die during the Tribulation. That is, believers who have come to Christ after the Rapture and non-believing Jews. As in Germany, where the Jew became the Nazis' scapegoat, so will the Jews again and the Christians be scapegoats when antichrist comes into the scene in the middle of the Tribulation. This alone might probably cause a holocaust that has not been seen since World War II, and never again will it be seen in this world. The Pale Horse again is here to play a huge part to kill with the sword, starve by famine, kill with pestilences, and use the beasts of the Earth to kill one-fourth of the planet's population, which translates to more than two billion people in today's census. Again, this is God's doing because of the sin in the world. But then again, fear not, for the Lord is in control.

In concluding this chapter, let's acknowledge the fact that it is God who has prophesied these things to happen. He is the Alpha and Omega, the beginning and the end. Let's beware that humankind has been tested and will continue to be tested till the end of this present dispensation. Philippians 1:6 (NKJV) says, "That he who began a good work in you will complete it until the day of Jesus Christ." Will you discipline yourself to get to that completion? Note that our God is looking for a pure, unblemished breed of people to reside with him through eternity. To be included into this group of people, you must become a believer in what the Bible has to teach, both in the Old Testament and in the New Testament. The bottom line is you must become a born-again believer in Jesus Christ. It's only through Him that you'll enter the kingdom of God. He's at the door. Knock, and it shall be opened unto you (Matthew 7:7).

In our next chapter, we'll look at the rest of the seals, a lawless character known as the antichrist, and the rebuilt Temple in Jerusalem.

CHAPTER 10

Seals – Five to Seven, the Antichrist and the Temple

Fifth Seal: In the fifth seal, we see the cry of the martyrs who are under the altar. "And they cried with a loud voice, saying 'How long, o Lord, holy and true, until you judge and avenge our blood on those who dwell on the Earth" (Revelation 6:10 NKJV). These are the martyrs who have been killed in the name of Jesus ever since the start of Christianity, and those being killed in the Great Tribulation. They're calling for revenge, but the Lord says no, not yet, for many more must undergo persecution during the Great Tribulation. Then the wicked will be judged and destroyed.

What about those martyrs that are under the altar? What does that mean? Some believe there is no altar in heaven but that the altar is here on Earth. The altar spoken of here might be Paradise, for even Jesus mentioned Paradise during the crucifixion. In Luke 23:43 (NKJV) we read, "And Jesus said to him, 'Assuredly, I say to you, today you will be with Me in Paradise.'" Jesus was speaking to one of the thieves from His cross; the man was also being crucified along with another thief. As one of the thieves defended Jesus after he was blasphemed by the other thief, Jesus rewarded him by making known that he was also going to Paradise with Him. But, where is Paradise? I've always thought that it meant heaven. But then again, we know that Jesus didn't go to heaven after He died because when He resurrected, He told Mary not to touch Him: "Do not cling to Me for I have not yet ascended to My Father" (Luke 20:17 NKJV). The implication here meant He didn't go to heaven, yet He went with the thief to Paradise.

Many scholars believe that Paradise is a place where the righteous go when they die. It's also been identified as the Garden of Eden. In Roman and Greek mythology, it is a place for heroes and gods, or a place for the blessed dead, also known as Fortunate or Elysium. The apostle Paul also mentioned the third heaven, referring to himself in Paradise in 2 Corinthians 12:2 (NKJV). The apostle said, "Such a one was caught up to the third heaven". I've even heard Paradise called Good Hell. My opinion is that if Jesus mentioned it, then it must exist.

Ask yourself, How will salvation come about during a time of persecution or tribulation? After all, won't the Church be silenced during this time in history, as many believe? I don't believe so. Jesus said, "And this gospel of the kingdom will be preached in all the world as a testimony to all nations, and then the end will come" (Matthew 24:14 NKJV). That means that even during the Tribulation, the gospel message will be heard whether by TV, radio, the Internet, books, Bibles, or missionary work, but it has to be done very carefully and in an almost subtle way. The remaining Church might have to go underground, especially when the antichrist takes over, and the message itself will have to go underground. But the message will survive right up to the end and beyond. The Bible says, "But the word of God endures forever" (1 Peter 1:25 NIV).

It was in Nazi Germany during World War II that books and Bibles were burned in large bonfires, but that didn't kill the Word. I also believe that the message doesn't have to stop because Jesus has come to Earth at the end of the Tribulation. There will be newborns during the millennium who will need to hear the message and be reminded of it, starting from Genesis through Revelation; it is the same way the Jews, for centuries, have been reminded of their exodus from Egypt. And it is also the same way that Christians are reminded through communion of Jesus Christ, and what He did for them at the cross. It was Jesus Himself who said during the last supper, "Do this in remembrance of Me" (1 Corinthians 11:25 NKJV).

I'm assuming or hoping the Rapture has already taken place by the time antichrist is revealed. The underground Church, which will comprise of new believers during the Tribulation, will unfortunately have to endure the antichrist's tactics, and many or most of these new believers will be martyred. But again, be joyful, for we're all coming back with the Messiah and the raptured ones, along with the "dead in Christ" ones.

The second way the gospel will get across is through 144,000 Jewish witnesses in Israel, who will materialize during the Tribulation; 12,000 will come from each tribe of Israel. We know this from reading Revelation 7, where these servants are mentioned as being undefiled, for they have never known (had sex with) women. Therefore, they are virgins who follow the Lamb (Jesus). Because of their service to the Lamb, many in Israel will be saved, even while the White, Red, Black, and Pale Horses are still at large. Apparently, no harm will come to these 144,000, for we see them later on standing on Mt. Zion with the Lamb in Revelation 14. This implies they will be alive at the end of the Tribulation, or that they have been resurrected and are now in their glorified state with the Lord. As believers, we must acknowledge that nothing is impossible with God; therefore, if God wills these 144,000 to remain alive, or spiritual, right through the Tribulation, then that's His business because these also "were redeemed from among men being firstfruits to God and the Lamb" (Revelation 14:4 NKJV).

Sixth Seal: In the sixth seal, we see a devastating disturbance that will send the remaining population of humankind to hide from the face of God. Here, a great earthquake will strike the Earth, the sun will become black, and the moon will turn red as blood. The stars also will fall from heaven, and the sky will recede as a scroll. Boy, that sure sounds scary. It's more like a sci-fi flick becoming reality. But then again, that's how God planned it. He's in control.

Exactly what does all this mean? Well, as you know from the prophetic Word, earthquakes will strike more frequently and more ferociously as we approach the end-time. But this particular one will be one of great magnitude, or should I say the Big One. It will move every mountain and island out of its place, thus causing the geographical map to change overnight. The rumbling will be felt worldwide, and it will seem as if bombs were being dropped from a far distance and echoing through the airwaves.

That brings to mind the pounding the city of Basra (Iraq) received during Operation Desert Storm, for it was felt as far as forty miles into Iran. This goes to show how the rippling effects of such pounding can travel through the ground and airwaves. Just think what the rippling effects will be like when this particular earthquake hits and moves every mountain and island out of its place. Will anyone or anything be able to stand? What about the sun turning black? Will volcanoes erupt and atomic bombs fall, causing a dust bowl effect that will block the sun's light and also the light from the moon, which will become red as blood? Will the term "nuclear winter" become a reality? I believe the sixth seal brings into view all of that and more. This is what the apostle John had to be witnessing.

As for war, the apostle's greatest hint had to be in the falling of stars scenario. I can't think of a better scenario than the first day of the Desert Storm campaign. After witnessing the battle scene on TV with Baghdad getting bombed, tracer fire from the Iraqis on the ground looked like stars being thrown to the sky and falling back to the earth when shooting at the allied bombers. It looked like the receding scroll mentioned by the apostle. Even the allied pilots were amazed at the visual effects.

The rest of the prophecy shows humans hiding and taking shelter from the intense judgment that is taking place. People know that God is speaking to them in His wrath, but they don't repent of their sins. If they repented, then maybe God would withdraw His bombardment of judgments. That's exactly what He did in Nineveh of Babylon in the book of Jonah. He relented from His judgment and didn't destroy Nineveh.

When looking at the book of Revelation, one must wonder whether all these events will happen in the chronological order in which they were written. If they are to occur in chronological order, then we know we must still undergo the seven trumpet judgments and the seven bowl judgments, which will climax with the battle of Armageddon, followed by the new millennium. But let us not get ahead of ourselves.

The sixth seal is an eye-opener because it shows the overall picture of God pouring out His judgments on humankind: the earthquake, the sun getting dark, the moon looking like blood, the stars falling, and the sky receding. Now compare this to what Jesus said in Matthew 24:29 (NKJV): "Immediately after the Tribulation of those days the sun will be darkened, and the moon will not give its light; the stars will fall from heaven, and the powers of heaven will be shaken." Both scriptures were spoken by Jesus Himself, and both give the scenario of the very end. "Then all will see the Lord coming on the clouds of heaven with power and great glory" (Matthew 24:29 NKJV).

As amazing as it seems, the sixth seal puts the icing on the cake. I look at it as an overview, or an outline, that God has beginning with the start of the Tribulation to the end of the Tribulation. From the sixth seal on, the book of Revelation will show how God will dispense His judgments on Israel and the rest of humankind. Hopefully at Messiah's coming, many will have repented and accepted Lord Jesus as their personal Lord and Savior, but as He said in Luke 18:8 (NKJV), "When the Son of Man comes, will He really find faith on the Earth." Was He being prophetic about this, or was He simply saying it in conversation as He spoke to His disciples? As is, for those remaining on Earth, their repentance will be their only ticket to salvation because at His coming, the Lord will immediately clean house to get rid of all unrighteousness. That means all nonbelievers will be done away with one way or another. We have to remember that the Lord is not coming alone but with an army of saints and angels.

Some theologians believe the Church will not be around during this time, for they believe the Lord will come and take away (rapture) the Church before the Tribulation. If this is so, then Israel will be left standing by itself, for the Christians will not be around to help them in their plight as in past times. The Christian help I'm referring to is America with its strong Judeo-Christian influence, who rescues Israel in times of trouble. Take away this Christian influence, and the Jews, who are hated around the world, will be left standing helpless by themselves—in other words, they will be sitting ducks. In contrast, America, without the Judeo-Christian influence, will suffer the same plight or doom as Babylon unless it repents, just as Nineveh did in the book of Jonah.

I once heard a preacher suggest that the sixth seal might be the war of Ezekiel 38–39. With all the activities going on in this seal, one must wonder whether this preacher is right. I am sorry that I can't agree with him, but with further study, we'll figure out this mystery. To begin with, I believe the two wars are separate events, and I've tried to the best of my ability to explain it in previous chapters. I believe these two wars might be separated by no more than a decade. I say this because of the temple that has yet to be rebuilt in Jerusalem.

I posed a question about the book of Revelation regarding its events happening in chronological order, so I will also pose the same question about the book of Ezekiel and whether its events are in chronological order. We're mostly interested in chapters 37 through 43. Let's review. As I mentioned before, chapter 37 deals with the rebirth of Israel becoming a sovereign nation again in 1948. Here, we're talking about a very popular chapter in the Bible known as the Valley of Dry Bones, where God puts this nation back together by calling the Israelites who were scattered (diaspora) among the nations. As we approach chapter 38 and 39, we see Israel getting into a great war with Magog (Russia) and all its hordes of nations. True, there were or are wars between chapters 37 and 38, but this particular one can't compare with the others because in my opinion, it's World War III. By the time we finish chapter 39, we are witnessing the cleanup of dead bodies from this war, which will take more than seven months.

The next chapter is 40, where the new Temple and the dimensions of the new Temple are being shown to Ezekiel in a vision. This continues through chapter 42. By the time we get to chapter 43, we are going to see the glory of God filling the temple, implying that God will be here on Earth by chapter 43. Not so. Remember that this whole vision is simply a vision that will come to pass at a later date. How later? I believe that the temple will be rebuilt after the war of Ezekiel 38–39—that is, if we are looking at it in a chronological order in the book of Ezekiel. This order of business will continue into the Tribulation when the antichrist sits in this very Temple in the middle of this seven-year ordeal, or at the three-and-a-half-year mark. Because the Messiah isn't here on Earth by then, once this happens, God will unleash His jealous wrath on the one who sits in the place of the Messiah.

In chapters 37–42, I see a chronological order. True, there is a time span between chapter 37 and chapter 38, but there is also a time span between chapters 42 and 43. In chapter 43, we see the glory of the Lord in the temple, but remember that Jesus doesn't enter the scene until chapter 19 of Revelation during the battle of Armageddon. After this ordeal, He enters the Temple through the Eastern Gate. The question here is whether He will take the same seat where the antichrist sat, whether the Temple will be refurbished, or whether we will see another new Temple built for Messiah. I believe the latter because of Armageddon, which might destroy most of Jerusalem, the Temple included. Only time will tell and reveal the real truth of the matter. Therefore, within the time span of Ezekiel 42–43, we're going to see the antichrist (beast), the persecution of the saints and Jews, God's trumpet and bowl judgments, Armageddon, and then the reappearing of the Messiah, Jesus Christ Himself, who will be entering a new or refurbished Temple that will be His dwelling place for a thousand years.

Now, let's elaborate on the rebuilt Temple of God. First of all, the rebuilding will begin in chapter 40 of the book of Ezekiel after the war. This is the temple that will exist during the Tribulation and into the Great Tribulation. How do we know this? Because we know that the antichrist will take a seat in it (2 Thessalonians 2:4). I believe this to be literal. Then again, the temple described here might be both the Temple of the Tribulation and the Temple of the new millennium, rebuilt or refurbished, as I mentioned before, to meet the Lord's needs and specifications.

Those who teach that the war of Ezekiel 38–39 is not the Battle of Armageddon see the Temple being rebuilt before Armageddon. Those who teach that the war of Ezekiel 38–39 is the Battle of Armageddon see the Temple being rebuilt after the "time of Jacob's trouble," or after the Great Tribulation, thus concluding that the Temple is the Millennial Temple. For the moment, let's conclude that both teachings might be right. But then again, there has to be a Temple where the antichrist will take his seat in the middle of the Tribulation. No one knows for sure because it's not stated, but it's hard to imagine that Lord Jesus will reside in a temple that was desecrated by the antichrist. It's only fair to conclude that a second Temple will be rebuilt after Jesus's return, or as I said before, it will be refurbished in order to accommodate the Messiah. But if the Temple is rebuilt after the Tribulation, then the Lord's entry into the Temple from the Eastern Gate will be delayed because it will take time to rebuild it, unless it can be supernaturally rebuilt quickly.

Let's elaborate further. From chapter 40 onward in the book of Ezekiel, we have a description of the building process with precise measurements and dimensions of the new Temple. The latter chapters deal more with the priestly works and laws governing the priests and the Prince (Messiah). It is this latter portion of Ezekiel that deals with the Millennial Temple, for the Prince comes into view here. Not only that, but the healing waters begin to flow. "And it shall be that every living thing that moves, wherever the rivers go, will live. There will be a very great multitude of fish, because these waters go there; for they will be healed, and everything will live wherever the river goes" (Ezekiel 47:9 NKJV). These same healing waters are referred to as "A Pure River of Water of Life" in Revelation 22:1 (NKJV) after the Battle of Armageddon. As we already know, the Messiah is here to stay at this point in history, and He will usher in the new millennium.

For the past few decades, there has been much talk about the rebuilding of the Jewish Temple. In fact, efforts, such as locating the priestly tribe (Levites), who are the only ones that can perform rituals in the temple, have been going on for a while. Not only that, but these twenty-first-century Levites have to be taught the practice because several thousand years have gone by since they last sacrificed in the Temple. The same applies to the red heifer, which plays a big role in the purification process. Without it, there is no completion of Temple rituals. Some even say these red heifers have been spotted in Ethiopia. Also, let's not forget that for the Jew to rebuild the Temple in Jerusalem, it has to be built almost on the same grounds of the second holiest shrine in Islam. We're talking about the Dome of the Rock mosque. This might pose a problem for both Jew and Arab Muslims. Some even speculate that it will take a war, or an act of God such as an earthquake, to demolish this shrine and make room for the new Temple. In all probability, the events of the sixth seal will take care of this problem, but then again, if the antichrist is going to sit himself there in the Temple in place of Messiah, then it goes to show that it will get rebuilt before Armageddon, or before the return of Christ.

Others have also suggested building a wall that would separate the Temple from the mosque. The Wailing Wall, which was left up by the Romans in AD 70 after the destruction of Jerusalem, currently separates the grounds between Arabs and Jews. Sharing these grounds with only a wall to separate the Temple from the mosque would be a disaster and a desecration unto the Lord. Humans cannot fix this matter. Only God can.

For the record, the Temple will get rebuilt only because it has been prophesied. Now, whether a wall will separate it from the mosque is yet to be determined. But judging from Ezekiel 43:8 (NKJV), one can see clearly that a wall will be constructed. Let's read: "When they set their threshold by My threshold, and their doorpost by My doorpost, with a wall between them and Me, they defiled My Holy Name by the abominations which they committed; Therefore, I have consumed them in My anger."

Why will God consume them in His anger? To answer this question, one must realize that the God of the Bible is a jealous God, and the God of Israel sharing the same ground as the god of Islam would be an abomination that will not be tolerated by the God of the Bible. In His own time prior, during, or after the rebuilding of the Temple, the Lord will take care of this matter. The rebuilt Temple will not stand next to the second holiest shrine in Islam (Mecca in Saudi Arabia being the first). An act of God will bring it down. Personally, I'm not trying to condemn the practices or shrines of Islam; I'm simply stating what the Bible has to say about it. When it comes to our Muslim brothers and friends, the God of the Bible loves them the same as any other human on this planet.

Many theologians believe that once this building project begins, it will usher in the Tribulation, and once the construction is complete, we'll be that much closer to the start of the Tribulation, if not into it already. At the beginning of the Tribulation, the antichrist will sign a peace treaty, or a covenant, of seven years with Israel, making him a friend of Israel. But don't be fooled, for then the real countdown begins.

It will take approximately three and a half years after signing the treaty with Israel before the antichrist will turn his back on Israel, attack them, and take a seat in the Temple to rule from it. Let's remember that the antichrist is a counterfeit to the Messiah. It is the Messiah, Jesus, who should be sitting in the Temple and reign from it, not the antichrist. And so at a later date, the Messiah will take the seat and rule the nations from the Temple in Jerusalem during the new millennium. As for the beast, he'll have to deal with a very hot situation (the lake of fire).

In concluding this chapter, let's keep in mind just how close we are to the end of this present age. The apocalyptic horses and their riders have already begun their trot, and a scramble for the preparation for rebuilding the Temple in Jerusalem has begun. This tells us, through discernment, that Messiah is virtually at the door. If He's knocking, why not open the door?

Jesus taught us what to look for prior to His second advent. The Old Testament prophets did likewise, for it was foretold that Israel would be gathered back again in the Ezekiel 37 "Valley of the Dry Bones" prophecy. This very feat began to come to pass in 1948 when Israel was proclaimed a sovereign nation again. This marked the beginning of the prophetic countdown toward the new millennium. Jesus said, "This generation will by no means pass away till all these things take place" (Matthew 24:34 NKJV). Friends, we are that generation that will see all these prophetic messages come to pass. Don't believe me? Research it for yourselves, or hang around a few more years. The events leading to the Tribulation are here already. The birth pangs have begun, and the Messiah will be making His second debut sooner than most think.

Friends, call on the Lord Jesus Christ today. He is the Lord and Savior of all. He's also the Messiah, the Son of the Living God, and the Deliverer of all. He said, "No one comes to the Father except through me" (John 14:6 NKJV). Accept Him now, and avoid the approaching judgments.

CHAPTER 11

Antichrist—Leader of a New Age Concept

Many of us have heard the term *antichrist*, especially those of us who have little knowledge in the Bible, whether in Sunday school, church, or even a synagogue. Maybe you've heard the term used on television or in a movie. If you've never heard it before, let me introduce you to it. The term, by definition, means one against Christ, usually referring to Jesus Christ, the Son of God. When broken down, *anti-* means against, and *Christ* means the Anointed One or the Messiah. Antichrist is therefore referring to anyone who is against, opposes, or denies Christ or Christianity.

The Bible does warn us to keep away and be on the lookout for antichrists, for they do exist. They come to devour, as birds do, the seed planted so as to keep it from taking root. That is, they come to discourage those who want to hear the Word of God, thus leading them astray. Many rock groups are known to do this very thing to our kids, for it is at this age that our young ones can be captured. That is why parents ought to pray for their young ones and bring them up in the admonishment of the Lord. Once they reach a certain age, they begin to rebel. And what a treat it is for the unrighteous to grab hold of one of these stray ones.

Antichrists can also be found in our very own churches, for they come in disguised as angels of light (2 Corinthians 11:14). History has shown us many antichrists—for example, Adolf Hitler and Napoleon Bonaparte, who both professed to be Christians but were very unfruitful, for they exalted themselves above all things, something at which Satan is a master.

In this chapter, we'll concentrate on a futuristic world system led by one who exalts himself above all things, including the Almighty Himself. This world leader, often referred to as the antichrist by theologians, will be given power directly from the beast (Satan). His ultimate plan will be to deceive as many nations as possible and to sit in the newly rebuilt Temple that has been reserved for God (the Messiah) Himself.

This practice of divine exaltation was used by several Caesars (antichrists) in the old Roman empire. One who comes to mind was Caligula, also known as Little Boots, because he exalted himself to the point where he declared himself to be a god. He also ordered the beheading of all statues of Roman gods so that the image of his head could be put on them. He went as far as ordering his statue image to be placed in the Jewish Temple in Jerusalem. Fortunately, this never took place, for the Roman and Jewish leaders in Judea feared a rebellion. Shortly thereafter, Caligula was assassinated. This is what an antichrist type attitude can do to a person, because he wishes to be worshipped. Unfortunately, this will be the attitude of the antichrist who is yet to come, for he will "Sit as God in the temple of God showing himself that he is God" (2 Thessalonians 2:4 NKJV).

In Daniel 7:25 (NKJV), we see him described this way: "He shall speak pompous words against the Most High, shall persecute the saints of the Most High, and shall intend to change times and law. Then the saints shall be given to his hand for a time and times and half a time." Deception will be his weapon of genius, and many will fall to his tactics and antics and respect him as a man of great stature. Many will even fear him because he'll appear to be demonstrative and convincing, having all answers to world problems, even from economics to war. No one on Earth will dare make war against him, because he'll appear to be a strong man with a very powerful and well-equipped military. Accepting him as Messiah will be no problem for many because in his mastermind deceptions, he'll even have them bowing down before him and accepting him as a god. His ultimate exaltation will come when he personally takes the seat in the rebuilt Temple in Jerusalem. This will happen three and a half years into the Tribulation. After that, God Himself will declare war on the antichrist. In His jealousy, God will kindle His wrath upon the kingdom of the antichrist, just as He did to Pharaoh's kingdom in Egypt during the exodus.

As for the saints of God (believers), they will not bow down before the antichrist, even though some will be fooled or give in to the antichrist's scare tactics. In my opinion, those who call themselves true believers (born again) will stand up to the antichrist. Unfortunately— and the Bible is very explicit about this—the antichrist will prevail over the saints (Daniel 7:21). A persecution will follow, but only after the antichrist is revealed three and a half years into the Tribulation. Then a fury will be unleashed against the saints, only because the saints will pay him no homage. In all, the antichrist will prevail for time (one year) and times (plural for two years) and half a time (half a year). It translates to three and a half years, or forty-two months. That means that all mayhem will break loose in the second half of the Tribulation, also known as the Great Tribulation. Are you ready?

Some have said that beheading will be reinstituted during the Great Tribulation, just as in the days of Napoleon when the guillotine was used. I don't believe this to be a literal scenario, but the end result will be the same, just as the Islamic terrorists did in the early 2000s by beheading their enemies. Once the persecution begins, it will continue right up to Messiah's intervention at His coming. True, it will be fearful for believers (if they are still around), for it will seem like a reign of terror, but there will also be an inner joy in knowing without a doubt that Messiah is near. By their study in the scriptures, they can begin the countdown because they know that the events coming to pass have already been prophesied. Therefore, their next grandest event is to meet the Lord, either by the Rapture in the air, martyrdom, or as survivors on the planet Earth at Jesus's return.

Once the antichrist takes his seat in the rebuilt temple in Jerusalem (referred to as the Abomination of Desolation) and claims himself as God, the Almighty's wrath will be kindled, and then the tables will be overturned. Remember that the God of the Bible is a jealous God, and for anyone to even try to take His seat or exalt himself above the Almighty, death will be his reward. Satan's ambition is to take the Temple seat, and he'll be successful doing it—but only because the Lord will let him. His success will be the result of possessing the physical body of a man we'll call the antichrist. Satan will work through him to actually sit in the physical seat of the Temple, and at the same time, he will also sit in the hearts of humankind.

Many will be tested by God during this time of the Tribulation. But they'll also be tested by the antichrist. The test will come in the form of a mark, often referred to as the Mark of the Beast. Antichrist will cause everyone to receive this mark either on their foreheads or on their right hands. Those taking the mark will instantaneously be incorporated into Satan's kingdom and will suffer the same punishment as Satan. Those refusing the mark, if they are believers, will remain in God's kingdom and inherit all the promised blessings. Those who are unsaved and refuse the mark will still be condemned unless they surrender their hearts to Christ Jesus. This includes Israel, who by now will hopefully have heard the true Word of God from the 144,000 converted Jewish evangelists. These evangelists will teach them all about the truth of the word during the Tribulation, including accepting Jesus as Messiah and Lord.

The mark that we're referring to is probably an invisible computer chip or barcode, which will be easily placed below or injected into the skin of the taker. The information on this chip will be easily retrieved by a scanner of some sort, which will read and transmit the account number into a main computer, thus enabling a transaction to take place, supplying information to the one seeking the information. What we have here is an invisible credit card and personal check system that will be needed for buying or selling, or for simply doing your banking. Without this mark or number, no one will be able to buy or sell anything (Revelation 13:17). The government will have total control of what you do: your health, your finances, your friends, and your whereabouts. It almost sounds like a book I read years ago, titled *1984*. So, watch out because Big Brother will be watching you if you take the mark. For those not taking the mark, in all probability they'll go underground to take care of all their businesses and needs.

Ask yourself, What about the almighty dollar? Apparently, the dollar as we know it will be done away with, because by doing so, the governments of the world will save billions by not having to produce and print these bills, which have a lifespan of only eighteen months. What we're talking about here is a cashless society, and that's exactly where we are heading. Today, millions of people do not carry cash because they have their credit cards and debit cards, and their checkbooks, to buy their needs. Their money is direct-deposited into their bank accounts. Even social security checks are being direct-deposited into retired people's bank accounts. What more do we need ?

How close are we to this system? I believe it is already here and is being done in a very slow and subtle way. It's simply waiting for the right time to be incorporated entirely into society. Back in the eighties, the term "rainbow money" was used to prepare the public about changes that were about to happen to our paper money. The whole idea was to color the paper money so as to keep it in one's own country, especially in America, where the greenback was a popular piece of legal tender all over the world. The idea of coloring paper money was supposed to eliminate greenbacks from leaving or entering countries illegally, for only rainbow money would be used nationally and not internationally. The greenbacks, in contrast, would be used internationally.

With the help of a magnetic strip, which would contain information such as serial numbers and who knows what else, metal detectors would pick up any illegal attempt to move it out of the country, thus leaving the colorful money in one's own country. The Europeans have been working on this monetary system for years, hoping that it would become the world's monetary system. So far the euro has proven to be successful with its citizens, with the exception of the British, who left the European Union in January 2020 (Brexit). They are now using the pound sterling as their currency, but they still accept the euro in certain places. What this will do to the plan of a one-world currency is yet to be seen.

Again, computerization with its complex information systems will play a big role during the end-time. The dollar will eventually be done away with and replaced with the Mark of the Beast system. This system will be masterminded by Mr. Antichrist himself. This is what has been taught for many years by prophecy scholars, and I agree with them.

With today's technological advances, I see no trouble with this system of the Mark of the Beast being developed. In fact, it sounds like a good and well-organized system, for it will keep an inventory on the census (head count), a close watch by the government on its citizens, the elimination of credit and debit cards, and best of all the elimination of carrying cash on one's person. That in itself will discourage the muggers.

Let me tell you, friends, don't be fooled for one moment. God has already warned us not to take the mark. Taking this mark will place you with the unrighteous, and damnation will be your fate.

For those believers who will still be here on Earth after the Rapture for one reason or another, or for those who were not raptured because of unbelief but are believers now because they came to Christ, remember how God took care of His people in the wilderness. He supplied them with manna to eat, and later on with quail. Also, the remaining Church will have to go underground to stay away from the antichrist's government system. For the Israelis, we already know that they're fleeing to the caves of Petra in Jordan. And yes, it will be a disaster for all, but just remember it's only for three and a half years, unlike the forty years for Israel's exodus from Egypt.

There are those who teach that the Church will not be around during the seven years of Tribulation because it will be taken away by God (raptured) just prior to it. I hope they are right, but my question to them is, What if the Church is still here at the beginning, for just part of the Tribulation? What a disappointment for some (or many). Shouldn't these teachers be assuring them or planning some kind of strategy to prepare them for this part of history just in case? Why not teach survival tactics such as setting up an underground marketing network where people can buy and sell without the mark? Or create an underground housing network, because many will lose their homes—again, by not taking the mark. As for payment, a barter system of some kind can be arranged.

During World War II, many underground hideouts were prepared for Jews and others who were persecuted by the Nazis. Also, underground black markets were set up for distribution purposes. I can see this same scenario happening during the Tribulation, for many will be persecuted by the antichrist, thus forcing them to hide for protection's sake. They will look for sympathizers to take them in just like the ten Booms of World War II, who helped Jews escape the Holocaust from Hitler and the Nazis.

Just how close are we to this Mark of the Beast? Closer than we can imagine. I remember reading an article printed by *USA Today* in 1991 titled "Microchips Could Rein in Lost Cats." The article stated that some household pets have been injected by vets with computer chips inside their skin and encoded with ID and other info. After checking it out, I found out this process started around 1988. If the pet gets lost, all that is needed is a scan on the chip to retrieve the owner's information. Just think if this can be done to animals, why not to humans? Why not to some seniors who might have dementia, go on walks, and can't remember how to get back home? That is just what's going to happen when the antichrist takes over the world during the Tribulation. Everyone on the planet will have to take the mark (a computer chip?) in order to survive the new system.

Let's read this truth: "If anyone worships the beast and his image and receives his mark on his forehead or his hand, he himself shall also drink of the wine of the wrath of God, which is poured out full of strength into the cup of His indignation, And he shall be tormented with fire and brimstone in the presence of the holy angels and the presence of the Lamb. And the smoke of their torment ascends forever and ever; and they have no rest day or night, who worship the beast and his image and whoever receives the mark of his name" (Revelation 14:9–11 NKJV).

The beast spoken of in verse 9 is Satan himself. I believe his image is the antichrist, even though some believe it to be a statue made by human hands or an idol such as Aaron erected when Moses climbed the mountain to speak with the Lord in the wilderness (Exodus). The rest of the verses (10–11) are self-explanatory concerning those who take the mark. It's Bible verses like these that give me the shivers. It's a do-or-die situation. If you take the mark, you'll suffer in God's wrath and die. If you don't take the mark, even though you'll suffer on Earth for a little while (three and a half years), you will live in eternity with Christ the Lord. How much plainer can this message be?

Friends, don't let the greatest liar of all time deceive you into believing the greatest lie. Be prepared by accepting Jesus as Lord and

Savior, for He will see you through. Don't hesitate to take that giant leap in your life. The greatest liar of all times is Satan himself, who is the beast and the devil in the book of Revelation. He goes by many names, and he is a mastermind at what he does and a great deceiver. Just look at what he did to Eve in the Garden of Eden—and we're still suffering today because of it. He comes to steal, kill, and destroy; and if you're not careful, he'll also devour you as a lion would devour its prey.

During the Tribulation, Satan comes as the counterfeit trinity—that is, the antichrist, the beast, and the false profit. Of course, he's mimicking the Father, Son, and Holy Spirit. Unfortunately, these deceptions will go on right until the end of the dispensation. That's when the Messiah will put an end to it, for by the breath of His mouth and the brightness of His coming, He'll destroy the antichrist, who's also known as the lawless one (the son of perdition) in 2 Thessalonians 2:8. Let's keep in mind that the lawless one is a man, and he's the one being destroyed by the breath and illumination of Christ, not the beast. After that, the Messiah will have the beast and false prophet thrown alive into the lake of fire (Revelation 19:20). Then the Messiah will have Satan bound in chains and thrown into the bottomless pit (abyss) for a thousand years. This will put an end to the counterfeit trinity for good.

As for the rest of humankind who side with the beast and his kingdom, they shall all be killed and fed to the birds, who will have a flesh-eating feast (Revelation 19:21) just as in Alfred Hitchcock's movie *The Birds*. Later on, unsaved humankind will be resurrected from the dead for judgment, only to be sent back to death, but this time to the lake of fire.

If people would only study scripture and believe in the God of the Bible, they wouldn't have to endure the havoc planned for them on Judgment Day. Unfortunately, they don't and they won't, only because they don't experience any miracles in their lives or any teachings from their parents or guardians. Satan and his hordes love this, and that is why they come to deceive even the elect of God with their works and wonders. A majority of today's teens fall into this trap because they're looking for fun, pleasure, and sex. With the Internet full of these things, it's no wonder why they serve other gods. This is exactly what happened to the Israel of old in the Old Testament. If you're familiar with these writings, you can see why time and time again they were in trouble with the Lord. Their biggest sin was putting God last and offering themselves to foreign gods. This led to God's chastisement and judgments against them, thus purging out the sin and bringing back the repentant remnant.

On the New Testament side, the Bible teaches us to be prepared at all times so as to withstand the trickeries of the devil. Ephesians 6:11 (NKJV) reads, "Put on the whole armor of God, that you may stand against the wiles of the devil." What is this spiritual armor? I'll list them.

1. Gird yourself with the belt of truth (God's Word).
2. Put on your breastplate of righteousness.
3. Take up your shield, which is faith.
4. Carry the sword, which is the Word of God.
5. Put on your helmet of salvation
6. Shod your feet with the preparation of the gospel of peace.
7. Pray. "The effective fervent prayer of a righteous man avails much" (James 5:16 NKJV). It is a very powerful weapon.

Again I say the devil comes to steal, kill, and destroy, especially those who take an interest in God's Word and become faithful servants. My friends, learn to protect yourselves by putting on this armor. It is your only assurance of salvation, for without it, you might as well take the mark because the forces of the underworld will take the seed that was planted in you and destroy it. Don't believe the lie. Satan wants to trick you into serving him. He'll even "transform himself into an angel of light" (2 Corinthians 11:14–15 NKJV). His ministers will come and infiltrate your churches and synagogues, and they will even preach from your pulpits.

The Bible tells the believers (Church) that they are the temple of God and that the Spirit dwells in them (1 Corinthians 3:16). Even Jesus called Himself a temple when He said, "Destroy this temple and in three days I will raise it up" (John 2:19 NKJV). What Jesus spoke here was the temple of His body, not the physical Temple in Jerusalem as the religious leaders thought.

In Satan's mastermind plan to have the antichrist sit in the Temple, he himself will attempt to sit in the temple of people's hearts, for it is his wish to knock out the Holy Spirit and take his place. God has given humans the power of choice, so unfortunately many will backslide, let in the evil one, and let the righteous one leave. That is precisely what's happening today. Church attendance is down and continues its downfall. They say in their hearts, Why go to church on Sundays, or why go to the synagogue on Saturday? What about midweek services? After all, we'll just miss out on the fun. What fun? Well, there's football, baseball, basketball, and other sports. There's going to the beach or picnics on Sunday. Or there's making up for sleep that was lost during the week. What about the Internet games and distractions with other technological toys?

My question in my heart is, Boy, if they only knew, would they change? Also, what if they're going to a New Age church that tells them they are their own gods and that they should live the lives they want? The Bible says, "For this reason God will send them a strong delusion, that they should believe the lie" (2 Thessalonians 2:11 NKJV)—a lie that tells them church is not important. Note: if the church or synagogue is not important to them, then God isn't either. If that's the case, then He will send them straight into the lake of fire on Judgment Day. The Word says, "There will be weeping and gnashing of teeth" (Matthew 8:12 NKJV). Ouch!

Many arguments have arisen over the issue of Satan, in the person of the antichrist, sitting in the temple (2 Thessalonians 2:4). I believe we should not only look at the physical side of it, which will come to pass; we should also look at the spiritual side of it, where Satan will be sitting in the hearts of unbelievers and those who backslide. Just how far will Satan get? It seems by this time, the Church will be plagued with apostasy—that is, a false gospel that will enter the Church. People will believe in it because they have no knowledge of God's truth. Along with his ministers, Satan will capture the hearts and minds of as many as he can with his New Age movement, which has taken a prevalent stature in today's society. It is sad to say we are now being bombarded by the forces of evil, who come to infiltrate our churches and synagogues to make us accept all or part of its occultic ways. These infiltrations come in the form of an ancient religion that was practiced in the Babylonian empire. They have been mingled and accepted by many who call themselves believers but know nothing of the teachings of the Bible, simply because they don't take the time to study scripture. Therefore, they accept what their churches or synagogues are teaching them and ask no questions.

Countless people are seeking ways to foresee the future. They seek the guidance of those who read tarot cards, crystal balls, and astrological maps. They check their horoscopes every morning and begin their day in satanic wisdom rather than biblical wisdom. Too bad people have to fall into this trap, for they do it out of ignorance and out of habit. They either defy the gospel message or have never heard of it. That is why it is so important to spread the Word of God all over the world: so that by hearing it, they can get faith, and with faith they can be saved. "So Faith comes by hearing, and hearing by the word of God" (Romans 10:17 NKJV).

The big craze since the Persian wars of the 1991 and 2003 campaigns has been the predictions of Nostradamus, a sixteenth-century so-called seer who made predictions in short paragraphs called quatrains. It amazes me to see so many interested in these predictions, yet they take little if any interest or notice in Bible prophecy, which is more precise because it is the true Word of God. God doesn't make predictions—He tells it like it is.

The Bible is loaded with end-time prophecies, which some might call predictions. Little do people know that Nostradamus came from a very religious background, meaning that he too had access to some Bible knowledge. If so, then he must have been aware of futuristic bible events, some of which he recorded in his quatrains. For instance, he wrote of futuristic climactic events that would lead to world wars. He wrote about a futuristic world leader who would terrorize the world. And finally, he wrote of a thousand-year millennium, all of which can be found in the Bible. True, some of his predictions might have come to pass. So did Jeanne Dixon, a psychic who predicted JFK's assassination. Were they good guessers?

People who seek these nonbiblical, so-called prophecies are also those who are, or will be, involved in the New Age movement. I'm speaking of those who should know better, for in all probability they're either Christian or Jew. If so, that makes them what the book of Revelation calls lukewarm. That means they will be spewed (vomited) out of the Lord's mouth according to Revelation 3:16. What it comes down to is whether these lukewarms will serve the Lord or serve the world's wisdom and riches. "For either he will hate the one and love the other, or else he will be loyal to the one and despise the other" (Matthew 6:24 NKJV).

One cannot serve the two kingdoms or try to mingle both into one concept. Unfortunately, with this New Age movement, countless will fall and serve Satan's kingdom. It is the anticipation of this movement to gather the whole world into believing a one-world, one-mind religious concept through its meditation techniques, and to focus on the "spirit guide" and "be your own god" concepts. Some believe that the antichrist will be very involved in this New Age movement along with his false prophet, who some speculate will be the leader of this movement during the Tribulation. The movement will be a one-world religious concept, which will require a leader. These two, the antichrist and the false prophet, will work closely together and deceive as many as possible.

By anticipating the deception, true believers and God's elect will be prepared for anything thrown their way, for they will know that greater rewards lie ahead. Knowing their scriptures will keep them from falling so that at the Messiah's coming, those who have done their homework well will receive their just rewards. Revelation 22:12 speaks of these rewards, and what are these rewards if not everlasting life with the King and a share in His inheritance? I've often heard preachers speaking about crowns as rewards at Christ's coming. That troubles me, because the only crown I expect, as a believer, is that of everlasting life. That in itself is the ultimate gift from God: "For it is by grace you have been saved, through faith—and this is not from yourselves—it is the Gift of God" (Ephesians 2:8 NIV).

It was almost two millennia ago that Jesus said, "I am the way, the truth, and the life. No one comes to the Father except through me" (John 14:6 NKJV). That truth still stands today, and for anyone believing otherwise, that means that the person has given in to the trickeries of the devil. It was Jesus who, by His crucifixion, paid the price (ransom) to free all humankind from their sins that have held them in bondage since the fall at the Garden of Eden. It wasn't Mohamed, Buddha, Confucius, a

New Ager, or any other entity that man worships. It was Jesus who rose from the dead to defeat death. No one else can make that claim.

Accepting this message means you'll be saved and accepted by the Father in heaven. His Son, Jesus, will stand up for you. He'll be your defense attorney or advocate and will plead your case before the Father when the accuser (devil) brings up his accusations against you.

In concluding this chapter, let's beware and take heed to what the Bible is teaching. It is warning us about a time when an evil person (the antichrist) comes into view during the latter days to disrupt the lives of God's elect if possible. His master plan will include forcing people to take a mark on their foreheads or right hand so that without it, they can't buy or sell anything. He also wants to excel himself before God, and proclaim himself as God and Messiah before the people of the Earth by claiming the Temple seat in Jerusalem and demanding to be worshipped. Also, a new world religion will arise, which many believe to be the New Age concept. This concept will be orchestrated by the antichrist and his false prophet. Together, they will devastate the whole world and bring it to war, even against God.

Friends, let's seek the kingdom of God first so that on that day of judgment, our advocate Jesus will defend us by telling His Father that we are His, thus letting us enter the kingdom of God, which has been prepared for us. Praise be His holy name!

CHAPTER 12

Prophetic Beasts and a Ten-Nation Confederacy

When looking at Revelation 13, we read of a beast that comes up from the sea with seven heads and ten horns. This is a vision seen by the apostle John while in prison on the island of Patmos. What he saw was a beast whose feet were like a bear's, whose body was like a leopard's, and whose mouth was like a lion's.

Keep this vision in your mind, for this is the beast on the New Testament side, which we'll call John's beast, because he's the only one to witness this vision. In contrast, in the book of Daniel, a similar beast was seen in a vision by the prophet Daniel in the Old Testament, which we'll call Daniel's beast.

In Daniel 7, we see four different beasts, whereas John saw only one. Daniel's first three beasts, incorporated together, will form the same beast that the apostle John envisioned in Revelation. Daniel's fourth beast is a little different. Let's take a close look at these beasts to determine the truth of both visions.

Beast 1—Daniel's first beast in chapter 7:4 (NKJV) was "like a lion and had eagle's wings." What we have here is a representation of ancient Babylon with its mighty king Nebuchadnezzar, the one responsible for destroying Jerusalem (586 BC) and causing the Israelites to be scattered all over the Babylonian Empire. Its wings represented the swiftness of its conquering power under Nebuchadnezzar's reign, which lasted forty-three years. Because Nebuchadnezzar exalted himself before God, this led to the wings getting plucked off, which meant that he couldn't perform in as swift a manner as before. Also, the king was brought down to Earth from his exaltation and given two legs to stand on, as well as a man's heart (welcome back to humanity). Let's read: "I watched till its wings were plugged off; and it was lifted up from the Earth and made to stand on two feet like a man, and a man's heart was given to it" (Daniel 7:4 NKJV). It seems here that Nebuchadnezzar thought he was like a god because he built Babylon into a great empire. This led him to exalt himself, even above the Almighty.

If you recall from Operation Desert Storm, Saddam Hussein, then Iraq's president, compared himself to this same Nebuchadnezzar of the ancient Babylonian empire. But little did he know that Nebuchadnezzar accepted the true God of the Bible after being brought down and humiliated by the Lord, who showed him that "the most High rules in the kingdom of men, and gives it to whomever He chooses" (Daniel 4:32 NKJV). After seven years of pain and humiliation, the Lord restored the kingdom back to Nebuchadnezzar. If you noticed, God transformed this man in seven years, because God works in sevens. That is His number of completeness and perfection.

Beast 2—The second beast Daniel saw coming out of the sea was "Like a bear. It was raised up on one side, and had three ribs in its mouth between its teeth" (Daniel 7:5 NKJV). This beast represents the kings of Persia (Iran) and Media (northern Iran). Together, they took over the Babylonian Empire, and became an even stronger empire; the Persian Empire. The three ribs in question here are Babylon, Lydia, and Egypt. Babylon fell to Cyrus the Great in 539 BC. Lydia also fell to Cyrus the Great in 547 BC in the battle of Thymbra, and Egypt fell to King Cambyses II in 525 BC.

Babylon falling to the Persians was foretold by Daniel the prophet when God gave him the interpretation of a dream that Nebuchadnezzar had (Daniel 2:39), and then Belshazzar, Nebuchadnezzar's daughter's son (his grandson, whom many mistake to be his son), when interpreting a writing on the wall of the palace, which was put there by the hand of God Himself (Daniel 5:28).

Some who look at these two beasts in Daniel's prophecy might think that the bear represents Russia, and the lion (because of its eagle's wings) represents America. This is not true. These two beasts represent the Babylonian empire (lion) and the Persian empire (bear). This part of the prophecy did come to pass in that the Persians did conquer the Babylonians in 539. The next beast in line will conquer the bear, and eventually the Persians will fall to Alexander the Great's kingdom, who is the leopard (third beast).

Ironically, America's emblem is the bald eagle, whereas the Russian's symbol (not emblem) is the bear, which for centuries was accepted by countries but not Russia itself. Finally the Russians gave in to the bear imagery and made it its symbol. In fact, they used the bear symbol, which is their national animal, in the 1980 Olympics. Its emblem is red with a two-headed eagle. In today's politics, people confuse the eagle and bear to mean the United States and Russia. This has no relevance to Daniel's prophecies. The bear of the twenty-first century is not fighting the eagle of the twenty-first century (unless they meet in a basketball game!). Ezekiel's prophecies in chapters 38–39 will take care of the Russian bear—that is, if the Russian bear is Magog. Then it will be destroyed in the mountains of Israel.

Beast 3—for the third beast in Daniel's vision, we read, "After this, I looked, and there was another, like a leopard, which had on its back four wings of a bird. The beast also had four heads, and dominion was given to it" (Daniel 7:6 NKJV). This beast, which is depicted as a leopard, is even stronger than the first two. It also has four wings and four heads, whose meaning I will explain shortly. Keep in mind that a leopard moves with more swiftness than a bear or a lion, for this is how this invader conquers.

This leopard represents Alexander the Great and the Grecian/Macedonian Empire. It was this very same Alexander the Great of Macedonia, son of Philip II, who exemplified his military genius and talents by masterminding strategies that brought him a conquered world while still in his early thirties. It was the rapidity and swiftness of his conquering drives that gave him the appearance of a leopardlike beast, a vision that God gave Daniel the prophet.

Alexander conquered practically the whole known Western world at the time. His leadership was limited to military genius and nothing else. Once the world was conquered, his boredom led him to severe alcoholism and depression, which ultimately resulted in his death at the young age of thirty-three. It was even speculated that he might have been poisoned, for after conquering India, his men wanted to go no farther. Some say he might have died of a fever. No one knows for sure. All that history reveals is that after his death, his entire family was terminated, and his empire was divided into four kingdoms.

The division of the empire into four separate kingdoms was a fulfillment of the prophetic meaning of the four heads and four wings on Daniel's third beast. This represented the breakup of the empire, which resulted in the depletion of strength and the makeup of four kingdoms: Turkey, Greece, Syria, and Egypt. Let's keep in mind that both Syria and Turkey are north of Israel, for in the latter days, according to Ezekiel's prophecies, people from the north will invade Israel.

Let's elaborate about these four kingdoms, because the breakup of Alexander's empire will eventually lead to the invincible Roman Empire—which, by the way, is not the fourth beast in Daniel's vision, nor is it John's beast in Revelation 13.

a. The first kingdom, ruled by General Seleucus, included much of the old Persian Empire, which includes present-day Middle Eastern countries such as Syria, Iran, Iraq, Pakistan, Afghanistan, and southern Turkey. This was known as the Seleucus Empire.

b. The second kingdom, ruled by General Antigonus, was Macedonia, which included present-day Greece, Yugoslavia (known today as the Federal People's Republic, composed of six republics and two provinces), Bulgaria, and northern Turkey. Because this kingdom's form of government was unstable, it led to war, which later split that kingdom into two other kingdoms ruled by two other generals.

c. The Third Kingdom was the result of the split of the second kingdom between Cassander of Greece and Lysimachus of Thrace, which is present-day Bulgaria. We now have three kingdoms because of the split.

d. The fourth kingdom is Egypt, and this fell to General Ptolemy, who was the first ruler in the Ptolemaic Dynasty, and whose last representative was Cleopatra. We've all heard of Cleopatra and her relationships with Julius Caesar and Mark Anthony. Even Shakespeare wrote about them.

Speaking of these four kingdoms that came from Alexander's empire, the prophet Daniel wrote, "And in the latter time of their kingdom, when the transgressors have reached their fullness, a king shall arise, having fierce features, who understands sinister schemes. His power shall be mighty, but not by his own power; he shall destroy fearfully, and shall prosper and thrive; he shall destroy the mighty and also the holy people" (Daniel 8:23–24 NKJV).

These two verses are speaking of the antichrist, who will come in the latter time. Also, it almost appears by these verses that the antichrist will come from one of these four kingdoms—that is, Syria, Turkey, Egypt, or Greece. Remember that the geographical boundaries have changed. I've stated this because there is much talk about the antichrist coming out of the European Union, created for the purpose of peace with a unified political and economic system. If unified politically, then it will need a leader at its helm. Many theologians believe this leader will be the antichrist spoken of in the book of Daniel.

Unfortunately, many fail to see that the empire of Alexander the Great extended all the way to India. So why look for the antichrist in Western Europe? Why not concentrate on the territories of the four kingdoms that resulted from the breakup of the Grecian/Macedonian Empire, which was Alexander's empire? True, we have Greece, which is located in southern Europe, but we also have a vast area in the Middle East to contend with before pointing to Europe as the empire of the latter days or the home of the antichrist. We'll reflect more on this subject as we proceed.

For now, let's reflect on Rome, because the Roman Empire was by no means an accident. This empire was already in the works during Alexander's time. What initially brought it into view was the downfall of Alexander himself, who chose four generals to split the kingdom among themselves rather than leave it to an heir. This downfall paved the way for the Roman Empire, which started off as a democratic republic but ended up as an imperial dictatorship ruled by the Caesars even though it had a consul and a senate. Had the Grecian Empire remained in tack, I doubt very much that the Romans would have challenged Alexander's superior war tactics, for the Romans were very inexperienced in warfare.

Little by little, the Romans gained ground by fighting two important wars, called the Punic Wars. It wasn't until the second Punic War that they gained the upper hand by defeating the Carthaginians (Phoenicians) in the Battle of Zama (202 BC). By the time Jesus was born, Rome had become an empire that was as strong as iron. Even the Caesars of that era exalted themselves as gods, along with their mythological gods. That is why Christianity became such a feared and conflicting doctrine, because it served the only true God of heaven and His Son, Lord Jesus (Yeshua). With that philosophy in mind, Rome's gods (Caesars included) were totally rejected and written off as false gods.

Rome's answer to Christianity was therefore persecution not only of Christians, but also of Jews, who had an intense hatred for Rome. Fearing this new doctrine called Christianity led the Romans to many encounters with both Christians and Jews. One that bears mentioning is Pilate's encounter with Jews when Jesus was tried. Here, the Jews reminded Pilate that "whoever makes himself a king, speaks against Caesar" (John 19:12 NKJV). Pilate, fearing what Caesar might do to him, sent Jesus off to His crucifixion even when he found no cause to put Him to death. Just a note here: Jesus never directly claimed in scripture to be a king, but He did mention something concerning His kingdom in John 18:36 (NIV): "My kingdom is not of this world." Judging from certain scriptures, including John 3:16, He is the Son of God and therefore the inheritor of all things, thus making Him the "King of Kings and Lord of Lords" according to 1 Timothy 6:15 (NKJV).

The fear incurred here for Rome was the fear that another king or god would be accepted, thus making the new king and his kingdom equal to Caesar and Rome. Therefore, Pilate had to be very careful. If he had released Jesus, that might have meant instant death for him for allowing a new king to penetrate Rome's defenses. Fearing his ultimate punishment, Pilate sent Jesus to His death by crucifixion and affixed a title on the cross that read, "This is the King of the Jews" (Luke 23:38 NKJV), thus eliminating the idea of another king in Rome's realm. The Jews rejoiced over this verdict because they also feared a new doctrine, which was really a fulfillment to theirs. Their biggest fear was that Jesus claimed to be the Son of God, thus making Himself equal to God. They also complained vehemently about the Romans calling Jesus the King of the Jews. It was Pontius Pilate who gave the order to write on the cross "Jesus of Nazareth, the King of the Jews" (John 19:19 NKJV).

In time, Rome's answer to Christianity was clearly exemplified by the martyrdom of those following this new doctrine. Nero Caesar's cruelty is especially noted in that he set fire to the slums of Rome and then used the Christians as scapegoats, blaming them for terrorist actions and the economic woes of the time. Sound familiar? Hitler learned well from this historical truth, for in his plight to get rid of the Jews, he blamed them for Germany's economic woes in the 1930s. Unfortunately, this led to a great holocaust that will always be remembered not only in Jewish history but also in world history.

Leaders such as Hitler, Stalin, and the Caesars of Rome were antichrists in nature. Yes, Hitler claimed to be a believer, but this man was definitely possessed by an entity of hatred and evil that needed exaltation and worship. And Stalin, as a communist, worshipped himself. The Caesars of Rome had a god for every letter in the alphabet. These antichrists were ultimately done away with, as history shows, but the ultimate antichrist has yet to show himself. I'm sure he's alive and well at this present time, waiting for his godly entrance—or should I say his ungodly entrance.

Unfortunately, many will look at the antichrist as a divine savior, or Messiah Himself, for he'll bring about peace and answers to all world economic woes. He will also downsize every nation's safety measures of protection. Beware, for the Word says, "For when they say 'peace and safety'; then sudden destruction comes upon them, as labor pains upon a pregnant woman. And they shall not escape" (1 Thessalonians 5:3 NKJV). Unfortunately, some say that the antichrist is the reincarnation of Alexander the Great because the antichrist will rise up from one of the third beast's kingdom's split.

Beast 4—Daniel's fourth beast represents the kingdom of the antichrist, which consists of seven heads and ten horns (ten kings of nations), three of which are subdued by the antichrist himself (Daniel 7:24). That means even though there is a ten-nation confederacy, only seven will have leaders, for the antichrist will oversee the other three and control all ten.

John's beast of Revelation 13 likewise has seven heads and ten horns. And like Daniel's fourth beast, it also shows a very strong leader (the antichrist) who blasphemes the God of heaven. This leader also prevails over the saints and all political matters for seven years, but with the worst of times in the last three and a half years. Now, with this information in mind, can we safely say that Daniel's fourth beast is the same beast the apostle John saw in Revelation 13? After all, they're identical in all respects.

At the beginning of this chapter, I requested a pictorial vision from the reader when I introduced John's beast. This was so one could visualize Daniel's first three beasts (lion, bear, leopard) in John's Beast, which is also Daniel's fourth beast, which is also the latter-day empire raised prior to the Messiah's return.

Can we now speculate that the makeup of this empire will also consist of some Middle Eastern nations? After all, the lion (Babylon/Iraq), the bear (Persia/Iran), and the leopard (Grecian/Macedonian Empire; Europe and the Middle East) are all incorporated in this latter-day frame. The Roman Empire is not John's or Daniel's fourth beast. It was Alexander's empire, and I'll repeat myself: it paved the way for the strong makeup of the Roman Empire, which included most of Europe and extended as far east as the Middle East and northern Africa. In other words, the Roman Empire came about by accident thanks to the breakup of Alexander's empire.

Even though Rome was spared the humiliation of defeat by the hands of Alexander, it did take on the characteristics of the Grecian ways. This resulted from Rome's takeover of the Macedonian kingdom, which included Greece. Whatever culture the Greeks left behind during

Alexander's time was mingled with Roman culture. This included politics and philosophy, which were major contributions.

The one thing that must be noted about the Roman Empire is that it did not come about as a result of an invasion. In fact, Rome had already been developing itself while Alexander was conquering the rest of the world. Fortunately for the Romans, Alexander did not turn his armies westward. If he had, the collision of both armies would have been one of the greatest battles of all times. As it is, this did not happen, and Rome developed itself into its own empire. It's breakup came about as a result of corruption in the system, with its final fall of the Great Empire in AD 284, when General Diocletian split the empire into two empires, eastern and western. From there on, it was downhill for the Western Empire, which lasted into the 400s, whereas the Eastern Empire (Byzantine) lasted until the year 1453, approximately one thousand years longer.

Not since the Roman Empire's existence has there been another of its kind. They tried with the Eastern Roman Empire but failed. Napoleon and Hitler tried, but they failed. But then again, an empire such as has never been seen will come into existence in the latter days before the return of Christ. It will have the characteristics of both the Grecian and Roman Empires. Most theologians call it a revived Roman Empire," but in reality, according to Daniel's and John's beasts, it is a revived Roman-Grecian Empire.

Some theologians have not taken into consideration the makeup of these beasts, which include Middle Eastern nations like Iraq (lion) and Iran (bear), as well as the rest of Alexander's conquered territories. Even when they speak of a revived Roman Empire, they must acknowledge the fact that this empire had within its boundaries territories like Syria, Egypt, Palestine (Israel/Jordan), parts of Iraq (Babylon), parts of Iran (Persia), and parts of Northern Africa (present-day Libya and Algeria). Yet they seem focused toward Western Europe, which consists of nations like the United Kingdom, France, Germany, and Italy.

When looking at Daniel's fourth beast, one can see that it has teeth of iron and nails of bronze (Daniel 7:19). Symbolically speaking, the iron teeth do represent the old Roman Empire. But the bronze nails also represent the Grecian Empire. How do we know this? From a dream that King Nebuchadnezzar had in Daniel 2. Let's summarize this mystery.

In Daniel 2, we see a vision given to Nebuchadnezzar in a dream. The vision was of a spectacular image, or statue, that had a head of gold, a chest and arms of silver, a belly and thighs of bronze, legs of iron; and feet of ten toes as part iron and part clay. Troubled about this dream, Nebuchadnezzar summoned his advisors to interpret the dream. They couldn't, so Daniel was summoned, and after praying to the Lord, he came up with the interpretation.

The image which Nebuchadnezzar saw represented the empires according to Daniel's interpretation from God. It started with Nebuchadnezzar's kingdom of Babylon as the head of gold, the Persian Empire as the silver, Alexander's Grecian/Macedonian Empire as the bronze, the Roman Empire as the iron, and finally the end-time empire of ten toes as partly of iron and partly of clay. Daniel dissected each of the levels of metal on the image to explain to Nebuchadnezzar his dream.

Daniel did not mention these empires by name because he did not know at the time who they were., Or maybe he did know but was kept from revealing their identities. What he did was merely label each portion of the image as a new kingdom, with gold signifying the softest and iron the hardest. The only time he ever revealed an invader by name during his captivity in Babylon was when interpreting the writing on the wall of the palace to Belshazzar, Nebuchadnezzar's grandson, who was their leader at the time. What Daniel interpreted from the writing on the wall was that the Persians and Medes were preparing to take over the Babylonian kingdom—something that happened almost immediately.

Our primary interest here in Nebuchadnezzar's statue image is the feet with the ten toes of iron and clay, for it represents the end-time empire that will break to pieces anything that gets in its way (Daniel 7:23). It's makeup will be former Roman Empire nations (iron) and former Grecian/Macedonian nations (bronze), which are depicted as clay nations. In my speculation, I'm led to believe these bronze (clay) nations are oil-rich Middle Eastern nations, which will form an alliance with highly industrialized nations of Europe to form this empire that will be controlled by the antichrist himself.

After putting this jigsaw puzzle together, how can one not see that Middle Eastern nations will be included in this end-time empire? The ten horns that Daniel and John both saw are the ten toes of iron and clay that Nebuchadnezzar saw in his great image dream. One must also consider the nails of bronze in Daniel's fourth beast (Daniel 7:19), which depicts Alexander's empire, or all of the Middle Eastern nations. Just a note here: Why are bronze nails mentioned in Daniel 7:19 yet are not seen in the toes of Nebuchadnezzar's great dream image? Yes, the bronze is mentioned as the belly and thighs depicting Alexander's empire, but it is not mentioned in the toes of iron and clay, unless the clay is a mixture of some of the weaker nations that Alexander conquered, namely those that we view today as oil-rich nations. In my opinion, these clay nations might just be the bronze nails in the prophecy. Also, though John's beast doesn't show these toes but ten horns, that doesn't change the formula. With this information in mind, why is there so much emphasis on the European community becoming this end-time menace? After all, aren't they strictly European nations? It makes sense for industrialized nations to team up with oil-rich nations (clay nations). After all, to run an empire of this magnitude, one must consider the energy source that will keep the empire on track and maintain the military hardware.

Greece, a southern European nation, fits into the formula because it is European and represents the leopard. But what about the lion (Iraq) and the bear (Iran)? These are definitely Middle Eastern nations, not European, yet they are incorporated in Daniel's fourth beast and John's beast in the book of Revelation. Daniel's first three beasts are seen in John's single beast—that is, the lion, the bear, and the leopard. Both Daniel's fourth beast and John's beast are almost identical: ten horns, seven crowns, and a man who blasphemes against God. That man who comes out of this confederacy is the antichrist himself.

A few years ago, I listened to a television evangelist talking and pondering about whether we were looking in the right direction for this end-time empire. As I observed him, he was carefully considering what the prophet Daniel had outlined about Alexander's empire splitting into four kingdoms, for he observed that the antichrist would come from one of these divisions. What he saw in the scriptures, and what he observed, inspired me to look further and study the scriptures with a more intense attitude. I forgot his name, but I truly thank him for his insight and for his drive.

Later on, during Operation Desert Storm, another evangelist questioned whether we were looking in the right direction, for all that was happening then was centered around the Middle East, especially Israel. He questioned whether those who study Ezekiel 38–39 were correct in determining whether Russia was that end-time menace that would attack Israel, or whether a Middle Eastern nation such as Iraq was the power that would lead the charge. This got me thinking again, for I already had accepted the teaching that Russia (Magog) would lead the charge of attacking Israel, and that the antichrist would come from the nations of Europe. As I mentioned in an earlier chapter, I'm pretty sure that Russia is the northern menace of Ezekiel 38–39. But consideration was also in order for other nations north of Israel, such as Syria, Turkey, or even the former Soviet satellites. Russia might not be the culprit, but it will surely be pulled into the arena.

Regarding accepting the European Union as the end-time empire, as you can observe by my writing, I don't exactly hold to that theory, and I have shown why. At present, with the Brexit situation, there's no telling whether other European nations will bail out of that union. Maybe that's a good thing, or maybe it's not, because the East might resent the West for its domination in world economics. It can still happen that way, which might contribute to one of the puzzle pieces of going to battle in the Valley of Meggido.

Instituting a setup by which Western nations will align with Middle Eastern nations is by no means impossible, for this very same scenario was seen in Desert Storm. America, along with its European allies, aligned themselves with Middle Eastern nations like Syria, Turkey, Saudi Arabia, Egypt, and Kuwait. Even the USSR sided politically with the West. President George H. W. Bush referred to this collective cooperation as a new world order, signifying that the world, as a united family, can deal with crisis situations.

Ezekiel 38–39 shows that the Arabian Peninsula will remain friendly with the West because it will have to fight a common enemy (Magog and his hordes). But what about the rest of the Muslim world? Will they set up a confederacy to fight against this newly established world order that promises to police the world? The answer is yes. We can see this in Ezekiel 38–39, for Western nations (Merchants of Tarshish with its cubs) will align with Middle Eastern nations (Arabian Peninsula nations). European Eastern nations (Gomer and others) will align with other Middle Eastern nations like Iran and Iraq. Each alignment is for its own common cause.

Let's face it: during war, fuel is the most important commodity because it keeps the war machines moving. Take this precious commodity away from the enemy, and you'll see victory for yourself. Such was the plight of the Germans in World War II when the Allies cut off their fuel supply during the greatest tank battle in history, the Battle of the Bulge. Here, the Panzer units were denied the luxury of fuel to keep their tanks operational. This made them sitting ducks when they ran out, leaving them no alternative but to surrender to the Allies. Had they not run out of fuel, God only knows whether the war would have been prolonged, thus adding more casualties to it.

Because oil plays a big role in keeping a military state in tack, one must see that the end-time empire of the antichrist will want its share of oil flowing from the Middle East. That means incorporating within its boundaries oil-rich nations. In all probability, the three nations of the confederacy being subdued by the antichrist (Daniel 7:24) will be oil-rich nations. That was Saddam Hussein's intention when he invaded Kuwait in the summer of 1990. His next target was Saudi Arabia. But thanks to the US-led allies' intervention, he was stopped; otherwise, he would have taken one Middle East nation at a time.

Whether speculating or not, my intentions are to capture the attention of those interested in what yet awaits them and humanity. If you're a true believer, then I don't have to convince you that God's Word is true. If you're not a believer, then it's time to get right with the Lord so He can direct your way through the Holy Spirit, who will point you to Jesus Christ. It was Jesus Himself who said, "I am the way, the truth and the life. No one comes to the Father except through me" (John 14:6 NKJV). In the latter days, which is now, many scoffers will come and preach a false gospel. The New Testament is loaded with warnings concerning these scoffers. To shield yourselves from them, you must know what the Bible has to say about truth and the future. You must become well informed with God's Word. That way, you will not fall into a situation where you'll believe a lie. Pray to God for wisdom, understanding, and knowledge. May He, through the Holy Spirit, direct your ways towards His truth. Praise His holy name!

CHAPTER 13

Alignments of Nations

Again, I have to stress to the Bible student, Please let the Bible be its own interpreter. Compare scripture with scripture. It's nice to read all kinds of books about prophecy, but not verifying the information to make sure of its truth will get you into trouble and mislead your Bible research. The same applies to Christian or Jewish TV programming. Many Bible prophecy teachers tend to speculate, including myself. But when I do, I let the reader beware of my speculating. I guess it's because of the excitement level in the mind, and also of what's going on in current events. For instance, how many times have you heard, "Oh, I don't know what this world is coming to" Or, if war breaks out somewhere, you might hear, "Is this it—the end of the world?"

As a Bible student, you should know the answer to these questions. Yet one might tend to speculate about the outcome of the event that's happening and jump into conclusions without really studying the situation or scriptures, which might lead to a correct analysis of the situation. In this case, the student is misled unintentionally, therefore passing along the misinformation to the next student. For example, to say that the European Union is John's beast with the ten horns is a premature conclusion, for not only was the European Union a ten-nation conglomerate for a short while, but in 2020 it numbered twenty-seven nations in an economic community. What's more, one has to take into account that most of the Bible is centered around the Middle East, not Europe. In fact, one might be bold enough to say that its fulcrum is Jerusalem. It doesn't amaze me for a moment that President Trump in December 2017 recognized Jerusalem as the capital of Israel. This by no means was an accident. This was God's doing because Jerusalem will become the capital of the world upon the Messiah's arrival. Even though the world had a problem with the president's recognition of Jerusalem as the capital of Israel, other nations followed suit.

Current events can lead to much speculating, but let's put our trust in God's Word, the Bible. It is a masterpiece authored by the Creator Himself, and it has to be taken literally in its entirety. Unfortunately, some will draw conclusions from this verse or that verse without really getting into the theme of its teaching. It really bothers me when secular people try to quote the Bible and mess it up. For example, they might say money is the root of all evil. It's not money but the love of it that is evil: "For the love of money is the root of all evil" (1 Timothy 6:10 KJV)

Many Old Testament stories, even though true, may still be considered as historical parables dealing with end-time situations. They should be taken seriously because history repeats itself. These historical parables are very important because they convey a message that should enable readers to confer with the tacticians before they commit themselves to an unwise strategy. Let's take David slaying a giant who in actuality would have single-handedly killed hundreds of Israeli soldiers when battling with the Philistines. Here, David, representing Israel (or a type of), takes down the enemy's best warrior while the enemy's army is staring down at him. Here, he cuts off Goliath's head, rallies the Israeli army to fight, and wins against the enemy. This reminds me of the war of Ezekiel 38–39, for here an alignment of nations will come against Israel and completely surround them, but guess who wins?

The beast with seven heads and ten horns is not one of what I call historical parables, but it is symbolic rhetoric used by the Apostle John because he had to be careful in his writings so as not to offend the Romans, who might have thought that his writings would spark a foreign invasion. Thus, John was kept prisoner in the Isle of Patmos for the rest of his life.

What the prophet Daniel saw coming out of the Great Sea (Daniel 7:2), which usually refers to the Mediterranean Sea, and what the Apostle

John saw from the Isle of Patmos, located near the Mediterranean (Aegean) Sea off the Greek shores was the future empire of the latter days, which I believe will be located off these waters. Why do I say a future empire? Because both Daniel and John saw the same beast in these same waters, which represents the empire of the latter days. Observing from the Mediterranean, one can see countries in Europe such as Italy, Spain, Greece, and France. One can also see Middle Eastern countries such as Turkey, Syria, Lebanon, and Israel. In Africa, one can see Egypt, Libya, Algeria, Morocco, and Tunisia. At the shores of these waters, one can see all these nations, which means that any combination of ten of these nations can be considered the end-time empire—that is, European nations mingled with Middle Eastern and/or northern African nations. Wouldn't it be a great strategy to be in the midst of three continents ? Let's think about it.

The makeup of the beast includes both Iraq (Babylon) and Iran (Persia), so some might dispute these as not bordering the Mediterranean. But when you look at these ancient empires, their borders reached the Mediterranean waters, especially during Daniel's time. To prove this point, let's look at Ezekiel 26. A scenario is described where King Nebuchadnezzar of Babylon invades Tyre (Lebanon), thus showing Lebanon and Syria, which is sandwiched between Babylon and Lebanon, as part of the Babylonian Empire. Both these nations border the Mediterranean Sea. Persia (Iran), as we know from secular history and the book of Daniel, invaded Babylon, thus acquiring these coastland territories, which later would be conquered by Alexander the Great from Macedonia (Greece) and then by the Romans.

Again, I have tried to show that the European Union is not this end-time empire—not with the makeup of what Daniel's beast is describing. Great Britain, Germany, Belgium, and other northern European countries do not come near these waters, whereas the three beasts of Daniel's vision do. The implication here is that the fourth beast, which is also John's beast, will be Mediterranean bound. This is my belief. Again, I'm speculating, but it makes sense because this whole scenario is like a jigsaw puzzle. I don't want to commit myself and say this empire will consist only of Mediterranean-bound nations. One has to consider the iron in this equation, which many believe to be on the European side only. But as I said before, this empire needs a fuel source to keep it going both militarily and economically. So why not incorporate these oil-rich nations into the formula? The clay nations, which I believe to be oil nations, will team up with the industrialized nations of Europe to form the greatest empire ever, one led by the antichrist himself. But then again, let's not leave God out of the picture, for He's in control and will have the last say.

As I mentioned before, Operation Desert Storm shows us how Western nations can team up with Middle Eastern nations to fight in a common cause. Too bad this end-time empire will side with evil, and anything that gets in its path will be destroyed—and that includes Messiah Himself at His second coming, if it were possible. Unfortunately for the antichrist, it won't be possible. The world has no idea what it's in for when Messiah arrives. Read on to find out.

Don't be fooled by false peace. There is no peace until the Messiah's return. All the peace conferences and meetings at the United Nations in New York will not solve anything, even though they might appear to. The believers know of this false peace, and they give no glory to it, for they already know without a doubt what the future holds: "For when they say 'peace and safety' then sudden destruction comes upon them" (1 Thessalonians 5:3 NKJV), a verse worth repeating. They know this because they read and study their Bibles on a daily basis. Ironically, some even say that the Bible has tomorrow's headlines already written in it, and I believe they're right.

The unfortunate thing for national Israel is that they will give in to this false peace, only because by then they will be tired and frustrated about all the peace talks that have gotten them nowhere. Therefore, they will accept anyone who can give them a guaranteed peaceful solution. This anyone will be a real person and a real deceiver who comes with promises and with a protection package. This anyone will be the antichrist himself, who is controlled by Satan the devil. He will talk and deceive Israel into signing a seven-year pact (treaty) that will be broken at the middle of that time span, after three and a half years, when the antichrist declares war on them. If Israel had only known this, they wouldn't have signed this pact. But because of their lack of knowledge from not studying their scriptures, they will become the antichrist's puppet.

Many obstacles will befall national Israel during this time before they realize who the true Prince of peace is, but thanks to God's merciful wisdom and compassionate love for them, He will save Israel (again) and bring them back to their land. This is the promise that was given to Abraham, Isaac, and Jacob in the Old Testament. It is also a promise for the meek: "Blessed are the meek, for they shall inherit the Earth" (Matthew 5:5 NKJV). These meek are true believers and humble servants of God who, together with Israel, will partake in the inheritance that God has reserved for them at Christ's coming. This inheritance will even include Arab Muslim brothers and sisters, and anyone else in the world who have come to recognize the true God of heaven and His Son, Jesus the Messiah. Ezekiel 38–39 shows us clearly where Arab brothers will aid in the rescue of Israel. This alone will reap for them rewards of salvation, thus making them inheritors too.

Let's not forget that oil is the most precious commodity coming out of the Middle East. That means the West will protect it, because it is in their best interest to do so. Therefore, Arab nations aligning themselves with the West (Sheba and Dedan) will be at a great advantage, for the West will become their protective shield. In contrast, goat nations from the West (Gomer and its hordes) will also align themselves with goat nations from the East—namely, Iraq and Iran (Persia)—to bring about the Ezekiel 38–39 scenario and, along with Magog, will invade Israel. These goat nations from the West will also depend on Middle Eastern oil to keep their war machines moving, but because they will align themselves with Iraq and Iran, there shouldn't be any problem.

The ten-nation confederacy, with the antichrist as its leader, is composed of goat nations, and therefore we know their final outcome. But what about other nations that might align themselves to become this end-time menace? Can the breakaway former Soviet satellites, combined with Middle Eastern nations, be this menace? What about Middle Eastern nations leading this confederacy with European industrialized nations to back them up? We've already eliminated the European Union because it needs oil-rich nations (clay) to back them up. Also, let's not forget that the antichrist will come from one of the four kingdoms that resulted from the four-way split of Alexander the Great's empire when he died. Any way you look at it, the prophecy of this ten-nation confederacy will come to pass as it torments the world and takes away the peace that was initiated at any of the prior peace conferences.

Another issue to consider during the end-time is economics. The European community alone can disrupt the economies of the world, even if it's not the ten-nation confederacy at the time, by dictating world trade strategies that will knock down the economic giants of the world. Presently, the United States holds the lead in world trade, followed by China and other giants. But that can change overnight once the antichrist takes over. It's no wonder why the kings of the East will war against the West in the Armageddon scenario, for a united confederacy of ten nations will have a prolific drive on its economy, which will force other economic giants to bow down to it, thus causing economic disintegration among the nations and having a devastating effect on the world scene.

Presently, in 2020, China holds the lead for car manufacturing, followed by the United States and Japan. Korea isn't that far behind and is becoming an economically prosperous nation. Just think what a unified Korea (North and South) can do for world economics. True, there are political obstacles that must be ironed out with its citizens, but the outlook for prosperity is there.

China, which has an open door now with the West, especially after acquiring Hong Kong, can finally learn its ways concerning economics and even government. True, the hardline attitude of the communist regime gets in the way, but what is to stop China from breaking away from it? If it worked in the Soviet Union, why not in China? That is the thought of many Chinese students who can see a more prosperous China if communism was done away with. Slowly this might become a reality, forced either by reform or by revolution. Then the Marxists' ways will be done away with, and the stumbling block that prevents prosperity will be lifted. Also, the pay scale will change, thus giving workers a higher wage, which will turn their lives around and transition them from a lower class to a more middle-class living situation.

As for Japan, they too pose a problem with the West, especially with their auto industry, which was second in the world in car exports in

2018–19; Germany was number one, and the United States was third. The United States has had to threaten Japan with import-export trade limits to slow them down. It seems that Americans look at Japanese cars as more reliable than the US counterparts. As a result, US auto manufacturers are aware of this and are trying very hard to manufacture a comparable, if not better, automobile for Americans.

Japan, along with Korea, has also been a menace in America in that it's buying everything from real estate to movie studios and more. I've often heard radio commentators say, "What Japan couldn't do in World War II, they are doing now by their economic onslaught on the West, especially America." So I ask, Where does it end? Or I should ask, When does it end? Does raising tariffs or setting import limits settle the problem? Not really, because they'll turn around and do the same to the West. And that applies to China, Korea, and other Indochina nations. Again, this conflict will be settled in the Valley of Megiddo.

Watching these Asian nations develop and compete with world markets will be exciting, for they too seek the same prosperity as the West. The problem here, as the future gets closer, is whether the West (European community, or the antichrist) will get in their way to prevent their markets from flourishing and deny them a lifestyle such as the West. Japan and South Korea are already there economically, but that can easily change. In my opinion, I see Japan and Korea, along with China, fighting in the end-time against the West. As for Japan, I feel they might still have a gripe against America for losing World War II.

I'm speculating that the new economic giant, the European community—if it remains intact—will supersede that which the East can develop. Only time will tell whether an economic war between the West and East will start the countdown toward Armageddon. As I mentioned in a previous chapter, who can raise an army of two hundred million? It's obvious the Asian nations can—and they will, according to prophecy.

Oil will play a big role in the Far East's quest to prosper as the West has prospered. It was during Operation Desert Storm that Japan was heavily criticized for not entering or contributing more toward helping the allies. Could it have been because they were importing 95 percent of their oil from the Middle East? If so, that goes to show just how dependent they are on the Middle East for their economy's growth and survival. Just think what reaction they would have if their oil supply was depleted. Would they instantaneously build up their fighting power and mobilize their troops for action? What about fighting partners, or an alignment with China and the rest of Indochina? It can happen just like that, for when a nation is threatened, that means war unless some kind of peaceful means can immediately resolve it.

I can remember the oil embargo against the United States back in 1973–74 because it disrupted the whole country. Middle Eastern oil accounted for almost 50 percent of America's oil supply at the time. Yes, America had its own oil, but not enough to run things as normal. Prices jumped 100–150 percent at the gas pumps. Even food prices went up. Price gouging became a household term. Now, what caused the embargo? It was America helping its little brother (Israel) when attacked by Muslim countries in the Middle East. To put it bluntly, Israel was losing that campaign known as the Yom Kippur War until America intervened by resupplying its defenses. That alone gave Israel the power to repel the enemy. America's reward by most Middle Eastern countries was an oil embargo meant to cripple America's economy. Luckily, America still got supplies from several Middle Eastern nations, namely Libya. Had the embargo continued, there's no telling whether the United States would have taken the oil by force.

I'm stating this to demonstrate what the United States, or any other nation dependent on foreign oil, might do if squeezed by a supplier. In the previous illustration that I used concerning Japan, in my opinion, an embargo against them might instigate a war. And because they have no nukes presently, I'm sure a supplier of nukes would be more than willing, if the price was right, to lend a helping hand. Again, an alliance might be in order for a successful campaign that might align Japan with China, Korea, and the rest of Indochina to head to the Middle East with their armies, for the kings of the East will cross the Euphrates River after it's dried up (Revelation 16:12). This is God's plan.

As in the Middle East, the kings of the East have to be taken seriously. It wasn't that long ago (the sixties and seventies) that America fought a bloody campaign in South Vietnam to no avail, because South Vietnam was taken by the communists after the Americans departed.

Prior to that, another war was fought in the fifties in Korea, again to no avail, because it left Korea divided (North and South). What about Japan? After World War II, Japan had to surrender unconditionally to the Allies, to their embarrassment and pride. This know-how of atomic weapons is not a mystery to the Chinese, for they already belong to the nuclear club and are making sure new members join because they are now in the business of recruitment. North Korea is a prime example of this. After all, they are allies. They were allies during the Korean War, and they still will be if, or when, war breaks out again.

Building up empires and alliances is no new mystery to the world because it has been going on since the book of Genesis, and it will continue through the book of Revelation with a new world order and a ten-nation confederacy led by the antichrist. History has shown that empires do not last forever because they eventually fade away as the Roman Empire did, or they get swept away by an invader wanting that position. But the Word says, "The kingdoms of this world have become the kingdoms of our Lord and of His Christ, and He shall reign forever and ever" (Revelation 11:15 NKJV). In other words, God's throne will last forever here on Earth.

The so-called new world order will be no different because this arrangement of policing the world, which started after World War I, will eventually meet its match, and then all hell will break loose. No one wants to be dominated by an outside force, not even the antichrist, who will have to deal with this new order at the beginning of his dictatorship; that is, if he's not part of it, which is the belief of many. His end will culminate with the Messiah's arrival at the height of Armageddon: "And then that wicked shall be revealed, whom the Lord shall consume with the Spirit of His mouth, and shall destroy with the brightness of His coming" (2 Thessalonians 2:8 KJV). Once the antichrist has been destroyed—and he will be destroyed—the Messiah, who is Jesus Himself, will usher in the new millennium, which will last one thousand years.

The end-time will be a fascinating time in history because the world as we know it will be transformed into a conglomerate of nations for the purpose of peace, or of war. The Almighty Himself will direct the traffic during these times, and He will put His angels in charge over the affairs of humans and will allow Satan to have his great finale here on Earth before his incarceration of one thousand years and demise.

In conclusion to this chapter, what we're looking at here is Middle Eastern nations teaming up with Western nations (merchants of Tarshish and the young lions), or with an evil northern empire (Magog and its hordes). This is the Ezekiel 38–39 scenario of the future. Then afterward, we're looking at a dictator (antichrist), who will take over the world and leave it open for all kinds of confrontations, especially with the Far East, who will muster up an army of two hundred million to march and confront the West. Also, let's not forget Egypt, which is a Middle Eastern and African nation and at the time of writing is still friendly with Israel thanks to the Camp David meetings during President Carter's administration. But that friendship can easily change overnight because of the Muslim influence in that country. Only time will tell.

As for the Far East, it will also align itself with other Asian countries to threaten world peace. In my opinion, it's overpopulation will make this threat a reality, for it must feed its multitudes and at the same time carry on economically to guarantee jobs for its massive population. An alignment of such a populace would not only guarantee an army of two hundred million but would also guarantee the war to end all wars, for the slaughter will be so great that the blood will reach the horses' bridles for up to about 185 miles (1,600 furlongs; Revelation 14:20 NKJV). Only the Messiah, who is the Lord Jesus, will be able to put an end to this slaughter; otherwise, "no flesh would be saved" (Matthew 24:22 NKJV).

Many believe the Battle of Armageddon will end the world, but on the contrary, the Messiah will issue in a new millennium of peace, for here is when He takes back His inheritance from Satan to share with His people. But before all this peace can come to pass, many nations will align themselves with other nations to bring about either peace or war. The ten-nation confederacy, led by the evil antichrist, will be the spotlight of the moment, but again to no avail, for it will be short-lived.

To believe or not to believe—that is the question. The way I see it, why take a chance, especially when the Bible has the answer? The answer is salvation through Jesus Christ. It is free, with no cost involved except surrendering yourself to the Almighty. So why go through this end-time ordeal? "The Lord is not slack concerning His promise, as some count slackness, but is longsuffering toward us, not willing that they should perish, but that all should come to repentance" (2 Peter 3:9 NKJV). The Lord is very patient and is waiting for you to make a choice. He doesn't want you to die and have to go to hell (the lake of fire) on Judgment Day.

CHAPTER 14

Time Out and Daniel's Seventieth Week

With all the emphasis that we've put on the Tribulation, we haven't figured out when in biblical history this time of trouble will occur. Yes, we discussed events leading to the Tribulation, but we want to take it a step further in study—that is, a study in eschatology, secular history, and current events. This will open people's eyes and minds to observe, through the study of Bible prophecy, a timeline and the truth of the Word. With this emphasis in mind, Bible students can discern approximately where and when certain events will occur.

To figure out the historical time period of the Tribulation), one must be aware of what time we're presently in. A good place to start is in the Old Testament book of Daniel, for by opening it, one can observe specific prophecies that have come to pass and specific ones that have yet to occur. What we're about to study here can be found in Daniel 9. Here, we have the prophecy of the Seventy Weeks. Keep in mind that we're presently in the dispensation of grace and are heading into a troublesome time between grace and the new millennium. This troublesome time is the seventieth week of Daniel's prophecy, also known as the Tribulation.

In this prophecy, the angel Gabriel, who might be an archangel according to the book of Enoch (Apocrypha) comes to Daniel to give him skill to understand a certain vision after a lengthy prayer to God.

He told Daniel, "Seventy Weeks are determined for your people and for your holy city, to finish the transgression, to make an end of sins, to make reconciliation for iniquity, to bring in everlasting righteousness, to seal up vision and prophecy, and to anoint the Most Holy" (Daniel 9:24 NKJV).

I love this verse because it's telling me that sin as we know it will be nonexistent after the seventy-week period. The word *transgression* means to go against the law, which is sin. The word *iniquity* means immoral behavior, which again is sin. Both words imply rebellion against the Most High, and that is why God is purging Israel for that period of time. But all of humanity will also be purged of their sins, especially in the seventieth week of this prophecy. It is God's intention to make believers of everyone in the world, for again He desires none to perish but to have everlasting life (2 Peter 3:9). Unfortunately, many will not want to repent of their sins because they love their sins too much, and that is why God will bring judgment to the whole world.

Remember that a week in the Hebrew is seven years. Therefore the prophecy states that seventy times seven, or 490 years, are determined to do away with all sin and unrighteousness that have encountered humankind since the Garden of Eden, when Adam and Eve committed the first sin and plunged humanity into a cursed situation. The prophecy also reflects a timetable of when the Messiah will initiate the millennium of peace, or the seventh dispensation in His calendar. That means 490 years will elapse before His coming and His enthronement in Jerusalem.

Now, one must keep in mind that Daniel was one of the captives during the Babylonian siege and destruction of Jerusalem in 586 BC, which means that 490 years to complete the prophecy, has already come and gone. Can this therefore mean that the prophecy was fulfilled in its entirety? I don't believe so because there is much sinning still going on in this world today. Also, the Messiah has not made His second debut on Earth as of yet, for there is no rebuilt Temple to speak of for Him to reside. The truth of the matter is Jesus (the Messiah) is still seated at the Father's right hand in heaven. It won't be until close to the end of the Tribulation that He'll come back to Earth to save Israel and the world. It almost seems like an interruption of time took place in the prophecy, and that is precisely what we're going to explain in a moment.

What we have in Daniel 9:24 is the entire time span of the prophecy (490 years). But if we proceed with the prophecy, we'll see how it's broken up to fit into the prophetic schedule of events, which ends at the end of the Great Tribulation. In verse 25 (NKJV), the angel Gabriel says, "Know therefore and understand that from the going forth of the command to restore and rebuild Jerusalem until Messiah the Prince, there shall be seven weeks and sixty two weeks; the streets shall be built again, and the wall, even in troublesome times."

The going forth of the command was a decree, signed by Artaxerxes of Persia, for the Persian Empire was now in view after Babylon fell to Cyrus the Great (539 BC) of Persia. In this decree, Nehemiah's request for going back to Jerusalem to begin the rebuilding process was granted to him (Nehemiah 2). What came about afterward was nothing but trouble for Nehemiah and his friends, and many enemies disrupted the rebuilding process. This did not stop Nehemiah, and he eventually put up the walls of Jerusalem and began the rebuilding process of the city. The trouble that pursued was a fulfillment of the latter part of verse 25 in the prophecy: "the street shall be built again, and the wall, even in troublesome times."

Now, what about "until Messiah the Prince"? Who is this Prince spoken of here who will be cut off after sixty-two weeks (Daniel 9:26)? Actually, He will be cut off after sixty-nine weeks because verse 9:25 words it as seven weeks and sixty-two weeks. Together, they add up to sixty-nine weeks. Some scholars believe the reasoning behind the seven weeks is that the whole construction of the wall and city took about forty-nine years (seven weeks) to complete. No one really knows why the separation of seven sevens and sixty-two sevens was put there, but it happens to be written that way in the prophecy. In determining this, let's take an approximate calculation and see where sixty-nine weeks takes us in biblical history.

As stated before, the Persians were in control at this time of the prophecy. It was Artaxerxes, the Persian king, who signed a decree that sent Nehemiah back to Jerusalem to rebuild the wall that surrounded the city. This happened twenty years into his reign. Ironically, it was also Artaxerxes who ceased the rebuilding project early in his reign due to letters sent to him with accusations against the Jews.

The rebuilding was not only for the wall, but also the city itself with a street as prophesied and explained by the angel Gabriel. Originally, it was King Cyrus who issued a decree to send the Jews back to Jerusalem to rebuild the Temple (Ezra 6:3), which was officially completed by 515 BC - again, with interruptions by adversaries who were against the rebuilding of the temple. It wasn't until the second year of King Darius that the construction restarted, then finished five years later. In all, the construction itself might have taken about seven years. Solomon's temple also took seven years to build. Some say that the project took forty-six years to complete, as stated in John 2:20, where some Jews told it to Jesus after He said, "Destroy this temple, and in three days I'll raise it up" (John 2:19 NKJV). But that was Herod the Great's (37 BC–AD 4) Temple they were talking about, which took forty-six years to rebuild or refurbish. Cyrus's edict went into effect around 538 BC, and the Temple was completed by 515 BC, so I can't see forty-six years of rebuilding.

Please note that Cyrus's decree was for the rebuilding of the Temple, not Jerusalem. Some scholars believe the clock started with Cyrus's decree, but it didn't. It started with Artaxerxes's decree with Nehemiah being sent to Jerusalem to finish the project that the Jews started with Cyrus's decree. As is, the Temple was completed in the sixth or seventh year of King Darius's reign (Ezra 6:15), which leads us to believe that it took twenty-three to twenty-five years to complete the project.

Ezra, who was a skilled scribe of the law of Moses, doesn't show up until chapter 7 of the book of Ezra. Here, he goes to Jerusalem on a teaching mission to teach the statutes and ordinances of the law. He reached Jerusalem in the seventh year of King Artaxerxes's reign. Thirteen years later, Nehemiah goes to Jerusalem, by decree of King Artaxerxes, to rebuild the walls and the city. Apparently, the walls were burned down with the gates between the reigns of King Darius and King Artaxerxes. It took fifty-two days to rebuild the walls only because of how Nehemiah strategized the whole building project, by putting sectional leaders in charge of their walled territories. The rest of the building project apparently took the rest of the forty-nine years of the prophecy (seven weeks total) to complete.

Again, it was Artaxerxes who signed the decree to send Nehemiah to Jerusalem to rebuild the city and the walls. The precise date of the signing is not available, but secular history records Artaxerxes's reign lasting from 464 to 425 BC, when he died. With this information in mind, and knowing from the Bible (Nehemiah 2:1) that the signing took place in the twentieth year of Artaxerxes's reign, we can calculate that this historical truth took place around 444 BC, assuming that secular records are correct.

Again, it's noteworthy to mention that the Temple was completed in the sixth year of King Darius's reign (Ezra 6:15). Because King Darius continued to reign another twenty-six years after the completion of the Temple according to secular history, and his successor to the throne (Xerxes or Ahauserus) reigned nineteen years. Here we have a total of forty-five years since the completion of the project. Now, let's add another twenty years to Artaxerxes's (son of Xerxes) signing of the decree to send Nehemiah to Jerusalem to give us a total of sixty-five years since the completion of the Temple. With this in mind, just think how much deterioration there had to be without proper maintenance of the Temple and its grounds, not to mention the wall itself, whose gates were burned down in all probability by the enemies of the Jerusalem populace.

Now, with the signing of the decree in 444 BC, let's add 483 years (sixty-nine sevens) into the future and see where it takes us. By predicating it upon the Jewish calendar of 360 days per year, we can clearly see the AD side of history around the year AD 32, which is approximately thirty-eight years before the destruction of Jerusalem by the Romans. It is also the completion of the "sixty-two sevens" part of the prophecy. The first part of the seven sevens, as we saw, dealt with the reconstruction of the city of Jerusalem, the streets and the Temple walls. The Temple itself had already been rebuilt prior to Artaxerxes's decree. We know this because it was completed seven years into King Darius' reign. The prophecy continues in verse 26: "And after the sixty-two weeks Messiah shall be cut off; but not for Himself" (Daniel 9:26 NKJV). The year AD 32, or thereabouts, was Jesus's final year of ministry here on Earth.

Biblical history reveals that the one cut-off around this period of time was Jesus Christ Himself, for even His crucifixion was unofficially recognized by Rome, who placed a title on His cross that read "King of the Jews," which strongly offended the Jewish religious leaders (the Sanhedrin). Not realizing it at the time, the Romans gave Jesus a title which to this day is still recognized and respected by all Christian believers, for he's not just the King of the Jews but the King of all humankind.

In Daniel 9:26 (NKJV), where "Messiah shall be cut off, but not for Himself," we are taught the concept of Christianity, by which Messiah (Jesus) paid the price for sin by the shedding of blood not for Himself but for all humanity. You see, He was the sacrificial lamb. This is how Israel atoned for their sins for hundreds of years: by sacrificing animals on the altar of the Temple for the forgiveness of sins. One might say this atonement ritual by the Jews was only a practice or rehearsal for the real thing. The real thing was Jesus, the Son of God, giving up His life as He hung on a tree as a bloody unblemished lamb who took upon Himself all the sins of humanity. This is what He did for you and for me. Believe this and repent of all your sins, and you're home free to an everlasting life with the Lord.

Once the Messiah was cut off, the dispensation of Law was terminated, and the initiation of the dispensation of grace began. This grace period has been interpreted as a time-Out period, reserved primarily for new membership into the community, or family, of God. It began at the end of the sixty-ninth week of Daniel's prophecy, and it will run through the Tribulation, or the "seventieth week." Again, we're speaking about the dispensation of grace, not grace itself. It was at the cross where the clock was stopped, but it will resume when God says so at the beginning of the Tribulation.

To illustrate this time-out period, let's compare it to a football or basketball game, for this is precisely what's taking place. In these games, a time-out is allowed, and the clock is stopped temporarily so that the coach can mastermind a play strategy to win the game. It also allows the players to take a rest before the clock runs out of time. In the seventy-week prophecy game, Jesus is the coach. The Holy Spirit is the assistant coach, and He plays a gigantic role in the training effort of all players. The Father in heaven is the referee who passes judgment on all foul plays. The team itself is the body of believers and those entering as rookies. As on any other team, each player has his or her own part in the strategy of plays.

After the sixty-ninth week, a time-out was granted by the referee (God the Father) that stopped the clock to enable the coach (Jesus), along with His assistant coach (the Comforter), to plan a strategy. This strategy, which is to carry the gospel message and to save many, went into effect after the resurrection of Christ, for up to that point of time, there was doubt, even among the disciples, that He would resurrect from the dead. It took His personal appearance and reappearance to convince them that He was really alive. Thus, the truth of His teachings began to spread all over Jerusalem, Judea and Samaria, and then the world (Acts 1:8). It took the miracle of the resurrection to make believers of all the disciples, and as a result many came to know Jesus as the Lord and Savior of the world.

Now, in order for this strategy to work, the coach had to send His assistant coach to Earth in the form of an invisible being known as the Holy Spirit—ghost, helper, or Comforter (John 14:26). His job is to reside in the hearts of the believers and guide them toward the will of the Father (referee). Today, He still resides in the hearts of believers. He's also in charge of drawing newcomers into the faith by empowering believers to spread the word. These newcomers, once they believe and accept Jesus, become awakened (quickened) in their spirit being, thus having what is known as the born-again experience. This leads them to have a personal relationship with Jesus Christ, thus making Jesus their personal Lord and Savior.

Friends, please take advantage of this time-out (grace) period, for it is a gift from God to the world: "For God so loved the world that He gave His only begotten Son, that whosoever believes in Him should not perish, but have everlasting life" (John 3:16 NKJV). This verse is worth repeating over and over again, for it not only seems to be everyone's favorite but is a sermon in itself.

Just how much longer do we have with this time-out period? No one knows for sure, but through the prophetic message, one can discern only an approximate time in history. For instance, the populace of national Israel, except a few, have not accepted Jesus as Messiah as of yet, but they will at a later time in history, when the Lord is finished with the Gentiles. That is, Israel will remain as is - right up to the time when the last Gentile on Earth accepts Christ Jesus. The apostle Paul worded it as "until the fullness of the gentiles has come in. And so all Israel will be saved" (Romans 11:25b–26a NKJV). The Living Bible reads, "Yes it is true that some of the Jews have set themselves against the gospel now, but this will last only until all of you Gentiles have come to Christ - those of you who will. And then all Israel will be saved" (Romans 11:25–26a TLB).

It seems to me that when the last Gentile is saved, then we'll see the beginning of the Tribulation, and later on the time of Jacob's trouble, especially when the Rapture (the next chapter) takes place and the Church is no longer there to defend the Jew. With the Tribulation in view, the Jew will turn to his God—that is, the God of Abraham, Isaac, and Jacob—and it will be another reawakening for Israel, or should I say a great revival for Israel. It will be the issuance of the seventieth week of Daniel's prophecy.

Another example of how much longer we have in this time-out period is Jesus's prophecy of the end: "And this gospel of the kingdom will be preached in all the world as a witness to all nations, and then the end will come" (Matthew 24:14 NKJV). As is, this gospel is being preached to the whole world, including national Israel. There are a few exceptions, as I mentioned in a previous chapter, but there will come a time when all nations will receive this gospel message.

The truth of the matter is - there are many who have received this message with open arms, and many will continue to do so. But then again, there are many others who have rejected the message and will continue to reject it. In Matthew 24:14, Jesus might have been referring to the end of time-out because He mentioned the whole world. But He might have been referring to those going through the Tribulation, implying that even during the Tribulation, the gospel message will be preached, and then the end will come. Unfortunately, Israel will have its hands full because of the antichrist, but God will send to them two witnesses who will turn the nation around. We'll look at those two witnesses later.

It is today's generation that Jesus spoke of when He said, "Assuredly, I say to you, this generation will by no means pass away till all these things take place" (Mark 13:30 NKJV). "All these things" referred to war, rumors of war, famine, pestilence, roaring waves (intense weather conditions), earthquakes, and finally the "Abomination of Desolation," which marks the beginning of the end, for it is a time when the world accepts the false one as Messiah. What follows afterward is God's wrath on the kingdom of the antichrist and all unsaved humankind.

Now, because ours is the generation that will witness the Abomination of Desolation and the second coming of Christ, we must wonder about the span of a generation. Exactly how long in years a generation is can be mind-boggling, because many have different definitions and opinions of a generation. Psalm 90:10 (KJV) tells us that a human's intended life's span is threescore and ten; that translates to seventy years. And if one remains healthy, this span can go to eighty years. In today's world, humans can live into their eighties and nineties, especially in Western societies. Does this mean that a generation nowadays can be considered to go up to ninety years? It's worth considering because Jesus was referring to the generation that began with Israel's rebirth in 1948. I believe we are that generation that will see all the Lord has listed in His end-time prophecies. Ironically, the genealogy in Matthew 1 shows forty-two years per generation, which shows just how far we've gotten in this twenty-first century.

With this information in mind, we can probably calculate with discernment when certain things will happen in our biblical trek. We already know by biblical history that a major phenomenon happens every two thousand years. For instance, Noah's flood occurred about two thousand years after the fall at the Garden of Eden. Two thousand years later, Jesus was born as the humbled, suffering Messiah. Two thousand more years have gone by since His death and resurrection. Can we therefore boldly say that two thousand years separates Christ's second advent from His days walking on this Earth? Maybe it's time for a rest. After-all, we are approaching, or might just be in, the third day (a day is like a thousand years in the heavenly realm). Jesus died and resurrected on the third day from the grave around the year AD 30. If we add two thousand years to that, we might be looking around the years 2030–2050 for His return, or the start of the Tribulation. We're that close. I'm speculating here, but again, it's worth considering. The

Jewish calendar might see it differently, but I don't like to get involved with numbers, for then it becomes a prediction on my part and strays away from the prophecy itself. But the truth of the matter is regardless when it happens, Jesus Christ the Messiah will return. He said it (John 14:3 NKJV), so therefore it's true.

It boggles my mind to see unrepentant individuals, especially those who have been somewhat indoctrinated in the gospel message, to lose their faith and remain in their comfort zone with the world. The world as a whole does not know, and does not want to know, what's in store for them in the future. They're too preoccupied with the now and the many technologies that the world has to offer them. This is even true for the young ones—and I'm speaking about adolescents, and even the younger ones like toddlers. I see this in my own grandchildren, who can retrieve anything they want off the Internet. Even my three-year-old grandson knows how to stream his kiddie channels on the TV remote. That worries me because they can too easily be captured in the worldly thing and forget about the spiritual thing. That's why it's important to pray for them.

The book of Revelation depicts a time of horrifying events in which God will express His wrath in a judgmental way. I don't believe anyone wants to experience God's trumpet or bowl judgments, found in chapters 8, 9, and 16, but they will unless they repent. Some might even say that they will not experience it if they die before the judgments. Let me tell you a mystery. We will all be resurrected from the dead at the end of time to be judged by God. The Word says, "Just as people are destined to die once, and after that to face judgment" (Hebrews 9:27 NIV). You see, God keeps records, and if your name is not found in His book of life, He will send you to a place where you will be tormented along with the devil and demons. That place is hell. Even Jesus spoke about hell (Mark 9:43). In fact, some say that Jesus spoke more about hell than about heaven.

I don't know about you, but I do not want to go to hell. How can anyone chance becoming a victim of God's wrath? I would rather be saved than be a partaker of His judgments, and these judgments will come to pass as prophesied because this is God's Word. All these things will happen in this generation, probably within the next thirty to forty years, if not sooner—that is, if my speculations and calculations are correct. We are already in the third day. Just as Jesus resurrected on the third day, so, shall we see him on the third day. A day is as a thousand years (2 Peter 3:8). Jesus compared this time in history as a woman in labor pangs: once the contractions begin, there's no stopping them. The woman knows that the baby's birth is near, especially when the contractions get more intense and less spaced apart, until finally the baby is born, and then the woman is relieved. The same logic applies to this present era. I believe the pangs have begun. Just look around the world. Famine is still prevalent, and wars and rumors of war are brewing among nations. There are earthquakes of great magnitudes, roaring waves (tsunamis and hurricanes), tornados in greater number (especially in the United States), and pestilence (AIDS, flu pandemics, COVID-19), and more.

Today, society has more corruption than it can handle. Their wants for getting richer can be considered idolatry and can lead many to thievery, robbery, murder, gambling, prostitution, and many other countless acts. There is no letting up. As the generations progress, so do corruption and immorality. Little do people know that their lifestyles and this present worldly system will come to an abrupt end. Even though God is patient and merciful, He is getting fed up seeing what is happening to His planet—the planet over which He gave Adam dominion. If you recall from the book of Genesis, God gave Adam dominion over the creatures of the Earth, the sea, and the air. Adam was in control over everything until Satan's temptation overwhelmed Eve and him. At that moment, Satan took dominion of the world, and look at what a chaotic world it has turned out to be.

Watching all these events coming closer together simultaneously shows us just how close we are to the birth of a new era, which we'll call the new millennium. This new millennium will bring about the Messiah's earthly reign after the end of the Great Tribulation. But for now, it is this very Tribulation that the Almighty will issue in, and He will give the order to restart the clock of Daniel's prophecy. No force on Earth will be able to stop it, for it has already been prophesied, and there is no going around it. The time-out period will come to an end, which will bring in the seventieth week in Daniel's prophecy. Once here, the world will suffer a time that has been labeled in the Old Testament as the time of Jacob's trouble (Jeremiah 30:7 KJV), or "a time of trouble such as never was since there was a nation, even to that time" (Daniel 12:1 NKJV). All this trouble will come as the result of an evil mastermind known as the antichrist, who wants to take the place of the true Messiah. Afterward, God will unleash His judgments on the antichrist and his kingdom. Not only will He purge Israel again, but also purge the whole world as well of all its unrighteousness, evil, and hatred, which means sin. But worry not because you, Israel, will eventually be saved out of it (Jerimiah 30:7).

Remember that God's number of completeness is seven. The seventh dispensation will complete God's plan of salvation in the dispensational era. I say this because even in the millennium, people will still have the will of choice—that is, whether or not to believe in the Lord. In this millennium, there will be newborns. The prophet Isaiah says that babies will not die. Older people will live to be over a hundred years old. In fact, at the age of one hundred, a person will be considered young. Only sinners will die young. There will not be weeping or crying anymore (Isaiah 65:20). I even doubt whether hospitals and doctors will be needed anymore. It almost sounds too good to be true, but it is God's promise to the believers.

With all these scriptural and secular hints all around us, can we not foresee that the time-out period is drawing to an end? Yes, the Tribulation years will be upon us sooner than we think, and It won't be long before we witness Israel's signing of a peace treaty at the start of these Tribulation years. This treaty is a seven-year pact between Israel and a ten-nation confederacy ruled by the antichrist. When we do witness this prophetic moment in history, or we witness the rebuilding of the Temple in Jerusalem, then we'll know that our redemption draws nigh and that Israel's time of trouble is at hand. Then we can begin the countdown to Armageddon, but before we do, let's elaborate on what is going on in Israel during this time of trouble.

Scripture is the true Word of God, so one must accept it as truth. Therefore when Daniel 9:27 speaks of a covenant or agreement being signed by all parties concerned, including Israel, one must adhere to this prophecy as truth. That means God will let the antichrist devise a peace plan that will benefit and be accepted by both the Arab Muslim and the

Jew. Unfortunately, as I mentioned before, the peace achieved will be a false peace, even though the world will recognize it as legitimate and trustworthy. The truth is we're dealing with the father of lies and the greatest deceiver of all time.

The signing of the seven-year pact will apparently guarantee Israel some kind of comfort and peace; at least for a short while—three and a half years, to be exact, as prophesied by the prophet Daniel. But don't be fooled, for again, once they say "peace and safety," then all chaos will break loose. At the midpoint of the pact (three and a half years), the antichrist will take his seat in the rebuilt Temple in Jerusalem. This is what he's wanted all along: to be worshiped as the Messiah will be. By sitting in the Temple, he'll proclaim himself as God. But because the God of Israel is a jealous God, this action will kindle God's wrath on the antichrist and his kingdom. Unfortunately, the antichrist will attack and prevail over anyone who believes in the God of Israel.

What we're witnessing will be the fulfillment of what Jesus prophesied in Matthew 24:15 (NKJV), for He said, "Therefore when you see the 'Abomination of Desolation' spoken of by Daniel the prophet, then …" He was speaking of the antichrist (Satan) sitting in the Temple in Jerusalem and proclaiming himself to be God (2 Thessalonians 2:4). This is the abomination that will not be tolerated or forgiven by God, for in His anger, He will destroy the antichrist (beast) and his partner (false prophet) by throwing them into the lake of fire reserved for the devil and his followers. The devil himself will be thrown into the fire at a later time, at the end of the thousand-year millennium and after serving a thousand-year sentence in the bottomless pit (abyss).

Some teach that the abomination of desolation spoken of by the prophet Daniel (11:31, 12:11) has already come to pass. Their reasoning comes from the fact that Antiochus IV Epiphanes entered Jerusalem in 168 BC and desecrated the Temple. If you recall from an earlier chapter, Alexander the Great's empire was divided into four kingdoms, and one of them went to General Seleucus, who founded the Seleucid Dynasty. Epiphanes, who is directly in line with this dynasty, reigned in this Syrian empire between 175 and 163 BC after his brother Seleucus IV was murdered. It was this very same Antiochus IV Epiphanes who plundered and desecrated the Temple, a practice which he was an expert at and known for. What he did was forbid the worship of Yahweh (the Lord's name) and all Jewish rites. Religious rituals such as traditional sacrifices, the Sabbath, and circumcision were done away with. For anyone caught practicing in these traditions, the penalty was death. Zeus, the Greek god, was worshiped in the temple in place of the true God of heaven. Even an altar was erected in the Temple for this purpose, and sacrifices to Epiphanes were made at the feet of a statue of himself. It has been said that pigs were sacrificed in the Temple during this time of plundering, a desecration unto the Jew.

Historically speaking, this event took place, but prophetically speaking, it will happen again during the time of Jacob's trouble, or during the Great Tribulation, because it is believed by many that the Temple will be rebuilt in Jerusalem during or prior to the Tribulation, thus bringing back the rituals of old. Let's remember that national Israel as a whole has not accepted Jesus as Messiah as of yet, and that's why the rituals will be reinstated. That includes the sacrifices of old.

Remember that a prophecy can be twofold. This is the case here, for the antichrist Epiphanes did take his place in history as the one desecrating the temple of Jerusalem. But later on, during the Great Tribulation, we're going to witness a similar scenario in that the antichrist will portray himself as an exalted entity and take the seat in the Temple (history repeating itself), thus igniting God's final wrath, which will be in the form of deadly plaques.

Just as the Temple was restored by the Maccabees, a Jewish dynasty of patriots, it will be restored again upon the Messiah's return. If you have studied your Jewish history or read the book of Maccabees in the Apocrypha, you will see that Maccabees, led by Mattathias and his five sons, brought back freedom to Judah. Known as the Maccabean Wars, the uprisings led by these Maccabees restored the Temple, which was desecrated by Epiphanes's abominations—but not after Epiphanes sent in a tax collector who took the spoils of Jerusalem, set it on fire, pulled down houses and walls, and took many captives, including women and children.

Again, we have a scenario of the end-time, when Israel will be attacked, Jerusalem will be trampled by Gentiles, women will be ravished or raped (Zachariah 14:2), and many will die in the name of religion. The antichrist will be the spotlight of attention during this time. He will give the orders, and many people, in their deceptive trance, will pay him homage by obeying his orders and instructions. He'll make war not only on the Jews but also on the Christians (those not raptured). But then again, we have a superhero who will come to the rescue of Israel and other believers. Never again will the Holy Scriptures be destroyed or harmed in any way. This superhero will come on a white horse, as mentioned in Revelation 19. He will be called "Faithful and True," and His eyes will be like a flame of fire; on His head He'll be wearing many crowns (Revelation 19:11–12). "And His name will be called Wonderful, Counselor, Mighty God, Everlasting Father, Prince Peace" (Isaiah 9:6 NKJV).

As Mattathias and his sons took revenge on the antichrist (Epiphanes), so will Jesus the Messiah. He will take revenge on the antichrist of the future and see to it that he is destroyed, for this time Jesus will come as a mighty warrior to save humankind, unlike His first time when He came as a humble servant to save souls. I believe the pivotal time of His physical return will be when the antichrist takes over the Temple to sit and rule from there. Also, the cry from His people to heaven will be such that He'll have to come to their rescue, or else no flesh will survive the onslaught.

Let me ask you a question. How can we be so sure that the scenario of the abomination of desolation (that detestable thing) will take place at a future time?

First, let's take a look at Matthew 24:15–16 (NKJV), for it says, "Therefore when you see the 'Abomination of Desolation' spoken of by Daniel the prophet, standing in the Holy place, then let those who are in Judea flee to the mountains." Here, the Lord is warning a future population of Israel (Judea) to flee to the mountains because of the atrocities that are about to come. This event has not come to pass as of yet, for He spoke it on the AD side of the calendar. The abomination that took place in Jerusalem during Antiochus IV Epiphanes's time was on the BC side of the calendar and has no relevance to the prophetic message that Jesus related to His disciples, for He said "when you see," implying time in the future sense. He didn't say "when you saw," implying the past.

What Jesus has done here is give ample warning to Israel—that is, the Jewish community and its offshoot, the Christian community—to run and hide from the evil one. Those who believe in this prophetic message will take heed and prepare themselves. Those who ignore the message will be trampled and crushed by the evil antichrist and his hordes. Let's face it: the Great Tribulation will bring into focus that leader called the antichrist. Want to know more about him? Just pick up your Bibles and study the Old Testament book of Daniel and the New Testament book of Revelation. These books will clearly show you who the antichrist is, where he's coming from, and how powerful he is. Also, 2 Thessalonians 2:3–10 will reveal the lawless one (the son of perdition) and what Christ intends to do to him.

The seventieth week in Daniel's prophecy will bring out the beast in humans. There will be countless atrocities, and the saints of God will be forced to war against the forces of unrighteousness. Though it'll seem like a loss for the saints of God, the ultimate climax will result in God sending His Prince (Lord Jesus) to the rescue. At that time, the unrighteous will be dealt with, and the Messiah will claim His inheritance, which is the Earth, and share it with His saints. Can you see now why the meek will inherit the Earth (Matthew 5:5 KJV)?

Before concluding this chapter, let's elaborate a bit on where America stands during the seventieth week of prophecy. If America is to be tested—and it will—then one must ask, What kind of test will it have to endure? After all, as many say, America is not mentioned in the book of Revelation. How can it? America didn't exist during the writings of the Bible, but it did in Ezekiel 38–39 as one of the cubs (young lions).

Let's face it: one must remember that America is like a big brother to Israel (at least during time of this writing). But then again, things can change overnight. I've often heard theologians say that America would be destroyed by this time in history, probably by a nuclear disaster. Some have even gone as far as to say that America is the Babylon of Revelation 18, which describes Babylon as being utterly destroyed by fire as a judgment from God. I can recall the 2001 attack on America (9/11) by terrorists who crashed planes into the Twin Towers in New York City and into the Pentagon in Washington, DC. As frightening as it was, the smoke in New York City reached the heavens; even the space station in orbit was able to observe what was going on below. The ships in the harbor stood in amazement. Those on the New Jersey side, across the Hudson River, watched in shock. I say this because of Revelation 18:17–18 (NKJV), where it says, "Every shipmaster, all who travel by ship, sailors, and as many as trade on the sea, stood at a distance and cried out when they saw the smoke of her burning, saying, 'what is like this great city.'" It almost seemed that this prophetic verse was coming to pass, but that wasn't the issue here regarding these verses.

The truth of the matter is New York City is not the Babylon in Revelation 18. New York City did not burn that day; only several skyscrapers did. The Pentagon survived its attack, and the plane that crashed in Pennsylvania, thanks to its brave and courageous passengers, never reached Washington, DC, where it was heading. But the solemn response by the whole country was felt worldwide. God was in the midst of the grief because His name was called that day by the inhabitants of America and abroad. Unfortunately, that's what it takes to get people's attention to seek out the Lord. Just check Israel's biblical history in the Old Testament to see for yourself.

Depicting this scenario of the destruction of Babylon as America is preposterous, for this chapter goes on to speak about finding "the blood of prophets and saints in her, and all who were slain on the Earth" (Revelation 18:24 NKJV). Yes, America will be judged one way or another. In fact, it was Reverend Billy Graham who said that God would have to apologize to Sodom and Gomorrah if America was not judged. I believe this to be true, but it will be done according to God's timing. America will also be purged of all its unrighteousness just as the rest of the world will be.

A plus for America is the fact that for many years, the gospel message has flowed not only in this country but also abroad. A second plus for America is the fact that it has been Israel's ally and friend since 1948, when Israel became a sovereign nation again. Now, whether this friendship diminishes before the Tribulation because of persecution or a takeover by the antichrist is yet to be determined. But as scripture says, "For with God Nothing shall be impossible" (Luke 1:37 KJV).

Once the Tribulation hour gets here, God only knows whether America will still be a big contributor to the gospel message. Presently, there is a diminishing of biblical integrity in America, yet many have not bowed the knee to Baal. Once the Rapture takes place, God will reprimand America for its sinful behavior, but I do not see a complete destruction against America. As is, God will do away with all unrighteousness not only in America but also throughout the whole world. One thing that the Godly world has yet to contend with still is spiritual warfare, because there are spiritual forces constantly working against believers and the gospel message. The Bible says, "We do not wrestle with flesh and blood, but against principalities, against the rulers of darkness, against powers, against the rulers of the darkness of this age, against spiritual hosts of wickedness in the heavenly places" (Ephesians 6:12 NKJV). Therefore, overtaking the saints, which will eventually happen, is Satan's goal for stopping the gospel message. That is why we must "put on the full armor of God" (Ephesians 6:13–18 NIV). But then again, as I've been saying all along, God is in control!

Friends, let's take advantage of the time-out period while it's still here. Invite your friends and neighbors to church because God has a gift for you and them. That gift is eternal in nature. It is the free gift of salvation, and you can get it only through the blood of Christ, who gave up His life for you and me on that cross. But praise His holy name, He was resurrected from the grave and now resides in heaven, seated at the right hand of His father. Believe it, and be saved. Deny it, and you'll experience God's wrath.

In the next chapter, we'll see how the believers will survive the plights of the Great Tribulation. We'll be discussing a very arguable doctrine in Christianity called the Rapture. Praise the Lord !

CHAPTER 15

The Rapture of Believers

With all the mass destruction going on in the book of Revelation, I've always wondered where the believers, or the family of God, will be during the seventieth-week trial, or the Great Tribulation. By believers, I mean those who have accepted the Lord Jesus Christ, the Son of God, as their personal Lord and Savior and washed themselves in the blood of the Lamb, whether Jew or Gentile. Being washed in the blood means accepting the fact that Jesus's blood was shed for us as he hung on the cross in order to cleanse us of our sins. In other words, He became the sacrificial Lamb. Believing this, and the fact that He resurrected from the grave, makes us born-again believers.

The question of believers enduring the Tribulation has puzzled many for ages, and one must wonder whether a merciful and loving God will see His people go through this disastrous nightmare in history without helping them somehow. To answer this question and more, one must realize that the Tribulation hour is a test for both believers and nonbelievers. Some say that believers won't be around during the Tribulation, whereas others say they will be around until the middle or even end of the Tribulation. As we progress with this chapter, we'll try to analyze the differences in this belief called the Rapture, a term not found in the Holy Bible.

Now, what is the Rapture? We'll define it as a state of being transported from one place to another, or being snatched and placed at another location. In Christendom, it is the snatching away of believers to heaven before, during, or after the Tribulation. Its purpose is to purge the Earth and rid it of all its evil and unrighteousness while at the same time protecting the Church from physical harm. Afterward, the Lord Himself will come back to Earth with angels, the resurrected (first resurrection), and the raptured believers.

Another term that may be used in place of rapture is translation, or being translated. It was Enoch who didn't experience death, for he was translated (Hebrews 11:5). He "walked with God; and he was not, for God took him" (Genesis 5:24 NKJV). That means he was taken or transported (raptured) to heaven without experiencing death..

We are therefore saying that the body of believers, whether Christian (Gentile) or Jew (because some Jews will accept Jesus as Messiah prior to the Tribulation, and many more during the Tribulation, thanks to the 144,000), will somehow be transported from this chaos in history to another location that points to heaven itself. The reason for this transportation is so God can deal with the rest of unsaved humankind through a series of judgments. Now, whether the unsaved take heed after the rapture of believers will be entirely their choice. The door will still be open for those who missed the Rapture, especially in Israel, for it is the consensus of many that 144,000, who are servants of God (Revelation 7 and 14), will evangelize the nation of Israel. As a result, many will give their hearts to the Lord. Afterward, the Lord (Messiah) will return to Earth with those who were raptured (Jude 14) and resurrected, along with His holy angels to destroy all unrighteousness. Because scripture tells us there will be survivors, we can only hope that some (prayerfully many) will be reached after the Rapture.

To illustrate this Rapture phenomenon, let's take an old but very popular TV series, and later motion picture, that sparked the curiosity in many as to what the future holds. I'm referring to the *Star Trek* series of the midsixties, where Captain Kirk and his crew would stand in a transporter room (in their spaceship) in tubelike, upright magnetic cylinders; energize themselves by breaking up into molecular energy; and beam themselves to any location outside the spaceship within their limits. Just imagine, as in this *Star Trek* drama, being instantaneously transported from point A to point B without leaving a trace behind. The

Rapture of believers will be just that. The only difference is that they will not have control as to where or when it will happen.

The Judge of judges will make that decision for the believer. That is why we must be ready for it at all times, for "the Lord will come as a thief in the night" (2 Peter 3:10 NKJV) and snatch us away. But comfort yourselves, those of you who are ready, for you are not in complete darkness thanks to the Word of God. Therefore, "you, brethren, are not in darkness, so that this Day should overtake you as a thief" (1 Thessalonians 5:4 NKJV). You see, knowing the Word will save you. In contrast, those who do not know the Word or aren't ready will have to deal with the antichrist and God's final judgment on humankind. For those who become believers after the Rapture, many of them will become martyrs because of persecution, but others will survive because of the grace of God.

I've always gotten a kick from bumper stickers that read, "Beam me up, Jesus!" They get this saying from *Star Trek*, when Captain Kirk or any other crew member would shout, "Beam me up, Scotty" (Scotty was the head of engineering) and be transported back to their ship. Unfortunately, believers will not know the exact time (or hour) of departure, thus hindering them from hollering, "Beam me up, Jesus." But when the Rapture happens, millions will leave the surface of the Earth to be united with Christ Jesus in the clouds for a short time before they return to Earth with Him.

This is the doctrine shared by most Christian, Bible-believing churches. There are a few denominations that do not believe in this phenomenon. But it is a comforting doctrine to believe in because it brings a hopeful outlook for those in fear and distress. In fact, the Rapture has been referred to as the "Blessed Hope, and the glorious appearing of the Great God and our savior Jesus Christ" (Titus 2:13 NKJV), for it will be a joyous and glorious time for believers. It will coincide with the first resurrection of the dead, thus enabling believers to be united with departed loved ones who have fallen asleep. "Fallen asleep" is a Christian term for being dead (deceased). In Christianity, Christians never die because when they fall asleep, they'll wake up again. This is the great "Blessed Hope" that Christians await.

In 1 Corinthians 15:51–53 (NKJV), the apostle Paul writes about the

Rapture in this fashion: "Behold, I tell you a mystery: we shall not all sleep, but we shall all be changed in a moment, in the twinkling of an eye at the 'Last Trumpet.' For the trumpet will sound, and the dead will be raised incorruptible, and we shall be changed. For this corruptible must put on incorruption and this mortal must put on immortality."

Can you imagine how quickly an eye twinkles? The twinkling of an eye is not a blink but a reflected particle of light that takes only a fraction of a millisecond (light travels at 186,00 miles per second). That is how quick the believers will be transformed into glorious beings at the coming of Christ. Those transformed will become like Him, never to experience death again if they came from the grave. For those raptured while alive, they will never experience death.

In 1 Thessalonians 4:15–16 (NKJV), we read, "For this we say to you by the word of the Lord, that we who are alive and remain until the coming of the Lord will by no means precede those who are asleep. For the Lord Himself will descend from heaven with a shout, with the voice of an Archangel, and with the trumpet of God. And the dead in Christ will rise first, Then we who are alive and remain shall be caught up together with them in the clouds to meet the Lord in the air. And thus we shall always be with the Lord."

Again, we have confirmation of this event called the Rapture, for we'll meet the Lord in the air immediately after the first resurrection. Also, let's keep in mind these trumpet blasts, for they will show up again during God's judgments in the book of Revelation. In my opinion, these trumpets in Revelation are significant with the timing of when the Rapture will occur. It is at this point in history when the Church will disappear from the face of the Earth to meet the Lord in the clouds, and where a marriage will take place. That marriage is between the Lord Jesus, who is the groom, and the Church, which is the bride.

Because we're looking at a "last trumpet" Rapture, we must assume that we're either near or within the Tribulation's time frame. If we are within the Tribulation's time frame, then we know that Israel is already at the hands of the antichrist, especially if the seven-year pact has been agreed upon (Daniel 9:27). Once the middle of the week (three and a half years) comes about, I hope that the Church will have already been raptured; otherwise, it will have to endure a war with the antichrist that cannot be won. But then again, that is how God has planned it.

Again, God will intervene to save Israel, and what remains of the world, by sending His Son, Jesus; His angels; all those who resurrected in the first resurrection; and those who were raptured to save Israel from the antichrist and his hordes. Now, what proof do we have that Jesus is coming back with His saints? Let's read Jude 14–15 (NKJV): "Behold the Lord comes with ten thousands of His saints to execute judgment on all. To convict all who are ungodly." Without a doubt, these verses show that Messiah is not coming alone but will be with His saints. And who are these saints if not those who were caught up to Him in the first resurrection and in the Rapture? It seems like these saints will participate with Jesus in the judging process, the liberation process, and the restoration process.

He's also coming with angels: "And He will send His angels with a great sound of a trumpet, and they will gather together His elect from the four winds" (Matthew 24:31 NKJV). Unlike Jude 14–15, Jesus is sending His angels but is not coming along with them. In all probability, we're looking at the Rapture in this verse, which takes place prior to His second physical coming. Take note also of the trumpet blast that accompanies the angels, because I believe the Church will be taken here.

Because immortality comes into the picture at the Rapture (we'll be like Jesus), the saints cannot be killed. Any weapon formed against them will not prosper (Isaiah 54:17), whereas the mortals can be killed. And that is precisely what is going to happen, for the saints (and angels in the spiritual realm) will do battle and prevail over the ungodly. The bloodshed will be so great that it will reach the horse's bridle for up to 180 miles (1,600 stadia), as I stated before.

It's apparent that the Messiah's arrival will coincide with the Battle of Armageddon, for He comes during a time where, if not shortened, no flesh would be saved (Matthew 24:22). Because we're looking at a battle scenario that is both in the physical and spiritual realms, the saints of God, along with the nonraptured believers, will be battling in the physical battle itself, whereas the angels of God, who are spiritual in nature but can be transformed to look like humans, will probably battle in both the spiritual realm and the physical realm. Together with the Lord Jesus, they will do away with all unrighteousness. Satan at this time will be captured and put in chains. Then he'll be thrown into the bottomless pit (abyss) for a thousand years. After the thousand years, he will be released to tempt the nations again (Revelation 20:2-3, 7-9). I believe this will be the last test from God to the human race. But again it is to no avail for Satan, because he'll try to attack and surround the camp of the saints. God will send fire from heaven to devour them. Then Satan will be thrown into the lake of fire prepared for him and his friends (Revelation 20:10).

The seventieth week, or the Tribulation, is a time no one wants to be in. Here the antichrist will bring havoc on not only Israel but also the whole world. It's also a time for God's judgments to be unleashed against unsaved humankind. The Book of Revelation informs us of twenty-one judgments: seven seals, seven trumpets, and seven bowls (or vials). These judgments are meant to purge the world of all unrighteousness and evil. There is no escape. To escape these judgments, God has invited all humankind to be saved from it. The formula is easy and simple. All you have to do is give your heart to the Lord right now and ask Him to forgive you of all your sins. Next, you have to follow Him by doing His will; that is, get yourself plugged into a Bible-believing church, read the Word from the Bible on a daily basis, and believe that the Lord Jesus Christ died on the cross for you and then resurrected from the dead to defeat death. Now you can make the Lord Jesus the Lord and Savior of your life. Do this, and be saved from the impending judgments that are coming upon this world.

Now, let's figure out when this Rapture will occur. We already know that the time-out period is over prior to the Tribulation. This will issue in the seventieth week in Daniel's prophecy, which will lead to the time of Jacob's trouble. We also know that the saints will return with the Lord Jesus (Messiah) at the end of the Tribulation, according to Jude 14-15. That means that the Rapture must occur sometime during a period just prior to the start of the Tribulation (Daniel's seventieth week) and the end of the Tribulation. That puts us in a premillennial view of the Rapture, which is the consensus of most Christians. With this in mind, we will show three different views of the Rapture within the premillennium.

1. Those who believe in a Rapture just prior to the Tribulation are known as pre-Tribulationists, or pre-Tribbers for short.

2. Those who believe that the Rapture will occur in the middle of the Tribulation are known as mid-Tribulationists, or mid-Tribbers. This belief evolves around the fact that the antichrist will be revealed midway through the Tribulation, and therefore the believers will escape him by being raptured.

3. Finally, those who believe the Rapture will occur at the end of the Tribulation are called post-Tribulationists, or post-Tribbers. These are the ones who believe the Church will endure all the trials of the Tribulation right through to the end of it.

Those who say that Messiah will come at the end of the millennium hold a postmillennial view. Then there are those who say we are already in the thousand-year millennium; these people are known to hold the amillennial view. In this book, we have emphasized the premillennial view. We have done this by taking the sequence of events in the book of Revelation and applying them in a literal chronological order to the prophetic message. The events that we're mostly interested in are the seven seals, seven trumpets, and seven bowls (or vials) judgments. Together with the Rapture, they are the most exciting events yet to happen next to the coming of the Messiah, who will issue in the thousand-year millennium.

Unfortunately, those holding a postmillennial view see the kingdom of God being won over by the believers, who will hand it over to the Messiah upon His return. I am sorry to say this teaching doesn't coincide with the chronology of the book of Revelation, where it shows the Messiah coming before the millennium in chapter 19. He comes to fight the forces of unrighteousness along with the saints (Church) and the holy angels. If this is so, how can anyone then foresee peace here prior to Christ's return?

The truth of the matter is the Messiah Himself will come to restore order before humankind destroys itself. Then He will make all things new again. In Matthew 24:22 (NKJV), we read, "And unless those days were shortened [note past tense], no flesh would be saved; but for the elect's sake, those days will be [future tense] shortened." How can those days be shortened if not by the coming of the Messiah before the end of the Tribulation?

You see, humankind cannot do it alone. We need a Lord and Savior who will come to the rescue when called. And believe me, Israel will be calling Him to save them from this chaotic mess. The whole world will be in such shambles that it will be impossible for people to put it back together again. It's just like Humpty Dumpty, who sat on a wall and had a great fall, and all the king's horses and king's men couldn't put Humpty back together again. Humans won't be able to put the world back together again. Only the Messiah will, for He is God's Son in the person of Jesus Christ. Only He can put the world back to its intended mode and restore all things.

With this philosophy in mind, let's conclude that the physical kingdom cannot be won over to Him by humans, as some may believe. But with the coming of Messiah, the kingdom will be won over to the Father. Jesus will lead the charge, for He will come on a white horse (Revelation 19:11–16) and strike the nations with a sharp sword. And with Him will be all the armies of heaven dressed in white linen. These are the saints, those who were raptured, and those who were resurrected from the dead, along with God's angels. Together with Jesus Messiah, they will fight the armies of the kingdom of the beast, and win!

The kingdom will eventually be won, but until then, the Word has to be preached all over the world. This will prepare the kingdom spiritually, and then at the Messiah's coming, a literal physical kingdom will be established. The Lord Jesus will finally take back that which was lost at the Garden when Satan deceived Adam and Eve.

Some denominations even teach that the raptured believers will dwell in heaven for a thousand years while the Earth restores itself from God's mighty destruction. I can't comprehend this teaching, because it took only six days to create the world, so why should it take a thousand years to restore? Isn't the God of Abraham, Isaac, and Jacob an awesome God? Why insult Him? A restoration of the Earth will take place only after Messiah arrives with His angels and saints at the end of Daniel's seventieth week, which is the end of the Great Tribulation. True, the Bible does speak of a new heaven and a new Earth, but this occurrence will take place after the thousand-year millennium; after

Satan is loosed again to deceive the nations again and test humankind. It isn't teaching about a thousand-year restoration as is believed by the postmillennialists.

Our business here on Earth is to get the message of the gospel out into the world to give all the lost sheep a chance to learn, repent of their wrongs, and turn to God. Once this is accomplished and the repentant process begins, then the believers are to make sure their lamps remain filled with oil at all times, for once that oil is used up and the light goes out, the Master might come and be seen only by those who still have their lamps burning. I use this analogy only because of the way Jesus spoke of His coming (Matthew 25). You see, no one knows the time of His coming. We can discern the time only by studying scripture. That is why one must be prepared at all times. "Watch therefore, for you know neither the day nor the hour in which the Son of man is coming" (Matthew 25:13 NKJV).

Let's keep the lamp lit so the illuminating light can shine on others. By doing this, the number of believers will increase, for by our fruits we'll be able to spread the message of peace and love, not the message of hate and violence such as is with the kingdom of darkness. This kingdom of darkness is being led by evildoers and angels of light who have been transformed to work with the evil one. "For we wrestle not with flesh and blood, but against principalities, against powers, against the rulers of the darkness of this world, against spiritual wickedness in high places" (Ephesians 6:12 KJV). Unfortunately, these evil forces will always be there to harass the elect of God until the Messiah's return. That is why we must put on the armor of God on a daily basis.

In 1 Thessalonians 4:18 (NKJV), the apostle Paul said, "Therefore comfort one another with these words." The comforting message was that of the Rapture, for no matter how much evil may encounter one's lifetime, that evil will come to an end. There is a time limit to the evil plan of Satan. There is no time limit to God's plan of everlasting foreverness. When the Rapture occurs, from that point onward, the saints will be with Jesus, who will comfort them and wipe away every tear. Evil will become nonexistent. Also comforting was the apostle's words of letting believers know that their believing loved ones, those who had fallen asleep, would also be with Jesus in the clouds along with them at the Rapture.

In my opinion, the premillennial view is the most logical view for the Rapture to occur. The other two views make no sense and have no scriptural backing. The Messiah's coming will occur at the end of the sixth dispensation (grace) during the Battle of Armageddon in the Tribulation. Then Messiah Himself will issue in the seventh dispensation, which is the new millennium.

Let's take a closer look at the three views of the Rapture in the premillennium. First of all, let's respect all three views, or concepts, of when the Rapture will occur. There are many arguments, with Bible scripture backing supporting all three concepts. What we'll attempt to do here is to give a short summary of each of the three views.

(1) In the pre-Tribulation view, the belief is that the Rapture will occur before the Tribulation. Now, you may be surprised to know how many denominations have spared themselves a breakup simply because it feels comfortable for believers to believe they won't have to go through the seven-year Tribulation. Some even teach that the war of Ezekiel 38–39 won't occur until the believers are raptured and in heaven with their Master. The reasoning is that a merciful God will not let them suffer through this time of trouble.

Most pre-Tribbers try to prove this concept by showing that the Church is not mentioned after Revelation 3. They also show where Apostle John is taken to heaven in the spirit (Revelation 4), which represents the Rapture of saints prior to the twenty-one judgments to come in Revelation. A good scriptural argument for the pre-Tribber is John 14:2–3 (NKJV), where we read the following: "In my Father's house are many mansions; if it were not so, I would have told you. And if I go and prepare a place for you, I will come again and receive you to myself; that where I am, there you may be also."

This verse definitely speaks of His return, and it also speaks of a dwelling place that He's preparing for the believers. In all probability, it's a place to spend time or take residence with Him in heaven. Some

Bible commentators look at this place as God Himself, where God will let the believer dwell in Him. The word *mansion* in this verse is not a luxurious mansion as we see in the twenty-first century but a room or dwelling place. In other words, God will make room for us in Him. This is what Lord Jesus meant when He said, "I go and prepare a place." Afterward, in this same chapter, He said He would give them the Spirit of truth (Holy Spirit) to dwell in them, and them to dwell in Him. I don't believe He was speaking about the Rapture in John 14.

Another place where pre-Tribbers go to is Revelation 3, where the Lord tells the Church of Philadelphia, "Because you have kept my word to persevere, I also will keep you from the hour of trial which shall come upon the whole world, to test those who dwell on the earth" (3:10). It appears that the church of Philadelphia will skip this terrible time in history. Or could it be that God is giving them warning so as to hide until this ordeal is over. In Isaiah 26:20 (NIV), we read, "Go my people enter your rooms and shut the door behind you, hide yourselves for a little while until His wrath has passed by." This verse could easily apply to Israel, but it could also apply to the Church if it should still be here on Earth during the Great Tribulation. Now, let me ask this: How many churches can say they have taken after the Philadelphia church, which is one of the seven churches in Revelation 2–3? Today's churches need to apply themselves to what the Lord saw in the churches of Smyrna and Philadelphia. They both got passing grades, unlike the other five churches that were admonished or rebuked one way or another. I like this verse because it tells me that the Lord will protect His elect. But then again, is this hour of trial the whole seven years (seventieth week), or is it from the time that the antichrist comes into the picture in the middle of the Tribulation and declares war on the saints?

Some Bible authors tend to take a strong stand on the pre-Tribulation Rapture concept. This disturbs me a bit because it seems premature not to look at all angles before coming up with a definite conclusion. It is not that they aren't looking for other clues for alternative concepts, but they seem to be surrounded, or stuck, by their past taught beliefs in the Pre-Tribulation concept, and this makes it hard for them to get out of that box. They go along with the flow to make sure the believers are kept happy.

Don't get me wrong. I'm not totally disagreeing with their Pre-Tribber concept, because they might just be right. In fact, I hope they are right because I don't wish to go through this nightmarish episode in history and watch my family suffer. The Bible specifically states that the antichrist will wage war on the saints of God (believers) and prevail. That means all believers, whether Jew or Christian, will suffer at the hands of the antichrist.

There are many lukewarm believers out there ready to grasp any belief that may come their way. If, for example, they grasp on the belief of a pre-Tribber Rapture concept and find themselves still here during the Tribulation, chances are they will pull away from their faith due to disgust and dismay for not making it. They might even take the Mark of the Beast in order to survive. This frightens me because I don't wish any sheep to go astray due to misinformation, not enough information, or bad teaching.

I'm no Bible scholar, but it seems to me more appropriate to teach all three concepts of the Rapture in the premillennial view (pre-Tribulation, mid-Tribulation, post-Tribulation) and let Bible students beware so as to keep their hope alive in case they should find themselves still here at the initiation of the Tribulation. At least they can still look forward to a mid-Tribulation or post-Tribulation Rapture. If for some reason they should go the distance, then I would stress God's love for them and reassure them that the Lord will guide them through the valley of the shadow of death, for once there, they'll be strengthened and comforted by God's rod and staff during that time of hardship.

(2) In the mid-Tribulation view, most believe in a Rapture that will occur during the middle years of the Tribulation, or around the three-and-a-half-year mark. This teaching evolves around the fact that the antichrist will be revealed, or unveiled, in the middle of the seventieth week. Because he declares war on the saints (both Jews and Christians), the consensus is that God will spare the believers (Church) that horrifying time of the second half of Daniel's seventieth week (Great Tribulation).

For some reason, many Christians believe that as long as the Church is around, the antichrist will not be unveiled for the fear of his exposure as the evil one. But because he is unveiled in the middle of the Tribulation, this proves without a doubt that the Church will have already been raptured, leaving those lukewarm and future believers behind to be rescued later by the Messiah's coming. If one can recall, a certain antichrist came into the scene back in the thirties. His name was Adolf Hitler, and he didn't have any concern about the Church. In fact, at the time he even challenged the Vatican, who backed off due to fear of being bombed and destroyed. Now, if Hitler had such power against the Roman Catholic Church, what is going to stop the antichrist from fearing it? The truth of the matter is the antichrist will persecute the Church of God, declare war on it, and prevail over it according to scripture (Revelation 13:7). Will He? Or will he simply prevail over the saints as it is written—that is, those left behind after the Rapture, and those becoming new converts? The truth of the Word is, "The gates of hell will not prevail over the Church" (Matthew 18:18 KJV).

Now what scripture do mid-Tribbers have to defend this view? The answer is none, but when we look at Revelation 11, we see something very interesting happening. It just happens that two witnesses from the past have come alive to guide Israel back to its God and also witness the coming of the Messiah named Jesus (Yeshua) Christ. These two witnesses are depicted as the two supernaturally sent by God who will witness for forty-two months in Israel. Some say these two witnesses are Moses and Elijah sent back to Earth to witness and reach Israel prior to the Messiah's coming. Others say these two witnesses are Elijah and Enoch only because both were taken (translated) to heaven without dying. In my opinion, I believe It's Moses and Elijah.

My reasoning for agreeing about Moses and Elijah is derived from Revelation 11:6 (NKJV), where we read, "These have power to shut heaven, so that no rain falls in the days of their prophecy; and they have power over waters to turn them to blood, and strike the Earth with all plagues." If I'm not mistaken, this verse describes both Moses and Elijah, because Moses did turn the Nile River to blood and strike Egypt with all kinds of plagues through God's power. Likewise, through prayer, Elijah was granted power to make it rain or not rain, thus causing droughts and famine. Also, these two witnesses are referred to as the "two olive trees" and the "two lampstands" (Revelation 11:4 NKJV).

The "two olive trees" can also be found in the book of Zachariah (4:11 NKJV). Let's read: "What are these two olive trees at the right of the lampstand and at its left?" The answer came back in verse 14 (NKJV): "These are the two anointed ones, who stand beside the Lord of the whole Earth." Now compare this with Revelation 11:4, "These are the two olive trees and two lampstands standing before the God of the Earth." These verses in Zachariah and Revelation are almost identical with the exception of the lampstands. In Zachariah we see one lampstand, whereas in Revelation we see two lampstands.

As for the two lampstands, some (including myself) say the two lampstands represent the Church. Why do I say this? Well, if you look at Revelation 1:20, it tells you that the seven churches, where letters were sent to, are the seven lampstands. What I'm doing here is comparing scripture with scripture. If you are familiar with these letters sent to the seven churches, found in Revelation 2–3, the Lord either admonished or rebuked five of them. The remaining two got an acceptable report from the Lord. These two were the church of Philadelphia and the church of Smyrna. I'm speculating that these two churches, or types of, represent the two lampstands in Revelation 11:4. Just remember that the number two represents the witness.

If you read this verse carefully, you'll see that a conjunction separates the two olive trees from the two lampstands. That conjunction is the word *and*, which implies that the two olive trees are not alone in the witnessing process. In fact, what I see might be two sets of witnesses. Set- one is the two olive trees that are witnesses to Israel, and set two is the two lampstands (Church) continuing their everyday process of spreading the gospel. Both sets of witnesses stand before the "God of the Earth," that is, the God of Abraham, Isaac, and Jacob. The Church as a whole is one step ahead because it has been acknowledging Jesus for centuries. The two olive trees, in contrast, are introducing Jesus to the lost in Israel and are doing a pretty good job at it, because it gets the attention of the antichrist and angers him to the point where he orders their assassination.

Many who read about the two witnesses in Revelation 11 see them as two Old Testament prophets (Moses and Elijah) come to life. Yes, they have come alive, but for a prime purpose: to prepare national Israel for its salvation. Personally, I see them as two very important witnesses for Israel (olive tree) who will stop at nothing to get through the gospel (good news) message, even devouring their enemies by fire that proceeds from their mouths (Revelation 11:5). I see the two lampstands (Church) as witnesses who, by the command of Jesus, have gone throughout the world, including national Israel, to spread the good news (gospel).

It's almost mind-boggling why Jesus included in this passage the two lampstands (two churches) with the two witnesses (olive trees). Or could it be that the two olive trees and the two lampstands are the same witnesses? Some commentators believe that. But one must remember what Jesus repeated to all of the seven churches in their letters: "For he who has an ear, let him hear what the Spirit says to the churches" (Revelation 2–3 NKJV). The lukewarm church (Laodicea), the dead church (Sardis), the loveless church (Ephesus), the compromising church (Thyatira), and the apostate church (Pergamus) are the five churches that were admonished by the Lord. Hopefully, these five types of churches will change their ways by the time the Church is raptured so as to qualify them with the two lampstands that stand faithfully before the God of the Earth. As it is, the Lord gave the five failed churches plenty of opportunity to overcome their obstacles and repent of their wrong doings.

Any way you look at it, the Church will be persecuted, paying a big price for its belief in Christ Jesus, especially those left behind after the Rapture. Satan will make sure of that. In fact, one might say that the persecution has already started. You might not yet see much of it in America, or other free countries, but it's there. It is this same persecution that was recorded in the book of Acts that caused the Church to spread out and grow. The book of Revelation, which shows countless martyrs standing before the throne, "are the ones who come out of the Great Tribulation and washed their robes and made them white in the blood of the Lamb" (Revelation 7:14 NKJV). In other words, these are the ones who were (or are) persecuted and killed by orders of the antichrist.

In today's world, we must realize there is persecution and martyrdom. Christian magazines report that some churches have suffered at the hands of terrorists. There have been instances of shootings and burning of churches, even churches filled with people. This has caused some churches to arm themselves. Some churchgoers even secretly carry guns to church to defend themselves, their families, and the congregation. If this is going on today, what do you think the Tribulation will be like? Scripture tells us that the antichrist will declare war on the saints (Christians and Jews) and prevail. I doubt very much that the saints will not fight back. Let's simply be careful. It was Jesus Himself who said, "For all who take the sword will perish by the sword" (Matthew 26:52 NKJV). Unfortunately, because of the times, many will take up the sword, but again the antichrist will prevail. He'll win this battle but not the war. Many saints will be killed, but fear not because these same saints are coming back with the Messiah to aid in the ridding of evil and unrighteousness. I can only imagine the faces of those who have persecuted and killed many, when they see their victims again in their glorified forms. Guess what? They can't be killed again.

The Bible does not give a clear picture of when the Rapture will occur. Most mid-Tribbers believe it will happen prior to the antichrist's unveiling because they believe God will not put them through this reign of terror during the second half of the seventieth week, known as the Great Tribulation. I believe the Church as a whole (believers) will not go, without being raptured, beyond the unveiling of the antichrist. At least I hope so. All I have to say here is, God help those lukewarm Christians and nonbelievers who become believers during the Tribulation, for they have to go through this disastrous time in history before the coming of Messiah. The Rapture occurs only once. Therefore, most of these new believers will be martyred. It's no wonder why the Lord told the Jews from Judea to "flee to the mountains." In other words: run for your lives and hide yourselves. And as we discussed before, Petra will be their refuge for a time being.

Because evidence points to a newly rebuilt Temple in Jerusalem, one has to take into account that many in the house of Israel will be worshipping in it as in the olden times. That includes offerings and animal sacrifices. These offerings and sacrifices will be done away with at the three-and-a-half-year mark of the Tribulation, or at the middle of the week as stated in Daniel 9:27 (NKJV). Once the order is given to do away with the sacrifices, the antichrist himself will take the seat in the Temple and proclaim himself as God. This will infuriate not only God

Himself but also the Jewish and the remaining Christian community, thus causing much animosity toward the antichrist, who in turn will declare war on anyone who even attempts to worship the true God of heaven.

If the remaining true Church thinks it can put an end to the antichrist, it is mistaken. Not only will they be outnumbered, but they must also realize that the antichrist has been prophesied in the Bible, and therefore the prophecy will take its course. The antichrist will prevail over the saints (Jews and Christians) and overpower them. But this overwhelming will only last a short while (three and a half years), because the cry will be so loud that the Messiah will be sent back to rescue Israel and the remaining true Church. Even though a true Church will exist because of new believers coming in during the Tribulation, a false church will also exist—that of a New Age doctrine led by the false prophet who works closely with the antichrist. The antichrist and the false prophet will be the first ones to get a taste of hell's fiery furnace, the lake of fire.

When Apostle Paul spoke of the Rapture in 1 Thessalonians 4:16 (NKJV), he mentioned the trumpet of God just prior to the first resurrection and the Rapture. He also spoke of the last trumpet, when he told the Church that "we shall not all sleep" (die), "but we shall be changed' from mortals to immortals, from corruption to incorruption" (1 Corinthians 15:51–53 NKJV). This is what will happen at the Rapture, at the last trumpet. There are no other trumpets in the Bible from this point on until we see seven trumpets in the book of Revelation. These trumpets in Revelation are God's judgments for the world, and you can hear them sounding beginning in chapter 8 and going through chapter 11. These trumpet judgments have a one-third destruction scenario, so there is still room for the survival of the Church if it should go through the trumpet judgments. It is in chapter 11 of the book of Revelation when we'll hear the last trumpet and see the two witnesses (olive trees) killed. But miraculously, we'll see them resurrect after three and a half days and then raptured after hearing a loud voice (an archangel?) shouting, "Come up here." They will ascend to heaven in a cloud (Revelation 11:12 NKJV). This all happens simultaneously—the resurrection of the two witnesses, the shout from heaven, and the rapture of these two witnesses.

Then the seventh trumpet sounds. I believe at this point, the Church will also be raptured, leaving behind the lukewarms, the apostates, the compromisers, the loveless, and the dead churches. It is at this moment when God claims the kingdoms of the world to Himself. Listen: "Then the seventh angel sounded: and there were loud voices in heaven saying, 'The kingdoms of this world have become the kingdoms of our Lord and His Christ, and He shall reign forever and ever!'" (Revelation 11:15 NKJV). From this point onward, the Lord will reclaim the world that was lost at the fall of the Garden of Eden to Satan. It's too coincidental that this scenario should happen exactly how the Apostle Paul stated it in 1 Thessalonians 4:16 (NKJV)—that is, the mention of the last trumpet, which doesn't appear after Revelation 11.

In conclusion to this segment of the mid-Tribulation, one might say that neither Christian nor Jew will stop what has already been prophesied about the antichrist. Only God Himself will do something about him, and that is to send His servant again for a second time in biblical history. That servant is the Messiah, who is also called "Wonderful. Counselor, Mighty God, Everlasting Father, Prince of peace" (Isaiah 9:6 NKJV). For those who dispute that Jesus is not God, take a close look at this verse, because it calls Him Mighty God and Everlasting Father. Ask yourself, "How can God also be a prince? Isn't a prince the son of a king?" Let's ponder on that one for a moment, but for the record, He also goes by the name Jesus.

(3) Finally, let's look at the post-Tribulation Rapture view. It is here where some say the Rapture will occur at the end of the Tribulation. That is, the Church and all other believers will have to endure the full seven years of the Tribulation. It was Jesus Himself who said, "But he who endures to the end shall be saved" (Matthew 24:13 NKJV). Enduring to the end won't be easy for anyone, but following the Lord's instructions to flee and hide yourself until His wrath is over and complete will be a blessing. And that is precisely what the Church and other believers have to do if the Rapture occurs at the end of the Tribulation. In other words, believers have to run and go underground, or hide in caves, to escape the antichrist.

When it comes to the Tribulation, the post-Tribulation is the most unpopular of the three views and is what most Christians fear. They ask questions like, "What if we have to take the mark in order to survive economically?" This question and more have boggled the minds of believers ever since the Rapture became popular. Also, some Christians believe that the seventieth week is only reserved for the Jew, because it is referred to as the time of Jacob's trouble (Jeremiah 30:7 NKJV), the consensus being that the Rapture will occur before the Tribulation. But let me tell you otherwise. Don't be fooled, because if there is a pre-Tribulation or mid-Tribulation Rapture, many so-called Christians will be left behind to endure the same tribulation as Israel, and that is to the end of the seventieth week.

In defending the post-Tribulation view, post-Tribbers look at Matthew 24:29 to show that the Rapture will take place at the end of the Tribulation. In this passage Jesus says, "Immediately, after the Tribulation of these days the sun will be darkened and the moon will not give its light." This is followed by verse 30: "Then the sign of the Son of man will appear in heaven." Verse 31 states, "He will send His angels with a great sound of the trumpet and they will gather His elect from the four winds" (NKJV).

There's that trumpet sound again. It almost appears as if the post-Tribbers are right because of this scripture spoken by Jesus Himself. But as I ponder about this verse, and the fact that there is that great trumpet sound for the angels to gather the elect, it seems to me that the Rapture is taking place here. Also, it could be that the Lord is recognizing the Tribulation's end for the elect but not for the unsaved, thus leaving the remainder of the seven years for the kingdom of the antichrist (world) to endure. That is my speculation. There are yet the final seven judgments, known as the bowl judgments, that still have to be unleashed. In other words, the Tribulation has ended for the believers, and the Rapture has taken place at this point. Those left behind (lukewarm), and those in the kingdom of the antichrist, will have to endure the rest of the seven years of the Tribulation, thus fulfilling the entirety of the seventieth week. This is my opinion concerning this verse, because I don't see the Rapture happening at the end of the seventieth week. One has to remember that the Tribulation is upon the whole world, not just on the saints of God. (For the record, a saint is a believer.)

What troubles me about this post-Tribulation concept is that Jesus comes back in person prior to, or during, the war of Armageddon. At that time, the Tribulation is supposedly still intact when He arrives with His angels and ten thousands of His saints (Jude). That is, Armageddon is still within the time frame of the seventieth week. If this is so the Messiah comes back with ten thousands of His saints, then the Rapture had to occur at a prior time before the end of the Tribulation. Upon looking at the seven trumpets judgments, which comes with a one-third destruction scenario, you know that there's plenty of room for survival for the believers. In contrast, the bowl judgments, following the trumpet judgments, are the ones that will devastate a greater part of the world and humankind. At this point of time, it's logical that we are still within the confines of the Tribulation, but the Tribulation will take a turn to come against the antichrist and his kingdom by its end, and with little room for survival. The Messiah will make sure of that.

It seems to me that after the last trumpet call, when the Lord raptures the Church, there comes a little break before the bowl judgments (see the next chapter) come into view. Within this break, (1) many left-behind, so-called Christians (lukewarms), who will give their hearts to the Lord, will be slaughtered by the antichrist; (2) Israel will be forced to flee to the mountains (Petra) for three and a half years or fewer; 3) many will be forced to take the Mark of the Beast for economic survival; and 4) nonbelievers hopefully will turn to God, especially after seeing the true Church disappear. It will be the serpent (Satan) himself who will wage war against the children of Israel at this time—that is, "for those who keep the commandments of God and have the testimony of Jesus Christ" (Revelation 12:17 NKJV). That is why the Lord tells them to flee to the mountains.

Because heaven has already proclaimed the kingdoms of the world unto God in the last Trumpet, now God takes over the remainder of the Tribulation by pouring out His wrath in the seven bowl judgments on the kingdom of the antichrist and all unrighteousness (Revelation 16).

There is no rapture after the Tribulation. It makes no sense because the Lord Jesus is already present here on Earth prior to the end. The purging process that God began in Genesis still continues but at a greater pace. This purging process will wipe clear humankind's home (the Earth). Then the Son of God, Lord Jesus (Messiah), will finish the cleanup and take over, with His credentials as King of Kings, Lord of lords, and Prince of peace. When that happens, all the nations of the Earth will bow down before Him and pay homage to Him in Jerusalem.

I don't believe the Church will be here on the Earth during the bowl judgments. If it is, God will supernaturally protect it. In fact, I believe the bowl judgments, seven in all, will be a quick "shock and awe" scenario. We might even want to compare this whole scenario to the judgments that were inflicted on the Egyptians prior to the Exodus. The Israelites were supernaturally protected in the land of Goshen while God bombarded the rest of Egypt with plaques. It was in the last plague in Egypt that God gave the Israelites instruction to remain indoors and put the slain lamb's blood on the two doorposts and lintels of their homes. They did this so the angel of death would pass over them. One can say the same about the true Church of God during the Great Tribulation, "for God did not appoint us [the Church] to wrath, but to obtain salvation through our Lord Jesus Christ" (1 Thessalonians 5:9 NKJV). It's also noted that the believers are sealed by the Holy Spirit. Ephesians 1:13–14 (NKJV) states that the believers are "sealed with the Holy Spirit of promise, who is the guarantee of our inheritance." Therefore, obtaining this salvation means being cleansed by the blood of Jesus and receiving everlasting protection from the Lord, even after the Rapture.

I know all this can be confusing, but what I'm trying to do is get the reader a bit more appreciative on how the Bible tends to symbolically interpret itself. Also, one must keep in mind that the book of Revelation and most New Testament books were written while the Romans were in charge. That means the New Testament writers had to be careful not to offend the Romans, especially when speaking about the one and only true God of the Bible. The Romans had many gods, including their supreme god of the state, the Caesar. They also had their invincible kingdom, which would have been a clash when speaking of a new kingdom for the believers—that is, the kingdom of God. Just how literal can we get with scripture? Let's illustrate for an example "gathering His elect from one end of heaven to the other," or "gather His elect from the four winds." Can we literally interpret this as heaven, or should we assume this to mean Earth? If Jesus had said, "From one end of the earth to the other," wouldn't the Romans of the time have gotten just a little suspicious and feared that He was gathering an army of nations against them?

In dealing with the book of Revelation, which is loaded with many symbols, we must take the same approach. The interpretation of scripture hasn't been that easy throughout the ages. Now, in the twenty-first century, we have the help of computers, the Internet, TV, radio, books of historical facts, archaeology, anthropology, and the discovery of ancient manuscripts (the Dead Sea Scrolls). And let's not forget the Bible itself. These tools have enabled Bible students to reach further than their predecessors.

Determining the exact time of the Rapture has been a challenge to many Bible students because there is no precise time to this phenomenon. But like the Tribulation, one can discern a probable time of departure by using the symbolic language that has been given in the Bible. For example: the four horsemen of Revelation, the trumpets, the bowls, the sword protruding out of Jesus's mouth, the red dragon (Revelation 12), and more. We can carry on throughout the entire Bible picking out symbols and interpreting them by using these symbols. Finally, the war to end all wars (Armageddon). It is during this war that Jesus will come back to us humans on Earth.

Again, I'm no Bible expert or scholar. I'm simply a very curious and observant student of the Word. If 1 Thessalonians 4:16 and 1 Corinthians 15:51 tell me that the Rapture will occur with a trumpet blast or at the last trumpet, my focus in the Word is to look for that last trumpet call in the Bible. As I mentioned before, the only place I could find with a last trumpet was the seventh trumpet in Revelation 11, the same chapter where the two witnesses of Israel are captured, killed, resurrected from the dead, and then raptured. The next scenario after the Rapture is the completion of God's wrath on the antichrist's kingdom and unsaved humankind. This will put an end to all unrighteousness. As for the way the Bible was written, I take it literally because I'm "looking unto Jesus the author and finisher of our faith" (Hebrews 2:2 KJV).

What I've been trying to say in this chapter is I don't see a pre-Tribulation, mid-Tribulation, or even post-Tribulation Rapture. What I see is a "last trumpet" Rapture, which can occur sometime after the middle, if not at the middle, of the Tribulation. I mean it will be around the time when the antichrist is revealed. For all we know, the Rapture might take place one year or less before the Messiah's arrival, thus leaving the remaining time of the Tribulation as God's final hour of wrath known as the seven bowl judgments, which will finalize the purging of all unrighteousness on this planet. In my opinion, once the trumpet judgments begin, then we can discern about when the Rapture will occur—that is, if the Church is still around, which I believe it will be.

When looking at Daniel 12:11–12 (NKJV), we read, "And from the time that the daily sacrifice is taken away, and the abomination of desolation is set up, there shall be one thousand two hundred and ninety [1,290] days. Blessed is he who waits, and comes to the one thousand three hundred and thirty five [1,335] days." Now, where did 1,290 days come from if the midway point of the Tribulation is 1,260 days (forty-two months)? Shouldn't the second half of the Tribulation also be 1,260 days (forty-two months)? In this verse, it appears that a month will be added to the calendar. One has to remember that the Jewish year is based on a 360-day calendar, whereas the Gregorian calendar is based on 365 days. That means that occasionally (every two or three years), a month is added to the Jewish calendar to catch up or synchronize with the lunar and solar cycles, thus giving it a leap year. That means within the last three years of the second half of the Tribulation, there will be a leap in its calendar that will make it 1,290 days instead of its traditional 1,260 days. In all probability, it will be on the final year in the calendar.

What significance does this have on the Rapture? I believe there is none, but what troubles me is the added forty-five days between the 1,290 days and the 1,335th day. It appears as if something big is about to happen in those forty-five days. It could be—and I'm only speculating—the Rapture itself, thus putting the Church close to the post-Tribulation view. Or it could be the time span of the seven bowl judgments. It could be the Messiah's arrival with His cleanup crew, who will be doing a lot of damage in the cleansing of the Earth. Time wise, it almost reminds me of Operation Desert Storm, which took forty-two days to bring about a cease-fire. For those who survive the Messiah's onslaught and restoration, they will be called blessed for waiting until the 1,335th day and not giving in to the antichrist's demands. Now, could these be the meek who will inherit the Earth (Matthew 5:5 KJV)? Or are they simply new believers who have escaped the antics of the antichrist after the Rapture?

Another possibility for the forty-five days is the wedding feast awaiting all believers after the Rapture, referred to as "the Marriage Supper of the Lamb." In Revelation 19:7 (NKJV), we read, "Let us rejoice and give Him glory for the marriage of the Lamb has come, and His wife has made herself ready." The bridegroom (Lamb) is Jesus Himself. The bride (wife) is the Church, or all believers, including our Jewish brethren. Together, they will inherit the Earth upon the Messiah's return. The marriage will take place regardless of when the Rapture occurs, for it is written. Therefore, it is truth, the true Word of God.

If the Rapture occurred on the 1,291st day (I'm just speculating again), that would mean God's final judgments, referred to as the bowl judgments, would last forty-five days, including the physical return of Christ and His Church during Armageddon. It is also the start of the new millennium shortly thereafter. His return will be glorious and worth watching, for it is said that "Every eye will see him, even those who pierced Him" (Revelation 1:7 NKJV). If the post-Tribbers are right, the Rapture might happen during this forty-five-day gap.

Regardless of when the Rapture happens—and it will happen—we must all be ready to partake in this glorious time in history. Believe me, you don't want to be left behind, because either the antichrist's hordes will persecute and kill you, or you'll get in the middle of the cross fire between the forces of unrighteousness and the forces of righteousness and be killed. God's judgments will devastate many lives. The Bible states that "there will be weeping and gnashing of teeth" (Matthew 8:12 NKJV) on the day the Lord has chosen to pour out His wrath. That means many will finally meet their destiny, which spells the lake of fire.

Friends, let's get right with God. It was the Lord Himself who said, "My people are destroyed because of lack of knowledge" (Hosea 4:6 KJV). Repent now, for now is the time of salvation. The Bible clearly states that the "Wages of sin is death but the gift of God is eternal life through Christ Jesus our Lord" (Romans 6:23 KJV). Wouldn't you prefer a gift? (Boy, I love Christmas!) Let's remember that God is merciful, and He'll give you that gift of salvation if you ask Him. It's free with no cost. It's already been paid for by the blood of Jesus. Think about it.

In closing this chapter, the point I want to emphasize is regardless of which premillennial view you have (pre-Tribber, mid-Tribber, or post-Tribber), the Rapture will take place, the last trumpet will blast, the believers (Church) will vanish in the twinkling of an eye and meet the Lord in the clouds, and they will be transformed into glorious beings just like Jesus Christ. Then on the Lord's Day, they will return to Earth with the Messiah to help in the restoration process. Let's also not forget the inheritance that awaits us all here on the Earth. It sounds too good to be true, but it is. The Bible says so. Friends, we are not reading or looking into a fairy tale. This information is found in your Bibles. Simply pick them up and read them. It has been the number one best seller for years. It might just save you from a very hot situation someday.

Some say in their hearts that they don't believe. My question to them is, Why take a chance? What if you died today? Where do you think you would go? Some think they would go to the grave, and that would be it. Just think: if the unbelievers are right, then they have nothing to worry about. If they are wrong and find themselves standing in the presence of God, they have a lot to worry about because they are going to end up in the lake of fire (hell). So why not give your hearts to the Lord now and be saved from the impending judgments that are just around the corner? The Word says, "Behold now is the time of salvation" (2 Corinthians 6:2 NKJV).

CHAPTER 16

God's Final Judgments

In finalizing the purging process, God has made no secret of His intentions as to how He will deal with unsaved humankind. A study in the book of Revelation will reveal that God has reserved twenty-one judgments that are designed to change people's way to conform to God's way. These twenty-one judgments, which I have mentioned and already touched upon in this book, are the seven seals, the seven trumpets, and the seven bowls.

In this chapter, we will be aiming toward the last fourteen judgments—that is, the seven trumpets and the seven bowls—because, together, they are designed to inflict pain on the unsaved. Who are these unsaved? They are unbelievers, lukewarms, and dead churchgoers; those who have taken the Mark of the Beast; those who have compromised themselves with other religions; and those who have been sucked into the apostasy of the church. Together, the trumpets and bowls will inflict such a blow to the unsaved that they will either be forced to change (repent) or spend the rest of eternity in damnation.

Though the trumpet and bowl judgments have some similarities, the trumpets are designed with a one-third destruction scenario as I have mentioned in previous chapters, whereas the bowls deal with a higher degree or proportion of destruction. In fact, one might refer to the bowls as God's last hour of wrath because they will claim countless lives on Earth. Their culmination will be in a battlefield called Armageddon in Hebrew, also known as the Valley of Megiddo, where many battles were fought in Old Testament times. There, as we'll see later, the forces of unrighteousness will meet their fate, because in finalizing His judgments, God will claim, "It is Done" (Revelation 16:17 KJV), thus issuing in the new millennium by the Messiah's arrival.

Unfortunately, the mass destruction will claim two-thirds of the population. In Zachariah 13:8 (NKJV), we read, "And it shall come to pass in all the land, that two-thirds in it shall be cut off and die, but one-third shall be left in it." Now, whether this one-third survival rate points to Israel itself or the whole world combined is a question worth debating, because the Rapture will already have taken millions (hopefully billions) thus leaving the unsaved behind. Can we then assume that the surviving one-third are all believers who gave their hearts since the Rapture?

We know from scripture that many will come out of the Great Tribulation saved, because even the Apostle John saw this vision in Revelation 7:13–14. But what about the surviving one-third left on Earth in Zechariah's prophecy? Are they newborn believers from all over the world who have finally come to their senses and accepted the truth since witnessing the disappearance of their true believing peers? Or are they Jews who have finally accepted Jesus as Messiah? The answer might just be both, because many will be saved either by the witnessing of the two witnesses (olive trees, the Church included) or by the 144,000 of Israel.

By the time the last trumpet sounds, millions will have been saved from God's wrath up to that point. But the final hour (bowl judgments) will still await those left on Earth, of which only one-third will survive. Their survival will not be luck but repentance and acceptance of a deliverer named Jesus, who is the Messiah. He comes for a second time in history; this time as a conquering Messiah. He is the Son of God, the deliverer, and a refuge for all who believe in Him. For those who do not believe, they will be dealt with in a very harsh way, and they will still await being judged on Judgment Day.

Believing in the Lord Jesus and accepting what He did for us on the cross—that is, dying, shedding His blood, being buried, and being resurrected from the grave—is the only survival kit available during this hour of despair. Believe this message, and you'll be saved. Deny it, and you'll be destroyed with death and then by fire after the millennium, on the Day of Judgment. This day is a day that the unsaved don't necessarily want to occur, because they will be resurrected from the grave, judged, and then thrown into the lake of fire along with Satan and all his hordes (fallen angels).

For some reason, there are those who believe that Israel will be totally destroyed, but Zachariah 13:8 confirms that it won't be, because even though two-thirds will die, one-third of the population will live. It saddens my heart today to hear certain church denominations proclaim themselves as Israel and deny even the very existence of national Israel, who has gathered up all the offspring of its original twelve tribes to fulfill Bible prophecy (Ezekiel 37). I've even heard that Israel has no place in the kingdom of God. This is an unfortunate and ridiculous idea that has propped up in some churches, because Israel has yet to experience a revival and receive the Messiah into their hearts. Also, let us remember that Christ died for all, not just for some.

The book of Revelation foresees a revival because of the two witnesses and the 144,000 who will be sent by God. But again, by the antichrist's declaration of war against the saints for their belief in Christ, they will be persecuted and put to death, therefore becoming martyrs.

The 144,000, the two witnesses (olive trees), and the Church (two lampstands) will play a huge role in the revival effort prior to the Rapture. Because these two (olive trees and two lampstands) will be raptured, it will be the 144,000 who will have to carry the role of propagating the gospel right to the end of the Tribulation. It is my opinion, and the opinion of others, that their role will be to evangelize all of national Israel. Some say they will evangelize the whole world. I disagree because of Romans 11, which implies that national Israel will not come to Christ Jesus until the fullness of the Gentiles. Then it will be their turn; that is, Israel will be the last nation on Earth to be evangelized. They will receive their Messiah.

To explore this further, one must take into consideration, by reading the book of Zachariah, that the feet of Jesus the Messiah will touch down at the Mt. of Olives, which is located in Israel itself (Zechariah 14:4). It doesn't show Him arriving in Rome's Vatican or in America, where a strong Christian influence is found. It even shows Israel mourning for the one they pierced (Zechariah 12:10) and led as a Lamb to the slaughter. And why do they mourn? Because they finally realize that this same Messiah visited them once before while they were under Roman rule about two thousand years ago. At that time, Jesus was rejected and handed over to the Romans to be crucified after three and a half years of ministry. Just think how much better off they would have been if they had only accepted Jesus then. But don't be fooled, because this is how God planned it. Again, I have to stress that God is in control.

When looking at the book of Isaiah, which was written approximately seven hundred years before Jesus's birth, one can see where Jesus was already prophesied as being the suffering Messiah: "He was wounded for our transgressions, He was bruised for our iniquities; the chastisement for our peace was upon Him, and by His stripes we are healed" (Isaiah 53:5 NKJV).

You see, Jesus died for both Jew and Gentile. The Gentiles, who are grafted into the "Olive Tree" together with the Jews, will serve God in His kingdom. When Jesus left Israel to go to be with the Father, it provoked Israel to jealousy upon seeing all those following the way. It was Jesus who said, "I am the way, the truth and the life. No one comes to the father except through Me" (John 14:6 NKJV). This caused the religious heads of Israel to persecute the Christians, who were Jews themselves, or the followers of the way, thus causing them to scatter. Little did the Jewish leadership know that as the Christians scattered, they also took the gospel (good news) with them wherever they went, thus growing this newfound faith in Jesus. This was God's plan all along: to have this scattering and, by doing so, to propagate the gospel message. God did not abandon His people at the time. In fact, it was the converted Jew, now a Christian, who would take the message to Jerusalem first, then to all of Judea and Samaria, and then to the world (Acts 1:8).

With this in mind, how can certain denominations not recognize national Israel and at the same time claim themselves as Israel, or they say national Israel has no part in God's kingdom? Let me just say that everyone on this planet has a chance and a right to be included in the kingdom of God, Jews especially. Romans 11 strongly warns the boastful of this very thing, for as Israel's branches broke off, so can the Gentile branches. Why not take heed and help those who will be grafted back into the olive tree at a later date? It is God's will for Israel to be grafted back; I've already mentioned this in a previous chapter, but it's worth repeating. Until they are regrafted into the olive tree, they will suffer much and go through tribulation such as they've never experienced. Many say that what they experienced during World War II will look like child's play next to the Great Tribulation.

The Tribulation is God's test to His elect, and at the same time, it is judgment against all unsaved. It will start off with the seven seals, some of which have already started, and which we have spoken about in previous chapters. The seven trumpets will follow, and finally the seven bowl (or Vials) judgments. As I mentioned before, the trumpet judgments are not as intense as the bowl judgments because they are equipped with a one-third destruction factor, thus leaving survival room for even the elect of God. That is why I see the Rapture at the seventh trumpet in Revelation 11 rather than at the beginning of the Tribulation. Once this last trumpet comes to pass, then the destruction scenario will change to a greater one, thus leaving very little room for survival. But there will be a small number, or remnant, of survivors, for the Lord said, "Blessed are they who endure to the end." Because the destruction factor involves all nations, I'm speculating that many nations will have survivors, especially those who come to the Lord in that last hour of despair.

Remember that it's not important when the last trumpet sounds, but it's important that we're ready at the blast. If we're not, then we'll miss the boat. Read Matthew 25 about the ten virgins, where only five of them made it. The other five had to wait till the end. If we miss the boat, then we will have to endure the terrifying last hour of the bowl judgments. That means running and hiding for our lives as instructed by Lord Jesus in Matthew 24.

For those studying prophecy during this time in history, the excitement level will be ecstatic, and they'll be able to count down the trumpets as the judgments are poured out. It is not that they'll be able to pinpoint the day of Rapture, but they will discern with close proximity as to when it will occur. Once the two witnesses (two olive trees) are killed in Israel, then we'll know that the Rapture is just around the corner. That is my opinion, because once the antichrist takes the seat and attacks God's people, God will retaliate, first with the trumpet judgments and then with the bowl judgments. Let's take a look at these judgments beginning with the first trumpet.

First Trumpet (Revelation 8:7)—In this first trumpet, we see hail and fire mingled with blood, one-third of the trees burned up, and all the grass burned up.

As scary as this may sound, we might be experiencing a nuclear war here. Many scholars believe this mingling of blood with hail and fire depicts such a war. Any way you look at it, whether nuclear or not, it does damage one-third of the world's ecology because the trees and the grass are burned up. In contrast, symbolically speaking, trees might be representing humans, because the Bible does use trees as a symbol for humankind. For example, after healing a blind paralytic man, Jesus asked him if he saw anything. His response was, "I see men like trees walking" (Mark 8:24 NKJV). Another example might be found in Isaiah 61:3 (NKJV), where those who mourn in Zion will be called "trees of righteousness." What we have here are similes used by the author (God) to symbolically compare humans to trees.

Now, whether these trees are literal and dealing with ecology, or implying a one-third destruction of humankind, one must consider and remember that a later judgment (bowl six, the Battle of Armageddon) will also claim a destruction of one-third of the world's population. Some say that the grass mentioned here is humankind itself, but I can't relate to that because if all humankind was to be burned, then that would be the end of the judgment. But because we still have six more trumpets and seven bowls, this interpretation cannot be. Therefore we must take the ecological approach and say that all grass literally will somehow be tainted, probably from a plague (radiation?) sent from the Lord Himself, thus reflecting the fourth seal's (pale horse) intention in the world.

Second Trumpet (Revelation 8:8)—As in the first trumpet, we have another one-third destruction scenario. This time it is one-third of the sea, which will turn to blood, thus causing a 33.3 percent loss of marine life. Also, one-third of ships will be destroyed, whether they be merchant or military (navy). Again, more blood will get spilled. All this is after a "great burning mountain" gets thrown into the sea.

Because the great burning mountain gets thrown into the sea, the implication here must be that of a missile falling from the sky with a deadly, destructive force (nuclear?). Apostle John's description of a burning mountain might simply be a description of a mushroom cloud from a nuclear bomb detonating upon impact in the sea, which might appear to look like a mountain. Remember that we're talking about a vision that took place about two thousand years ago. This is the apostle's best description about what's going on. Now, the question must be asked: Which sea ?

When you look at today's current events, you see the Middle East as the most troublesome spot on the planet. We can therefore almost discern this second trumpet's sea to be the Mediterranean Sea (Persian area) because the Bible is mostly focused on this region. In contrast, the sea spoken of here might include all seas in the region, including the Atlantic Ocean. I say this only because all bodies of water interconnect to one another. A nuclear blast in the sea can kill and contaminate the rest of the waters in that region easily, not just the Mediterranean.

As for the ships in these waters, one must take into consideration all the military, oil tankers, and merchant ships that go to and come out of the Middle East. The United States alone has many ships, especially naval ships, in these waters patrolling the region twenty-four seven, but at a distance, respecting the territorial waters of a foreign nation, which is usually twelve nautical miles. They do this in case of war breaking out in the region. The Russians, the British, the French, and other nations also patrol these waters along with Middle Eastern countries. Just think about how many ships are in these waters. The blast from the "burning mountain" will destroy one-third of the ships, most assuredly those which are close to the blast. Think how aircraft carriers, which in some cases are the size of about three football fields, won't be able to stay afloat after this massive blast. Also think of the number of seamen from many nations, which can number to the tens of thousands of deaths. A US aircraft carrier alone can house a crew of over five thousand men and women.

Third Trumpet (Revelation 8:10)—Again there is a one-third destruction scenario, this time the world's water supply. Rivers, streams, dams, and more will get struck with a falling star called Wormwood, which means bitter. These waters, as in trumpet two, will also turn to blood, thus causing many to die from not having any drinking water due to all the contamination from whatever falls into the waters.

Ironically, the Russian nuclear reactor that blew up in the mideighties was located in the town of Chernobyl, which means *wormwood* when translated into English. Wormwood is a bitter herb used in medicinal medicines. It can be used in tea but is fatal in large amounts. This prophecy specifically mentions that "a third of the waters became wormwood, and many men died from the water, because it was made bitter" (Revelation 8:11 KJV). The blast at Chernobyl miraculously killed about fifty people, but later on, because of the radiation, many more died, numbering in the thousands. Many firemen at the scene died later due to being exposed to radiation.

With this in mind, think what a terrorist group might do in formulating a plan that might contaminate the world's rivers, reservoirs, and streams. Throwing some kind of contaminant into the waters to make them bitter and poisonous would be expected of them. But this is not the ordeal here. This is part of God's judgment against the unsaved world. Remember that He still gives humankind a chance to repent by destroying only a third of what He targets. If this destruction ever came about because of terrorism, it's because God will allow it.

Fourth Trumpet (Revelation 8:12)—Here we see darkness, for a third of the sun, moon, and stars will not give light, thus disrupting one-third of daylight. And what will cause this darkness? It will be God's doing, and I believe He will darken the whole Earth. A darkened Earth means a cooler Earth because the sun's rays will not be as illuminating upon the Earth. Let's also keep in mind that a nuclear disaster can do the same thing, especially if the disaster is coming from previous trumpet judgments.

If you recall back in 1991, during the Desert Storm campaign, the Iraqis set many oil wells on fire, thus causing darkness in the region. It was the soot in the air (atmosphere) from the burning wells that blocked the sunlight, thus causing darkness. Also consider volcanoes, such as the one in that very same year in the Philippines that forced the closing of Clark Airforce Base (June 1991) in the region. That alone devastated the atmosphere, including the Hawaiian islands, with darkness. Again, God can, by His almighty power, set the stage where such phenomena can occur overnight. These two disasters were responsible for the emitting of tons of soot into the atmosphere that blocked the sunlight for thousands of miles. Just think if the planet as a whole was to be darkened in such a way. Scientists claim that a nuclear exchange can easily cause the darkening of the planet, thus causing what is termed as nuclear winter. The prophecy ends with a flying angel hollering, "Woe, woe, woe to the inhabitants of the Earth, because of the remaining blasts of the trumpet of the three angels who are about to sound" (Revelation 8:13 NKJV). Let's keep in mind that with God, nothing is impossible. Apparently the three woes might have been an indication or warning of three more incoming trumpet blasts.

Fifth Trumpet (Revelation 9:1)—At the fifth trumpet, we encounter a most unusual situation. Apostle John goes on to describe a horrifying episode, where locusts are released with smoke from a bottomless pit after a fallen star (angel) is given the key to this abyss. These locusts are commanded to torment (sting) the unsaved for five months but not to kill them. The torment is aimed at the unsaved, so the implication here must be that the saved, or those sealed by God, are still at large. The apostle then goes on to describe these locusts as horses prepared for battle with women's hair and teeth like a lion's. They also have breastplates on them, wings that sound like chariots, and tails with stingers on them.

I've never heard of a locust described this way, but in his own terminology, not knowing exactly what he was looking at, Apostle John might have been describing what some scholars and some military personnel believe to be a combat helicopter. I might be inclined to agree with this, because after watching the Apache combat helicopter on TV during Operations Desert Storm and Shock and Awe, they do look like locusts from a distance.

It also seems that during this time, people will look for ways to commit suicide due to the pain inflicted by the locusts' stings. Unfortunately for them, they will not succeed, and their failure to seek death may be God's supernatural intervention. God may yet be planning their salvation. Hopefully they'll take heed to the call, or else they will suffer with death at a later time.

In this prophecy of the fifth trumpet, we are also introduced to the angel of the bottomless pit. He goes by the name of Abaddon (in the Hebrew) or Apollyon (in the Greek). To the Bible student, angels are real spiritual beings, they are invisible to the human eye most of the time, and they serve God day and night. But this particular angel is different. He is a king over these locusts. Does that mean these locusts are also spirits and invisible? Remember that an angel can transform itself to look like a human (I believe this phenomenon is called shape-shifting in sci-fi flicks). So why can't these stinging demonic locusts do likewise? I'm sure they'll be seen by unsaved humans for five months. They will look horrifying, and their sting will be painful, more painful than bee stings—and believe me, I've had my share of bee stings!

Some might contend that Apostle John was actually witnessing spiritual warfare that has been going on since the fall of humans at the Garden of Eden. Unfortunately, many today do not believe in a spiritual dimension that focuses on destroying humankind. Believe me, it's true only because the Bible speaks about it. You can read about spiritual warfare in Ephesians 6, which I touched upon in a previous chapter. Spiritual warfare is real, and it will intensify to a point, or climax, which will be termed spiritual Armageddon. It's finality will come when Satan is thrown into the bottomless pit after or during the Battle of Armageddon. You see, if you're a military tactician, you will always focus on taking down your opponent's leader to end the battle. This is precisely what's going to happen after spiritual Armageddon—that is, the takedown of Satan. Don't get me wrong, because there will also be a physical Battle of Armageddon.

Back in the mideighties and nineties, I became a fan of Frank Peretti's novels on spiritual warfare. Novels like *This Present Darkness* and *Piercing the Darkness* were favorites of mine because they showed spiritual warfare at work. Here, Peretti attempted to present the reader the reality of a dark spiritual kingdom actively at work against all that was, and could be, called Godly. He showed the evil side, which is Satan's kingdom; and he showed the good side, which is God's angels at work coming to rescue those in need. True, these novels were fictional, but again it showed the spiritual side of an ugly warfare at work.

You see, God put us on this planet to worship Him. He didn't put us here to worship ourselves or Satan, who is the god of this world. Satan wants to be worshiped, and in his deceptive ways, he succeeds in many ways by alluring those who are not knowledgeable of the things or Word of God. But thanks to God's grace, the elect (saved), who are knowledgeable of the Word, do not give in to Satan's tactics or deceptions. As a reward, God spares the elect the torment that is described in Revelation 9:5—that is, a torment that has been prophesied to last five months within the Great Tribulation's time frame.

Unlike the first four trumpets, the fifth doesn't have a one-third destruction scenario in it. What it does have is this verse of warning: "One woe is past. Behold, still two more woes are coming after these things" (Revelation 9:12 NKJV). What we see here is one-third of the woes coming to pass by the end of the fifth Trumpet. Now, whether this woe spoken of here relates to just the fifth trumpet or all other trumpets combined up to this point is not clarified, but I will speculate that it is a combination of the five trumpets up to this point. So let's stand by for the next two woes.

Sixth Trumpet (Revelation 9:13)—In this trumpet judgment, the angel sounding the trumpet is ordered to "Release the four angels who are bound at the great river Euphrates" (Revelation 9:14). Their mission is to gather up two hundred million horsemen for the purpose of killing one-third of humankind with three plagues: fire, smoke, and brimstone. The mere description of these plagues implies a war scenario that will involve, in my opinion, nuclear weapons.

What we are witnessing here is the beginning of the end. I say this because this trumpet judgment precedes the last trumpet that, again in my opinion, includes the Rapture of believers. It seems like the Lord will get the Church out of the way before disaster strikes. That means the final hour has come for the unsaved. What follows after the seventh trumpet will be the bowl judgments with no escape. The gathering of two hundred million horsemen will be the most awaited time in history because it will bring in what the secular world describes as Doomsday. In the Bible, it's the most awaited battle of all times and the one that will end all wars. This is the Battle of Armageddon.

Again, this trumpet judgment has the makings of a one-third destruction scenario, because one-third of humankind will perish. Ask yourself, Will this battle actually be fought here in the sixth trumpet? My answer is no, and I'll tell you why. You see, what Apostle John saw in his vision was just the preparation for the battle by the release of the four angels from the Euphrates River. In other words, their release makes it their duty to build up this army of two hundred million, which will come from this region of the world.

John's vision also includes a death headcount of one-third of humanity. That means billions, not millions, of lives will be snuffed away by the plagues of this war. The actual battle itself will be fought in the sixth bowl judgment and not in the sixth trumpet. I'll show you when we get to the bowl judgments.

To illustrate what I'm trying to say, let's take a step back to the Desert Storm campaign in 1991 as an example. If you recall, when Kuwait was invaded in the summer of 1990, the battle did not take place right away to free Kuwait. Instead, prior to the battle's confrontation, after many meetings at the United Nations over a period of five and a half months, the United Nations, with the leadership of the United States, took military action against Iraq to force them out of Kuwait. Prior to this action, during the time span of the UN talks, the preparation for the battle, known as Operation Desert Shield, enabled allied troops to mass five to six hundred thousand military personnel for the invasion. Once the invasion started, its code name became Operation Desert Storm.

As I mentioned in an earlier chapter, the only nations capable of massing an army of two hundred million in today's world would have to be the nations of the Far East, and we don't see this gathering again until we get to the sixth bowl judgment. The way I see it, the army of two hundred million from the kings of the East will amass at the sixth trumpet (compare this to Operation Desert Shield) and then fight it out later during the sixth bowl judgment in the Battle of Armageddon (compare this to Operation Desert Storm). One must also take note—and

I'm jumping ahead—that the kings of the East cannot cross over to the Middle East until the waters of the Euphrates River are dried up in the sixth Bowl (Revelation 6:12). That's a jump of six judgments before we see the gathering that will head to the plains of Megiddo for the Battle of Armageddon.

Revelation 6:18 (sixth trumpet) gives us the results in advance of the casualties of this war: one-third of humankind will die. If this prophecy were to come to pass today, in a world approaching nine billion in population, the results of the dead would be three billion people from the three plagues (fire, smoke, and brimstone).

Confused? Don't be. What I'm saying here is the Lord Jesus, through Apostle John, has already given us tomorrow's news headlines in advance. He reported that a mass gathering of two hundred million troops around the Euphrates region were heading west toward Israel (Valley of Megiddo), but they were waiting for the River Euphrates to dry up for the crossing of its military. He also reported a futuristic battle (war) taking place around that time that would claim one-third of the world's population.

As in the Persian War of 1991, Desert Storm, Apostle John also implied a time span between the gathering of the two hundred million and the battle itself. Just think: if the Far East is contemplating on raising this army of two hundred million, then the rest of the world has to be contemplating also raising its military to meet the challenge. Both sides are nuclear ready, so the only conclusion we can come up with is the end of the world. That's scary, but that's the way the Lord planned it. Just as He destroyed the world in Noah's time by flooding it, He will do it again, but with a great boom this time. His intention is not to do away with humanity, but just as there were survivors from Noah's flood, so will there be survivors after the purging of the world. The Messiah's return will repopulate the world and restore it just as it was during Adam and Eve's days in the Garden of Eden.

Seventh Trumpet (Revelation 11:15)—By the blowing of this trumpet, all kingdoms of the world will be proclaimed as kingdoms of God. In other words, God will take back the Earth that Adam lost to Satan when he and Eve gave in to temptation. But first, He must complete the purge, or the cleansing, of the world with the remaining judgments known as the bowl (or vial) judgments.

Up to this point in history, Satan has ruled the world. That's why there is much hatred against the Jews and Christians. True, Jesus inherited it by paying the price (ransom) on the cross, but that inheritance has not been claimed as of yet. The Lord has taken His time so His flock could get bigger and bigger. The seventh trumpet takes care of that inheritance when the Lord makes His reentry back to Earth and when the proclamation is announced by the seventh trumpet angel. Jesus, who is the Messiah, will claim His inheritance and share it with His followers. Who are these followers? They are those who have resurrected from the dead, those who have been raptured, and those who will survive the onslaught that God has planned—that is, if they have given their hearts to Him. This includes the Jews of national Israel.

Because it is the last trumpet, we already know from the previous chapter that it will result in the Rapture. By now, at this point in time, the two witnesses (olive trees) will have completed their three-and-a-half-year mission, and the antichrist will be at the height of his war against the saints (believers). The only thing remaining will be the final purging process, which will come in the form of seven more judgments. These seven final judgments will be God's literal declaration of war against the evil one (the antichrist), his kingdom, and Satan himself. Let's take a look at the rest of the bowl judgments, because we've already touched upon the seven seals and the seven trumpets.

In some of the trumpet judgments, we saw disasters of a one-third destruction scenario. The bowl judgments will prove to be more devastating. These judgments are meant to complete God's wrath toward unsaved humankind and rid the antichrist's kingdom forever. That means new plagues, though similar to the trumpet plagues; these will be stronger, more effective, and more intense than ever before. Because God's wrath will be completed with these plagues, Satan's kingdom will be totally destroyed, including those who have taken the Mark of the Beast and all other nonbelievers regardless of whether they took the mark. They will be destroyed for not accepting the Son of God (Jesus) as their Messiah and for going to war against Him. All this suffering will happen during the last seven plagues of God's wrath.

God's purpose here is to purge all unrighteousness from the Earth and restore it to its intended righteous mode—that is, as it was at the Garden of Eden. His judgments will be like in the days of Noah, when violence and unrighteousness ruled humankind. Back then, God's only solution was to destroy the known world at the time by flooding it with water and killing every human with the exception of eight who entered the ark. In fact, by entering the ark, one might even look at that scenario as a type of the Rapture, where God put His people in a safe place while purging the Earth.

As God's righteous servant Noah and his family were saved from the flood by entering the ark, so will the believers at the Rapture by entering a safe place prepared by the Lord Himself. Afterward, God will finish the work that has to be done here on Earth. The final mop-up will be finished by the Messiah (Jesus), His angels, and those who were raptured, including the resurrected saints.

I don't know about you, but this excites me because once God restores the Earth, it will again belong to Him and His followers (believers), who are also heirs. That means all His people will get a piece of the rock. But that comes with conditions: you must accept Christ Jesus as your personal Lord and Savior and become a born-again believer (John 3:3).

You must put your trust in Him to get through part of the Tribulation until the Rapture occurs. Can you do this for yourselves and your family? It might not be easy, but the Lord said that He would be with us until the end of the age. As I've stated before, there is room for survival during the trumpet judgments, but there is very little room in the bowl judgments (the last seven plagues). Let me show you these judgments, which are in the book of Revelation beginning in chapter 16.

Bowl 1 (Revelation 16:2)—The first bowl judgment is that of a malignant sore that will come upon those who have taken the Mark of the Beast. It will be painful and horrible just as Job's were in the book of Job, when God gave Satan permission to inflict painful sores upon him. But, unlike that situation where Satan did the damage, it will be God Himself who will send forth His angel to pour out the wrath of this particular bowl.

The reality of such a plague happening cannot be undermined or denied, especially with today's deteriorating ozone layer, which has many scientists dazzled and which is causing many harmful rays to reach the surface of the Earth. These rays alone can cause skin cancer because of the increase of UV rays on the surface. And as we already know, cancer itself can be considered a plague, especially if it increases, thus becoming an epidemic or even a pandemic. Again, this judgment is only for those who have taken the Mark of the Beast, and for those who worship his image. That again translates to maybe millions of people, if not billions.

Bowl 2 (Revelation 16:3)—In the second bowl, an angel throws its vial into the sea to destroy all living creatures in it and turn the sea to blood. This prophecy is almost identical to the second trumpet judgment, but, unlike the second trumpet's one-third destruction scenario, it now becomes a 100 percent destruction scenario. That means those dependent on the sea for a food source, whether to sell or eat, will no longer have that luxury. The result will be that of a more famished environment, especially in Asia, where so many are dependent on the sea to supply them with their everyday nutritional needs.

Unfortunately, the famine caused by this judgment will hurt billions of people worldwide. It will raise food prices to an unbearable amount of money (seal three,– the Black Horse). It might even lead to a stock market crash. The planet will look like Mars from outer space because of the waters turning to blood (red). It will be a complete chaos for all of humanity. It's no wonder why the kings of the East will march westward in quest of food supplies for their people. For this reason and other economic ones, the Eastern kings will war with the Western nations (the antichrist), eventually forcing the greatest battle of all time, Armageddon. We're looking at the Black Horse at work here, as well as the Red Horse (war).

Bowl 3 (Revelation 16:4)—The third bowl judgment is similar to the second bowl judgment in that the rivers and springs of waters also turn to blood after the angel pours out his vial (bowl). That means that drinking water, which many take for granted, will be scarce. unlike the third trumpet, which contaminated one-third of the water supply of the world, the third bowl will contaminate most, if not all, water supplies, including reservoirs. This contamination, noted as blood, doesn't necessarily imply literal blood, but it surely implies death, because as the third trumpet showed us that the waters were made bitter and undrinkable, which caused many to die, so will the third bowl, but with a greater impact on humanity.

What we have here is a judgment that will affect not just part of the planet but also the planet as a whole, because drinking water will be cut to a minimum, thus causing many to fight and war over this precious commodity, which is a necessity for the survival of the human race. It is noted that a person going without water for three to four days will dehydrate and die because the human body needs to replenish its water due to sweat and urination. The Egyptians went without water for seven days when God, through Moses and Aaron, struck the rivers, streams, ponds, and pools of water (Exodus 7:17–25). I don't believe they died, because God wasn't done with them yet. Also, that was only the second plague. Eight more plagues remained before the exodus.

The necessity for such a plague to take place in the third bowl judgment is God's avenging judgment for the saints who have been martyred since the start of Christendom, and also for the prophets of old. God reminds us through scripture that He is the avenger. He states in Deuteronomy 32:35 (NKJV), "Vengeance is Mine, and recompense." In other words, He's saying, "It's time to pay back for the blood spilt. Now it's My turn to avenge." Our God does not mess around. If He says it, He'll do it. Praise be His holy name!

When looking at this bowl judgment in Revelation 16:4, one must wonder how God will ignite this judgment. Will He make nuclear reactors melt down as in Chernobyl, thus causing bitter waters? Or will He cause humankind to throw biological weapons of mass destruction at each other's water supplies? Any way you look at it, it will be done only because it has been prophesied. I often wonder about it, but I'm not overly concerned, because I know my God has it all under His control. When the time comes, He'll rapture His people, and then He'll bombard the world with His last seven plagues.

Bowl 4 (Revelation 16:8)—In this bowl judgment, God will have His angel pour the fourth vial on the sun so as to intensify the heat. The effects will be that people will be scorched from it, and the heat will be so intense that humans will drop from heat exposure, heat exhaustion, and dehydration. We're not talking about a bad sunburn day here. We are talking about death by heat.

In the Middle East and some Asian countries, people are used to intense heat getting into the triple digits, especially in the summertime. But even this heat will not be tolerable to these people. And if it should coincide with the second and third bowl judgments, where waters are to be contaminated, people will drop like flies from the plague this judgment brings. With all this going on, the Bible says that people will still refuse to give glory to their Creator. Not only that, but they will continue cursing God for the pain that is being inflicted upon them. That brings to mind Job's wife, who told Job, who was being afflicted with pain by Satan, to curse God and get it over and done with. Job refused to curse God, but these people in the fourth bowl judgment will curse Him because they love their sin too much.

With global warming today, one can see this very situation of intense heat creeping into view in today's world, for the ozone layer in the atmosphere is deteriorating. That is the consensus of many scientists who say this layer, which acts as a filter for deadly sunrays, has been deteriorating for years. Its cause? No one knows, but the consensus points to the pollution trend that has hampered our breathing air for decades. Once this layer is destroyed, the heat will intensify, thus creating what has been termed the greenhouse effect.

Again, doctors have warned many as to the effects of this deterioration. Many will die of cancer and heat stroke caused by the severe heat. Thus, prophecy will be fulfilled in the fourth bowl judgment, which reads, "And men were scorched with great heat" (Revelation 16:9). For those who think this bowl judgment is just symbolic jargon, just keep up with the scientific news, especially that which deals with the weather and climate change.

Bowl 5 (Revelation 16:10)—Again, God will give His angel instruction to pour out more of His wrath. This time, as during the plagues against Egypt in Exodus, God will plague the kingdom of the beast (antichrist) with darkness. This darkness, in my opinion, will probably last through the duration of the Tribulation, unlike the ninth plague in Egypt during Moses's time, which lasted three days. If you have read Exodus, then you will recall that the ninth plague was aimed at Pharoah (a type of antichrist) and his kingdom, but not at the Israelites who were residing in Goshen at the time. It appears this same scenario will exist here in the fifth bowl because this darkness is aimed only on the kingdom of the antichrist, not on Israel or new believers, although some new believers will still reside in the kingdom of the antichrist. But I think the Lord will still protect them in the supernatural. Now, let's ask a question here: Will God use humankind to inflict this plague among themselves?

As I mentioned when discussing the fourth trumpet, looking back to the Persian Gulf War of 1991 (Operation Desert Storm), one must wonder whether the burning oil wells of Kuwait was a scenario of things to come, because the immense fires that ensued blanketed the skies of the Middle East for months, allowing very little sunlight to penetrate through. This brought about not only darkness but also life-threatening concentrations of gases, such as sulfur dioxide and hydrogen sulfide.

Along with the darkness, in this plague comes pain. "And they gnawed their tongues because of the pain" (Revelation 16:10 NKJV). But what pain? Does darkness cause pain? Again when looking at Exodus 10:21 (NKJV), one reads, "Then the Lord said to Moses 'stretch your hand toward heaven, that there may be darkness over the land of Egypt, darkness which may be felt'."

Not only will God bring about a plague of darkness, but He'll also make sure that the kingdom of the beast feels every misery that the darkness has to offer, whether it be in a physical realm, a spiritual realm, or a psychological realm. The magnitude of it all will focus much pain upon those who, even up to this plague, will not repent of their unrighteous deeds. It's no wonder "they will gnaw their tongues because of the pain." After all, along with the darkness, they'll have to deal with the first bowl (boils), which will lead them again to blaspheme the Lord. Just imagine being with boils (bowl 1) with hardly any water to drink because of its contamination (bowls 2 and 3), in pain because of the scorching of the sun, and then being plunged into darkness with no light. To top it off, you can't even commit suicide because God won't let you. It's no wonder why there will be weeping and gnashing of teeth

(Luke 13:28). I'm glad I'm right with the Lord. That alone will spare me the judgments that God has planned at this time.

Bowl 6 (Revelation 16:12)—This bowl judgment brings us to the battle that will end all battles and wars. We're speaking here of the Battle of Armageddon. It is here in the Valley of Megiddo where the forces of righteousness will fight with the forces of unrighteousness. I'm sure by this time the Church and true believers will have been raptured. This battle alone, as I stated in the sixth trumpet, will claim one-third of humankind. We're talking billions of lives, not millions, with the majority being nonbelievers. I'm saying this because the remnant of believers might also get in the cross fire of things and find themselves in the same plight as the nonbelievers if they don't take heed of Jesus's warnings to flee to the mountains or hide. It's shameful that these nonbelievers might have believed at one time but then indoctrinated themselves in other religions and other idols that made them stray from the true God of Israel and His Christ (Parable of the Sower; Matthew 13).

If you recall from our discussion of the sixth trumpet, Apostle John envisioned the preparation for Armageddon when the four demonic angels were released at the River Euphrates (compare this to Operation Desert Shield, which took place in 1990). By the time the sixth bowl strikes, which might be weeks or months later after the sixth trumpet, these forces are prepared for battle (parallel to Operation Desert Storm in 1991). But, there is one thing missing in the puzzle, and that is a means for getting the Eastern troops into Israel. You see, Eastern and Far Eastern nations have no enormous navies or air forces, even though they're trying, especially China. In reality, they are trying to beef up these militaries so that someday they might get closer to the American and Western allies' might. In all probability, they will achieve this goal in size, but the truth of it is they do not have the West's experience in dealing with naval or air battles. The Japanese are the only ones with such experience from World War II. The biggest threat these Eastern nations have is the size of their armies. And to move these enormous armies, they must do it by land. The sixth bowl judgment prophecy solves this mystery by allowing the reader to see how these troops will move toward Israel. Let's read: "Then the sixth angel poured out his bowl on the great Euphrates River, and its water was dried up, so that the way of the kings from the east might be prepared" (Revelation 16:12 NKJV).

Back in the early nineties, Turkey boasted about being able to dam up the Euphrates River and dry it up. Even the *New York Times* reported this drying up of the Euphrates in an article on July 13, 2009, because of a dam-building project in Turkey. This has brought about tension with Syria and Iraq, who are dependent on this river. With this idea becoming a reality, what's going to stop Eastern nations from mobilizing their troops and letting them cross the Euphrates with ease and speed once this drying up takes place? Will the United Nations (the new world order) be able to stop them? I doubt it. Will America? Again, I doubt it. But I bet they'll lead the charge to try to stop this enormous army from crossing the Euphrates—that is, if they still have their military superiority and capabilities. Again, I would doubt it, but there's another empire that will take the challenge, and that is the empire of the antichrist.

The reality is that these enormous armies from the East crossing the Euphrates might have as strong a military force as the antichrist, America, and all allies combined. And because both sides have nuclear capabilities, then we know what the outcome might or will be. But militarily speaking, I still give the West the edge because of its technology. I remember back in the early eighties when President Reagan proposed a Star Wars program designed to shoot nuclear missiles from space. After spending thirty billion dollars on the program, it was discontinued during the Clinton administration. If this program is reenacted, then it will be a plus for whoever has it, namely the richer Western nations of the world.

No matter how many nations are involved in this final destruction scenario, there will be no winners except the one who will claim His inheritance. This is the Lord Jesus Christ, who comes for the second time in history as the conquering Messiah. He alone will claim the victory, for He alone is the Champion.

Bowl 7 (Revelation 16:17)—This is the grand finale before the issuance of the new millennium. Here, the seventh angel will pour out the seventh vial, and the whole world will tremble with an enormous earthquake, which will level many, if not all, great cities (New York, London, Paris, Tokyo, etc.; Revelation 16:19). Thunder and lightning will also join in, and great hailstones the size of talents (an ancient Greek measurement equaling about 25.8 kilograms, or 56.75 pounds—about the weight of a medicine ball) will fall from the sky. To summarize it even more, take a look at the sixth seal again, because it's practically saying the same. The seventh bowl mentions the fact that "It is done" (Revelation 16:17 NKJV). The sixth seal mentions, "For the great day of His wrath has come, and who is able to stand?" (Revelation 8:17 NKJV). Both verses have scenarios of the very end.

It is during this shake-up that the Messiah makes His appearance in Israel, touching down on the Mount of Olives, the same spot where He was lifted up into a cloud two thousand years ago. Upon His touchdown, the Mount will split in two, from east to west, causing a valley to form. Half of the mountain will shift northward, and the other half will shift southward (Zechariah 14:4).

For those geology students interested in Israel's landscape, there is a fissure (crack) in the Earth's crust that runs the length of Israel from north to south into the Gulf of Aqaba, and into the Red Sea. What amazes me about this prophecy is the fact that Bible writers of that time had no idea that a crack existed and runs right through the heart of Israel. Apparently, the valley formed by this split will provide an escape route for those fleeing from Jerusalem. Zechariah 14:5 (NKJV) implies this: "Then you shall flee through the mountain valley." It almost seems as if the Lord has purposely formed this valley and given escape instructions to His people Israel, because He continues the verse this way: "Yes, you shall flee as you fled from the earthquake in the days of Uzziah king of Judah."

Once this escape takes place, the Lord (Messiah) will take action against those who have come against Jerusalem (Israel). Along with His saints and angels, He'll hit the enemy with a plague the prophet Zachariah describes this way: "Their feet shall dissolve while they stand on their feet, their eyes shall dissolve in their sockets, and their tongues shall dissolve in their mouths" (Zechariah 14:12 NKJV). I believe what the prophet has described here is a nuclear explosion of great magnitude in Israel. As I said in a previous chapter, God did not give humankind nuclear toys in vain. Again, I believe what we'll be witnessing here is a nuclear holocaust. Those surviving will apparently be those following the Lord's instructions to flee through the mountain valley, which might act as a shield against the plagues that are about to strike Israel's enemies. If it's a nuclear plague, those surviving will not have to worry about a radiation aftermath. I'm sure the Lord will take care of that once the new millennium is issued in.

In concluding this chapter, let's take a close look at these plagues. Believe me, you don't want to experience these plagues. I can't believe that the hard hearts of humans will not take heed to what has been discussed here. It's all in God's Word in a book called the Holy Bible. This book has tomorrow's headlines already. Maybe some believe in Nostradamus' predictions, but God's prophecies are not predictions. They are the truth, the whole truth, and nothing but the truth. The truth is God's Word, and that Word became flesh (John 1) in the person of Jesus Christ, who is waiting for your surrender unto Him. Friends, let's wave that white flag of surrender today and give our hearts to the Lord. Don't wait until tomorrow. Tomorrow might be too late.

CHAPTER 17

Conclusion: A Time for Peace and Rest

It's been a long trek for Israel since 1948, when it became a sovereign nation again. In fact, it's been a long trek since the days of Exodus, when Egypt finally let Israel go after holding them captive in slavery for 430 years. To take it even further, one might say that it's been a long trek for the world (humankind) and all its nations since creation, or since the Garden of Eden. Yes, it's been a long and at times harsh journey. But God has seen it all. As Father and Creator of His children, He too has journeyed with His children, and He has kept up in the histories and eras of His creation.

It was God Himself who built the framework of the seven economies, or dispensations, beginning with innocence and going right on through to the new millennium. He has traveled through the entirety of the Bible—that is, from Genesis in the Old Testament to Revelation in the New Testament. He has seen the death of His Son, Jesus, who is really Himself in the flesh. And He has seen the resurrection that He himself planned long before it happened, even before creation. He prophesied, through His prophets, on events that occurred in the Old Testament and on events that would occur in the future on the AD side of the calendar.

At present, it is this same Jesus, God's Son, who sits at His right hand in heaven, even making intercessory prayers on behalf of His people here on Earth (Romans 8:34). This goes to show that God Himself hears us through our prayers. It's also amazing how many millions or billions of prayers the Father receives in heaven on a daily basis. It's more amazing that He answers them even though some think He doesn't. But for those who think He doesn't, He might be saying no to their requests, or He might be saying, "Wait."

The Father also has appointed His Anointed One (Messiah) to inherit all things here on Earth. Upon claiming this inheritance, Lord Jesus will share it with all His followers (Romans 8:17): those who have shared in His sufferings, those who were resurrected, those who were raptured, and those who were survivors to the onslaught that occurred during God's final judgments during the Tribulation—that is, if they were believers washed in the blood of the Lamb.

Because God works in sevens, and because He rested on the seventh day of creation, we must look at the seventh dispensation (new millennium) as a time of rest and a time of total peace. It's like the calm after the storm. The storm is the Great Tribulation, with its climax of Armageddon destroying everything in sight, and the calm is the return of Christ, who initiates peace and rest by the issuance of the new millennium.

At this time, the Messiah, who is Jesus, will have absolute reign here on the Earth. He and His bride (the Church) will rule over the whole entire world with the righteousness that God has given them through Christ Jesus. One might even say that there will be no foreign governments because all governments will be under the supervision of God's people. In fact, all nations (not some) that have come against Jerusalem will have to visit the King (Messiah) at least once a year to pay Him homage and worship Him. For those who don't, a curse of no rain will be levied upon them. Such a curse will bring about famine because of the lack of rain (Zachariah 14:16–17 NKJV).

They will also be required to keep the Feast of Tabernacles in obedience. Why the Feast of Tabernacles? Because the Lord has commanded it. The Feast of Tabernacles, also known as the Feast of Ingathering, is held in the fall to celebrate the gathering of the harvest and to spend time with God for seven days. It's also a time for Jews to celebrate the Jewish exodus from Egypt when they spent time in tents, or booths, out in the wilderness. Today, Jews and some Christian groups celebrate this feast, which is considered one of the three pilgrimage festivals in the Jewish faith; the other two are Pesach (Passover) and Shavuot (Pentecost).

In Luke 4:17–30, when Jesus was handed the book (scroll), He quoted Isaiah 61:1–2, "The Spirit of the Lord God is upon Me." But He never finished verse 2. He stopped short when He said, "To proclaim the acceptable year of the Lord." Had He continued with the verse, "And the day of vengeance of our God," it would have come to pass at that very moment because after taking His seat in the synagogue, He said, "Today this scripture is fulfilled in your hearing." This alone infuriated those at the synagogue, and they chased Him out because He made Himself look like God in their eyes.

Just think what would have been if he had quoted, "And the day of vengeance of our God." I believe the timeline would have instantaneously jumped to the plagues in the book of Revelation. But because He was God in the flesh, He knew exactly what to quote and what not to quote. Had the timeline jumped, all prophecies from that point onward to the end of the Tribulation would have been erased—that is: the death and resurrection, the growth of the Church, the destruction of Jerusalem by Rome in AD 70, Ezekiel 38–39, the Rapture, and probably the Tribulation itself with the antichrist as leader, leaving God's wrath on humankind just prior to His return. As it is, it didn't happen that way because that's not the way God planned it. God is all-knowing (omniscient) and all-powerful. His plan, which was initiated before creation, had to stand no matter what because it was already spoken into the destiny of the world and of humankind.

What follows after these verses in the book of Isaiah 61, starting in verse 3 onward, is a beautiful and comforting message of what the millennium will look like and who will rule in it. Yes, the Messiah will rule in it with an iron rod and an iron fist if He has to, but His reign, unlike any of humankind, will last forever. The world as we know it will be one of no war, no bickering, no arguments, no pollution, and no pain. Just imagine a world of no cancer, no heart attacks, and no strokes. Like I said in a previous chapter, I wonder if the world in the new millennium will even need doctors and hospitals. Maybe a few can be here and there to take care of the mortal population if needed. But then again, God's plan of peace will prevail.

What happens toward the end of this millennium will be a test of nations again to finalize God's plan of salvation for humankind. This plan, which has been put on a silver platter for people to choose from, will finalize humankind's destiny. He will either accept it or deny it. In this test, God will set Satan free, who has been bound in the bottomless pit for a thousand years (Revelation 20:7). Again Satan will go out to deceive the nations of the world. In his deception, he will gather a multitude of peoples (Gog and Magog again) who will number in the hundreds of thousands, as many is as the sands of the sea (Revelation 20:8). These peoples, under Satan's leadership, will surround God's people and His city, but to no avail. God will send fire from heaven that will devour them and destroy them forever.

Is this another war? No, it's just God's final cleanup of His enemies. These enemies came about during the new millennium, for God, in His merciful and good ways, will still give humankind (those born during the new millennium) the power of choice. It will be in their choosing as to whether they want to serve God or serve an idol (Satan). Because Satan will be successful in his deception again, he will take many with him into the lake of fire, because that's where God will send him: "The devil who deceived them, was cast into the lake of fire and brimstone where the beast and the false prophet are" (Revelation 20:10 NKJV). This same torment will also be a forever place for those not found in God's book of life (12).

Let's make a note here. It is said that God never intended for people to go to this lake of fire. This setup was reserved for Satan, the beast, the false prophet, and the demons. And let's not forget those angels chained in captivity (Jude 6 TLB) who will also join their master (Satan) in hellfire. For evil humankind, or those not found in the Book of Life, they too will suffer the same torment as Satan and his hordes. But that won't happen until the white throne judgment after the second resurrection (Revelation 20:11). At this time, all the dead will be called, judged after the books are opened, and then sent to their just rewards, which might include hell itself.

With a message so explicit as this, how can humans not take heed to what the Bible has to teach and refrain from evilness? The lake of fire is a real place of torment that will separate humans from God. Also known as Gehenna In the Hebrew Bible, that was a valley near Jerusalem in its time where some of the kings of Judah would sacrifice their children by fire to the false god Moloch. It almost seems like a popular place (lake of fire) because it's mentioned so many times in the Bible. But the truth of the matter is no one has gone there yet. Even Jesus spoke of hell over seventy times in the New Testament. He did it to give warning to the unrepentant sinner. But then again, this unrepentant sinner still has until his very last hour to make amends with the Lord. Thank God for that.

In looking beyond this millennium, we are looking at a new heaven and new Earth. The old one will be destroyed, unlike the first time when it was flooded. This time it will be destroyed by fire. Apostle Peter writes about this: "But the day of the Lord will come as a thief in the night, in which the heavens will pass away with a great noise, and the elements will melt with fervent heat; both the earth and the works that are in it will be burned up" (2 Peter 3:10 NKJV).

Science has already predicted the demise of the sun, which means that someday, eons from now, the sun will cease to function. It's feeding of hydrogen will be depleted, thus leaving it to burn helium instead. That will turn the sun red, and it will burn with more intensity. This in itself will dry up the Earth of its waters. The oceans and seas will cease to exist, thus causing surviving humans, animals, and vegetation, to become extinct. The helium will be exhausted in time, thus causing a downhill approach to the demise of its surrounding planets, including the Earth. In fact, science claims that by the time this happens, the Earth will already have been burned to a crisp.

It's no wonder the Lord will recreate the heavens and the Earth, for the old Earth, as Apostle Peter prophesied, will be burned up with such an intensity of heat that it will melt all elements known to humankind. The sun itself will burn itself out, and the universe as we know it will be rearranged by God Himself. Although science claims this demise might take eons to come to pass, the reality of it might just occur after the new millennium.

When looking at Revelation 20, we are witnessing judgment against

Satan after being captured. Then we see a thousand-year period, which this chapter doesn't really elaborate on, but the book of Isaiah (chapters 60–65) does mention some of the highlights. Afterward, we see Satan back on the scene before he's sent to the lake of fire. Those who were resurrected from the dead (second resurrection) have to stand judgment and experience their just reward, whether of hellfire or something else, because there will be varying degrees of punishment for all. By the time we get to Revelation 21, we see something different: Apostle John sees a new heaven and a new Earth, for the old heaven and Earth have passed away.

Not only will there be a new heaven and Earth, but there will be a new Jerusalem that will come from heaven and be lowered onto the new Earth. This new Jerusalem will be the new home for those who are in Christ Jesus. It will have twelve gates, and its adornment with gold and jewels will be a sight to behold. It will be God's dwelling place. The glory of God and the Lamb (Jesus) alone will illuminate the city, which means the city will have no need for electricity, lamps, the sun, or the moon. Also, the river of life will flow from the throne of God and of the Lamb. It will flow down main street with trees of life on each side of the river bearing twelve different fruits every month. Even the leaves on the trees will be used for the healing of the nations (Revelation 22:2).

As I conclude this book, let me invite you to become a member of the family of God, as I have done with almost every chapter in this book. First, you must be born again in order to enter the kingdom of God. Jesus Himself said, "Unless one is born again, he cannot see the kingdom of God" (John 3:3 NKJV). That means your spirit must be quickened, or woken up from its dormant state. This quickening happens when you accept Jesus Christ as your personal Lord and Savior. You must also accept the fact that He died for you to wipe you clean from all your sins. That means you must ask Him to forgive you of your sins. One last thing: you must accept the fact that He resurrected from the dead and now sits at the right hand of the Father. You see, Jesus is part of the Trinity: Father, Son, and Holy Spirit.

After you have accepted Jesus, plug yourself into a Bible-believing church if you haven't done so yet. Most of all, read your Bible on a daily basis. Start small, with maybe a few verses per day, and then increase it to a chapter a day. My motto has always been "A chapter a day keeps the devil away." I made it up in the early eighties when I gave my heart to Jesus and began reading the Bible. Once I began reading it, I couldn't put it down. That made me hungry to search and seek more of the Word. I began to read books, watch Christian programs on TV, and listen to Christian programs on the radio. But most of all, I got plugged into a Bible-believing church. I have fellowship with my church family and am looking forward to an eternal relationship with the Lord Jesus Christ. He is my first love, my God, and my friend. I'll finish with this verse: "For I am persuaded that neither death nor life, nor angels nor principalities, nor powers, nor things present nor things to come, nor height nor depth, nor any other created thing, shall be able to separate us from the love of God which is in Christ Jesus our Lord."

Let's keep the faith, friends. The Lord loves you more than you can even imagine. May "the Lord bless you and keep you; the Lord make His face shine on you and be gracious to you; the Lord turn His face toward you and give you peace" (Numbers 6:24 NIV).

Printed in the United States
by Baker & Taylor Publisher Services